THE PLANET RENAISSANCE AND GLOBALISATION OF SOCIALISM

THE PLANET RENAISSANCE AND GLOBALISATION OF SOCIALISM

Constanlin Gruicci Vitali

GYAN

The Planet Renaissance and Globalisation of Socialism

ISBN : 978-81-212-1145-1

Published in 2013 in India by
Gyan Publishing House
23, Main Ansari Road, Daryaganj,
New Delhi - 110002
Phones : 23282060, 23261060
Fax : (011) 23285914
E-mail: books@gyanbooks.com
website: gyanbooks.com

Laser Type Setting : Rajender Vashist, Delhi
Printed at : G. Print Process, Delhi

Dedication

This book is dedicated to the militants and sympathisers of socialism, as well as to its opponents, to those who, in their memory and conscience, bear feelings of social justice and progress.

Contents

Preface

Many of the everlasting ideas of Victor Hugo, author of the historical novel "Les Misérables", who said that "there is something stronger than all the armies in the world, and these are the ideas for which the time of implementation has come", were for me an inspiration to gather my thoughts, my observations, analyses and ideas in a book that is a compendium on the revival of the new world of solidarity, democracy and humanitarianism: the revival of socialism.

When I discovered, in the international arena of confrontation of the left-wing and right-wing forces, the new phenomenon of the revival of socialism in many countries in Europe, Asia, Latin America and Africa, I could not imagine that the financial bankruptcy and the deepest economic crisis since the 1929 breakdown would shatter and weaken the capitalist world, that the malignant growth of imperialism signaled the nearing end of an age.

I could not imagine that neo-colonialism, the main pillar of imperialism, would crash down irrevocably and so fast.

I could not imagine that the revival of socialism would take on such global dimensions in such a short time.

Nor could I imagine that the direction taken by China and India onto the road of social market economy, the road of revival and modernisation of socialism, would arouse so fast the awe of the entire world.

Moreover, I could not imagine that Russia would rise again from its ruins and clearly drift to the left, pushing again into the international area with such great force and authority.

I could not imagine that in most countries in Western Europe, it would be possible to witness the flying flags of the left-wing political parties ascended to power.

Even less could I imagine that in the presidential and legislative elections in most of the Latin American countries, their populations would extend their confidence to the left-wing political leaders, thus heading on their way toward independence, democracy, freedom and socialism?

And, finally, I could not have imagined that the struggle of the African people for independence, democracy and humanitarian socialism would expand to Pan-African dimensions.

When analysing the new historical turn of the balance between the worldwide right- and left-wing forces on global level tilting in favour of the latter, I came to the understanding that, in fact, the actual praxis had overtaken my theoretical analyses. This is a unique circumstance for the pace of change of our history. The more I was pushing forward in the preparation of my surveys, I understood the growing need to alter the extent and nature of my research.

The present title of my book – "Worldwide Revival and Globalisation of Socialism" – is in accordance with the historical turn of the 21st century. At the end of 2008, in 56 countries, the power was being detained by the left-wing political forces, representing nearly 4 billion people – that is over two-third of the population of our planet, leaving alone the 26 countries where the left shares power with the right, or where the left is more powerful in the opposition. I am referring here only those states which have already chosen to walk the way of progress, freedom, independence and socialism.

It may happen that, reading this introduction, some readers will come up with the following question: OK, revival of socialism, but what kind of socialism, the state socialism of Marx and Engels, the bureaucratic socialism of Lenin, the egalitarian socialism of Mao Zedong, the totalitarian socialism of Stalin, Chervenkov, Rakosi, Tito, Ceau°escu, Jaruzelski, the socialism of the already dead and buried nomenclature, or the anthropological, democratic and humanitarian socialism arisen from the roots of the evolutionary, self-managing Marxism, the socialism rising from the roots of the constantly changing society, the socialism summarised in the ideas of Deng Xiaoping, of Mahatma Ghandi and Jawaharlal Nehru, of Jean Jaurès and Olof Palme, Salvador Allende, Nelson Mandela, Hugo Chavez or Lula da Silva, Evo Morales, Thomas Sankara, Dos Santos, Laurent Kabila, and of the new star of African freedom – Laurent Gbagbo, or of other militants and visionaries of social progress?

The answer does not lie in the formal logic of the idea movement, but rather in the very real logic of the social progress movement of the 21st century. The idea of worldwide revival and globalisation of socialism, as a new phenomenon of social progress, represents the idea for the implementation of which the time has come – obviously, but which has not yet found its proper place in the contemporary literature of social sciences. Up to date, there have been written hundreds of books, as well as thousands of studies and tens of thousands of papers on the globalisation of capitalism. Lately, more and more papers and books are being published on the subject of the actually concealed face of globalisation, studies which originate in the absolutely negative results of this globalisation for the social progress. Practically, the repercussions of this phenomenon trigger a new reaction of the civil society – which, in the haze of researching the alternatives, can get a glimpse on the reconsideration of socialism at the global level.

Now-a-days, an ever greater number of analysts of the novel social movements, more and more political party leaders and leaders of left-wing political movements write and speak about the evolvement of an alternative to the financial and monopole globalisation, an alternative desired and promoted by the population. They mention a type of globalisation which would bring about the development of new trends which contribute to social betterment; they speak about the identification of new government methods and forms, and even about the emerging of new relations between peoples, nations and states on our planet. In fact, what we are witnessing now is a process of bringing again before the eyes of the entire world the ideas of socialism, a development occurred in the late 20th and the early 21st century. This is the time when socialism seems to be the forerunner of globalisation of the new social relationships, a process that grows more and more in the underdeveloped countries of the South, of the medium developed and the flourishing West.

Socialism could not re-emerge in the world either by attempting to push again into the present picture the old concepts, theories and programs of the eastern totalitarian socialism or of the western reformatory social-democracy, or else by evolving based on such ideas. It has to demolish the old edifice both as theory and practice, as this is obviously largely outdated; only then, on this old foundation, but on a clear ground still preserving some of the yet unaltered old values, will the new modern structures be able to evolve, along with the new concepts and the new strategies of social development.

Undoubtedly, rediscovering and development of socialism in the entire world represent a historical turn in the evolution of the leftist political movements; consequently, we could say that we witness, on the one hand, the debut of an irrevocable crumbling of the very ancient ideas, theories and social systems that were the origin of the former, and, on the other hand, the erection of an adequate alternative of social development.

The reconsideration of the capacity of socialism to face the challenge of the globalised society is part of the endeavours to look for suitable solutions to the present requirements. The new historical process is on the lookout for the answer to a number of basic issues, regarding the fate of left-wing political currents: What. in fact, is the phenomenon of rediscovering and the globalisation of socialism? Where should we look for its historical roots? Which are the new economic and political laws of social development? What comes after the revival and globalisation of socialism in the field of structural, economic and humanitarian changes? Which are the new elements of the theory and practice of social progress? Which is the relation of the left-wing parties to the state structures, to the revolution of society and to democracy? What is their relation to reformism, reforms and revolutionary evolution of society? What is the nature of the changes effected in the class structure in the highly developed capitalist countries? What are the changes occurred in the strategy of class conflict and of cooperation between social classes? What are the relationship changes between social ideology and conscience of civil society?

What are the new relations between the Church, the State and the left-wing parties? What could be said about the relations between left-wing parties in the pursuit of a common way to revive socialism? Well, there are more such questions which are raised in the social practice and are awaiting appropriate answers!

These are the questions, and many more, regarding the social development, that I have tried to find more or less precised answers to. I am not entirely sure that such extremely extended issues could be assimilated without major turmoil in the field of interpretations on the nature of social movements. The revival and worldwide expansion of the area of implementation of socialism is no mental and intellectual figment of my own. This process belongs naturally to the reality of the IT and biotechnological revolution which destroys all the ancient social relations.

The development of socialism evolves from the latent social revolution, which corrodes all the outdated social relations of the highly developed capitalism of the West, the medium developed East and the feebly developed South. Both the revival and the spreading of the socialism originate in the globalisation process of the market economy, of the neo-colonialism, fostering not only the development of the production forces in the underdeveloped countries, but also the development of the working class, of the new intellectual category, the emancipation of the peasants; all these are incentives and enhancement of the pursuit of peoples and nations for national independence and social freedom, for their breaking free from the dullness of never-ending poverty. We could say that such a course initiates and amplifies the new democratisation trends and describes the re-development of the socialist ideas as a unique direction and as the only positive alternative for the social development. The revival of socialism can be identified as the only answer or solution for the solving of the issues of the oppressed classes, devoid of their right to a reply in connection with their future, with the future of our civilisation.

The age of the violent revolutions is past and gone, as well as that of reformism and spontaneous evolution of social movements. A new age is coming into being, an age of latent and peaceful social revolution, an age of transition of our civilisation from capitalism, from totalitarian socialism and from neo-colonialism to democratic, liberal and humanitarian socialism. No doubt that the 21st century is the age of transition of the most peoples and nations on the way to democracy, socialism and humanism.

The ideas, principles and considerations comprised in this survey do not originate in already written books, although the latter are the documentary support of the former. These ideas are the results of investigation, observation and summarising the actual social progress movement in the great laboratory of the totalitarian socialism in Eastern Europe (where I lived during the years of my youth), in the great social laboratory of the left-wing movement in the highly-developed West and of the national freedom movements of the underdeveloped South (where I lived as a grown-up, where I had the opportunity to share the bread and salt, the good and the ill of all the three social systems). The scientific truth can not be researched in the libraries in Paris, London and Berlin. Truth can not be found in any library, and, even less so, in the minds of the research scientists, but rather in the practice of social development.

The vital ideas and concepts of my research on the historical truth of the future of the human race are based on certain basic discoveries of the 21st century. It is the task of those critics who hold in their hands the balance of scientific justice to pass judgement on their scientific value. The duty of my conscience as an investigator of social truth is to draw the readers' attention on the fact that my efforts were focused towards synthesising a number of fundamental processes and laws of the social progress, such as:

- Worldwide revival and globalisation of socialism,
- Decline and metastasis of the developed capitalism in its imperialistic stage and transition to a democratic, liberal, humanitarian and socialist society
- Failing of neo-colonialism and stepping of the under-developed countries on the way of national independence and social, socialistic emancipation

- Simultaneous action – in the developed countries – of the laws of both capitalist and socialist accumulation, on the one hand, and simultaneous action of fundamental economic laws of both capitalism and socialism, on the other hand
- Gradual socialisation of production means, via an increase of the involvement of the state and the civil society among the shareholders of the main companies
- Complicity of the Church, the state and the left-wing political parties in the achievement of the general welfare
- Political principle of power alternation of the left-wing and the right-wing political parties on the path to social progress

Such are the processes and laws of the movements of society, on the basis of which I have tried to imagine a projection of our common future. No matter if this endeavour of mine was able to reflect the permanently evolving and changing reality, or if it was no more than a utopia resulting from too much optimism, my readers will be free to pass the final judgement on this book, as will the objective political professionals, ideologists and critics. As for those ideological analysts, critics and judges who will not be able to assimilate the new ideas of social progress, I will quote them again the famous words spoken by Galileo Galilei before the judges of the Inquisition: "And yet it moves." And yet, we acknowledge the worldwide revival and globalisation of socialism.

While writing these lines, I am aware not only of the ideological hardships of my adventure, of the scientific value of some of my analyses and discoveries, but also of the possible opposite, of the imperfection of certain summarised conclusions. I am sure that I have not to be relegated to the box of defendants having to face the partisans of the "purity of Marxism", but rather that I am standing in the vast research laboratory which, following multiple essays, will lead to the discovery of scientific truth.

Based on the logical historical method in exposing my thoughts and ideas, in the five chapters of my book I have examined the crucial issues of social progress which could be of interest not only to politicians, but also to professional analysts, and to militants and sympathisers of socialism and for those opponents who, in their memory and conscience, harbour feelings of social justice and progress. In the process of explaining the economic processes, phenomena, categories and laws, I have avoided to make use of the methodology of such analysts as consider pedagogy to be an exclusive feature of secondary and higher teaching.

Finally, taking into account the fact that the book is meant for a wider readership (not because of my university professional practice), my explanatory method exceeds the frame of scientific research norms, explaining the processes and phenomena in a pedagogical manner, a fact which professional analysts consider simply common, but which is absolutely needed for the understanding of the complexity of the economic, political, sociological and philosophical issues of the described phenomenon. Most important is not as much the expression form, but rather the understanding of my concepts via communication with the readers who, in their mind and conscience, keep great expectations for the evolvement of a new world.

Constanlin Gruicci Vitali

Acknowledgements

Most part of this book was written in Abidjan (Ivory Coast), a part of it in Paris, and the rest in Bucharest. The indispensable documentation was researched in the "François Mitterrand" and "Georges Pompidou" libraries, in the New York National Library, as well as in the National Library in Bucharest. So that I have to extend my thanks to the staff of the said libraries, who guided me in researching the necessary material.

First of all, I have to thank my wife, Maria Prune Gruici, for her invaluable help in classifying the documentary files, for her patience and her passion in working through every version of the manuscript. But, foremost, I am grateful to her for having accepted my "marriage" to this book, resulting in sacrificing much of our family life.

I also thank my old friend from way back when we were both students, namely George Vrcelj, professor at the University of Economic Sciences in Bucharest and Chief Scientific Consultant with the Economic Research Institute in Belgrade, for his advice in the economic, ideological and political reading of certain issues in connection with the worldwide revival of socialism. His reasonable suggestions, particularly of macro-economic nature, were a great contribution to the improvement of the scientific contents of the book.

Also, the suggestions brought by Milan Petrovic, press correspondent of the newspaper "Politica" in Bucharest, former student of the Military Academy in Moscow, helped me greatly in the philosophical and sociological interpretation of the great social movements all over the world.

My very special thanks are extended to Ms Diallo Adam, professor of Sociology and French in Abidjan, who undertook the task of language stylisation and spell-proofing the manuscript.

"Ideas may be considered great in as far as they are able to implement, particularly when they are able to bring some benefit to reality, starting from the actual situation, and when they come to show, in a practical way, the course of the actions by which the undertaking of an organised collective will can highlight (generating them) such benefits or, by their highlighting, can destroy them by replacing them."

Constanlin Gruicci Vitali

1

Collapse of Totalitarian Socialism and Neo-Colonialism, Opening of New Ways Towards Social Progress

1. Contemporary Approach to the Study of the Theory of Emergence and Evolution of Socialism. Relativity of Historical Truth

We are living now in times of great economic, technological, social and cultural changes; many of whom will fail to be integrated in the memory of the future. We have entered he 21st century, the century of informational and bio-technological revolution, which brings changes not only in the technological production system, in the social relations, but as well in the relation of human beings to nature, to their peers, and in our theories on the past, the present and the future.

We are stepping into the 21st century with great expectations for our future, for the future of our children, grand-children and great-grand-children. Nevertheless, what kinds of future are we talking about, a future which, first of all, we do not know appropriately? Yes, that's right; we are not familiar enough with our future. Yes, we wish to learn more about the kind of age that may come, not by simple curiosity, but out of the anthropological yearning of human beings to consciously build up their own becoming, that is the common future of the entire society. Such a future can not be projected blindly, on plain sand, in the absence of the knowledge of the past, of our historical, anthropological and ideological roots, lacking the knowledge of our errors and failures, with no knowledge and mastery of the economic and social laws of evolution.

"The forces acting in society, wrote Engels, act as natural forces: blindly, brutally and destructively, as long as we lack in their knowledge. When we come to understand their actions, directions, effects, and then it is up to us to subject them more and more to our own will and, with their help, to achieve our goals."[1]

Knowledge of the blind forces of economic and social development in the present stage of capitalism, of neo-colonialism, their taming and submitting to our common will, in view of the liberation from exploitation, alienation and poverty, the erection of a new socialist society and the diverse blooming of mankind, such are the main goals of my paper.

It is not the fruit of the research of the huge literature on social processes which, certainly, is the working base of my considerations. It did not come out of a comparative summary of the vast material needed for making up such a study and which is also one of the sources of my research work. It results from my own scientific research work of the authenticity of the real processes of social reality in observing the developed Middle East, the underdeveloped South and the developed West.

My research in the great laboratory of social conflicts in the second half of the 20th and the early 21st centuries made me understand that the great turns of civilisation changed certain general principles of socialism into obsolete concepts, relegated to the history museum, since the informational and bio-technological revolution alter the circumstances of their emergence. Such process does not encompass the universal theories, as defined by Smith, Ricardo, Marx, Engels, Lenin and Keynes.

If now-a-days we are witnessing strong remainders of the ancient, presently disappearing social relations, in the coming 50 years the new generations will learn about the traces of their existence from school books. And, while attempting to envision our future over the next 100 years, we are overwhelmed by confusion, uncertainty and doubts on our capacity to project at least approximately realistic predictions.

However, scientists and exponents have been forever trying to project the future more or less successfully, starting from the existence of written civilisations. Therefore, my attempt will be no exception, but rather the general law of social science evolution. To implement our wishes and intentions which, in fact, may be lacking in perfection, we will have to start with a critical analysis of the emergence roots of socialism, as a concept, as a movement, and to pursue this analysis up to its embodiment in the social relations, so as to let us set up our theory on the future based on such critical assertions.

According to the general theory, socialism has its roots in the utopian socialism of Robert Owen, Saint Simon, Charles Fourrier, Campanella, Tchernychevski and other famous (or less famous) philosophers of the utopian socialism, emerged from the incipient capitalism of the second half of the 18th century and the first half of the 19th century. Such theories are but partly verified, because the present evaluation of old time historical processes is quite relative to a great extent, except for the great eternal historical truth. The great leaps forward of science and technology always throw a new light not only on the present and future changes, but also on the interpretation of our past, meaning that the extent of the historical research is getting ever wider and deeper, so as to impart to our knowledge new values and new references from the past, as a part of the dynamics of our present and future.

The great French sociologist and philosopher Raymond Aron explained in his scientific interpretation essays on the limitations of historical objectivity: "Do we think now that the science of history, as such, may escape all relativity? It seems, however, that there still remains a factor of renewal: the present situation, which dictates the organisation of the past, often imparts a new value to the old results, at the same time as finding a new place to occupy in building up knowledge."[2]

Therefore, if we intend to stay within the scope of the objectivity of our ideas, in the analysis of the history and the theory of the emergence and evolution of socialism, we have to update the social processes, our concepts on the research in the field of the historical roots of socialism, in connection with the new dimensions of social knowledge. Yet, it is true that utopian socialism came forth as a result of the industrial revolution, of the emergence and development of early capitalism.

However, it is equally true that the natural, historical roots of its primary constitutive elements reside in the anthropological formation of the primitive community, in the philosophical processing of the ancient Oriental social progress and in the Christian, Buddhist and Islamic theological socialism.

Exceeding the narrow European area of the emergence origins of socialism, in order to integrate the history of our civilisation on the road of great changes, we attempt to disclose new prospects on the historical roots of the diversity of social progress on the way of worldwide revival and globalisation of socialism.

Moreover, the relative character of historical truth imposes the need of rather entirely, not partially reconstructing the capabilities and limitations of Marxism and social-democracy, so as to open a new outlook on our future and on that on our children and grand-children.

2. Scientific Socialism, Strong Points and Limitations of Marxism and Social-Democracy

(a) Strong Points and Limitations of Marxism

The gradual transition of social concepts, theories and movements from utopian socialism to scientific socialism is the stepping stone for a historical turn in the evolution of our civilisation. The founders of the scientific socialism, Marx and Engels, have instilled to the utopian visions of their predecessors the scientific spirit resulted from reality and perpetual changes. Thus, they offered the working class the ideological weapon in their struggle for liberation from exploitation, alienation and poverty.

For more than 150 years, the revolutionary ideas of Marxism have inspired and led the progressive humans on the path of breaking free from ancient social relations. In this time span, Marxism advanced on the ascending road of attracting the conscience of world estranged subjects and marked achievements unprecedented by any other ideology in history.

In his book "Karl Marx or the Spirit of the World", Jacques Attali, one of the most proficient French analysts, wrote: "No author had more readers, no revolutionary produced more reports, nor, except a few founders of religions, did any other man exert upon the world such influence as Karl Marx in the 20th century."[3]

However, in its ascending spiral, like any other process of social development, Marxism has known low tide as well. In the 1990s, after the failure of totalitarianism in the former Soviet Union and in the countries of Eastern Europe, Marxism survived in retreat. The left-wing political parties and their political leaders, confused by the failure of totalitarian socialism, referred less and less to Marxism. After the dissolution of the totalitarian regime in the former USSR and the Eastern European countries, the ideology of the ruling class and its powerful machinery for moulding public opinion made ever more reference to the decay and extinction of Marxism.

How much of it is true and how much is false?

Which is and which can be the relations of political parties and of left-wing political movements with Marxism?

We are in no position to issue any answer to this question, without a previous brief examination of the way Marxism understands life. If we see Marxism as a Biblical doctrine and a glorification of its predictions, then its critics are truthfully right. Nevertheless, the present day scientific theory of Marxism totally contradicts its glorification. As per the doctrine of Marx and Engels, Marxism represents the scientific critical theory of capitalism, a doctrine that defines the laws of evolution of capitalism and replaces the latter by a new social order – the socialism, as an inferior stage of communism.

Marxism is not exclusively a philosophical or economic doctrine or just a social-political one with respect to the evolution of society. Marxism represents the only doctrine in the world which encompasses almost every social science.

According to the Robert Dictionary, Marxism is the "Philosophical doctrine (dialectical materialism), social doctrine (historical materialism) and economic doctrine worked out by Karl Marx, Friedrich Engels and their followers".[4]

Having the doctrinary understanding of Marxism as a starting point, Miladin Korac, a former Yugoslav professor of political economy, wrote: "Marxism, in its widest sense, as a unique outlook on the world, represents the complex investigation method of social reality and human thinking, the method of revolutionary transformation of society ...".[5]

However, in the evaluation of Marxism, of its historical values, we have to go beyond the methodological and practical estimation of its dimensions. We have to reassert its essentially universal philosophical, sociological and anthropological values, precisely those dimensions that touch the humane character of the human race, its psychology, conscience, spirit, ethics and great expectations for a better future. That hope, which is the last to die, that hope which keeps us alive, which makes us more resilient, as an anthropological dimension of the human race, our hope in a better future, as outlined by Marxism, this is the unbreakable social and human force which becomes the main catalyst of social progress.

In his characterisation of the essential universal values of Marxism, Jacques Barros wrote: "Marxism is a vision of the world, a global reflection on the human beings and their place and role in life. It is that which the Germans name "Weltanschauung", the Greek "theory" and which I would define as "existentialism", would this term not have been already employed in a different meaning; to cut it short, it is a reflection on the essential, a system that explains and combines with the adventure of life and the destiny of mankind."[6]

This means, ipso facto, that Marxism is not a common formula for the erection of a future socialist society, nor a utopian (imaginary) structure of a never before existing society. Marx set the human being in a crucial position in his early works (as late as 1936), printed under the title "Manuscripts of 1844". He says that man should be in the centre of every social analysis and political action, of humane and anthropological dimensions of social progress. "Communism is the natural way of life of man", "a compendium of the entirety of human passions and typical features."[7]

Still, wrote Marx, communism does not originate from the ideas and concepts of thinkers, philosophers, economists and sociologists, but rather from real social progress. Therefore, the construction of the future and its final processing for all times is no concern of them. What the founders of scientific socialism have conceived is a ruthless criticism of all which is in existence. From the general criticism of the actual situation at that time of capitalism still under way of formation, Marx and Engels projected solely the fundamental outlines of the progress of the future society. Their scientific discoveries were restricted to the given times. Therefore, just as any other social science, Marxism has its historical limitations.

By setting the historical limitations of Marxism, our considerations lead us to the answer to an overall basic question on the historical limitations of sciences generally, not of social sciences alone. The question is whether the scientific truth, generally, not the social sciences alone, but the exact sciences as well, is finally objective or do our discoveries and knowledge evolve depending on the evolution and development of the human mind, in connection with the evolution and development of our capacity of knowledge?

There is a single objective answer. Nothing lasts forever, except the constantly changing matter. Consequently, there is no final reality, there is only the historical truth. Science as such is a historical category under perpetual movement and change. "If historical truth were final, wrote Antonio Gramsci, science would have ceased to exist as such, as research, as novel experience, and scientific activity would have been reduced to the disclosure of what had already been discovered. Which is far from being true, for the good of science."[8]

Present day scientology, this science of sciences, makes us understand the difference between exact sciences, which discover the universal laws of the movement of matter and the social sciences, of which certain discoveries have more than universal character alone, but also the limitations of a certain age, of a certain time.

That is why, in the name of dialectical Marxism, of scientology and historical verity, we will attempt to make a synthesis of these principles of Marxism which, in those times, were a reflection of actual development, of social progress and which, because of the present social progress, are replaced with the new ones. Not raising any claim to be exhaustive, now-a-days, more than 150 years after Marxism has been proven in practice, we may state that some of its basic concepts are outdated. The principles stating the inception of the socialist revolution first of all in the developed countries, rather than in the underdeveloped ones, the concept of the need for a violent revolution and for the establishment of the dictatorship of the proletariat, the concept of the downfall of the old state institutions and their replacement with new ones, the concept of the consolidation of the executive, legislative and judiciary powers into one united force, the idea of the complete nationalisation of the main production means in the primary sector and of the collectivisation of agriculture in the secondary sector, as well as other less important concepts, have disappeared in the flood of history a long time ago.

The evolution of the social progress has shown us the limitations of Marxism, the need of its restructuring and updating and, at the same time, the need to investigate the new roads of social evolution in the spirit of Marxism; thus, we are denying such obsolete principles and we concentrate on the assertion and scientific concentration of the new concepts risen from the buds of their practical implementation and proving in the society. The new phenomena and processes of social progress must be concentrated and, meanwhile, the diversity of circumstances will be the tireless source of the moulding and expansion of scientific socialism.

(b) From Democratic Socialism to the Crossroads Between Surrendering Reformism and Revolutionary Evolutionism

The capital issue of the international left-wing movement is to find out whether Marxism remains the starting point of our ideology or if, after all, we should forsake it and replace it by a new, not yet existing philosophy. This central issue is somewhat dividing the socialist and communist, the Marxist and non-Marxist movements. Most of the communist, socialist and working-class leaders declare that they do not accept the reformist ideas, although they swallow some of the pills of the European social-democracy.

Generally, all of them tend to converge again, on different ways, around the same goals. If we see Marxism as a Biblical philosophy, then Marxism has outlived its time and has no future at all. If Marxism is considered as the starting point of our ideology, a starting point of the working-class and the socialist movement, then it means that, in the galaxy of all other left-wing philosophies, Marxism still has an important influence on the evolution of social progress. But for how much longer? The practical implementation alone, in the actual society, will be able to give a certain answer to this issue.

In the actual combat between Marxism and social-democracy on a number of issues relating to the paths of social progress, history has passed once again a judgement in favon of social-democracy. In the developed countries of the West, in the emerging countries of the East and the underdeveloped ones of the South, the ways of social progress, the roads to socialism, do not quite interlock with the Marxist principles concerning a series of issues of social progress, rather fitting with the concepts of social-democracy.

Consequently, reconsidering and revaluating their teachings, cleaned of the rust and dust of the opportunistic era, is not only a task for the politicians, but even more so of the ideologists of socialism especially.

The contemporary social-democracy is on the right way to get rid of the surrendering reformism and of the cosmetic reforms. It will follow the way of revolutionary evolutionism, so much cherished by Jean Jaurès, one the most famous politicians of the French left-wing movement.

Marxism and social-democracy have the same goals, but follow different ways they deem are granting them the possibility to reach those goals. These ways are the expressions of the pluralism of social progress.

Based on their understanding of the pluralism of left-wing ideologies, the international working-class, social-democratic, socialist and communist movements, as well as their ideological interpreters, undoubtedly will find, and practically find right now the right answers to the basic issues of social progress.

Social progress objectively follows its road to the future. Social sciences are entrusted with the task to discover new ways to an effective development and to place the ideological weapons in the hands of the political movements which, encompassing the conscience of people crowds, may evolve into the great material forces of social progress aiming towards reclaiming the ideal of social equality and justice, as well as of the general good and welfare of all socicty members.

3. Leninism, Stalinism and Totalitarian Socialism

(a) Leninism and Totalitarian Socialism

Unlike Marxism resulted from the developing capitalism, with certain fundamental principles having the universal character, Leninism resulted from feudalism and from emerging capitalism had an oriental Russian character. The attempts of the Russian schools to raise Leninism to a degree of universality similar to socialism and to show the twosome "Marxism-Leninism" as being the theoretical source of socialism are an expression of subjective interpretation and, at the same time, an expression of the wish to force the experience of one country alone to the international left-wing movements.

In his attempt of a creative implementation of Marxism within the specific Russian circumstances, Lenin, the great architect and guide of the October Revolution, as well as of the erection of the first Socialist State in the world, contributed to the development of Marxism but, to a certain extent, imprinted it with a dogmatic character, and developed a theory of socialism that did not always equal the essence of Marxist ideas, a theory which, in the age of Stalin, degenerated into a totalitarian system and in a Jacobinian dictatorship against those who were the great expectations of Marxism.

"Because Lenin had not appropriated the concept of social evolution, such as, interpreted by Marx, stated Vladislav Inozemtsev, Russian university professor, it would be naïve to assume that the Marxist doctrine of revolutions had been transposed suitably into the Leninist theory. Relentlessly pointing out the role of class struggle in the social evolution and the role of proletariat in the contemporary times, Lenin set up a doctrine of revolutions which is in clashing contradiction with Marx' ideas and he ignored the main principles relating to the causes and the very course of the social revolution."[9]

Based on his erroneous reading of certain principles of Marxism in the Russian background, and following his mechanical absorption of Marx' concepts on State and Revolution, on demolishing and destructing the old bourgeois state apparatus, Lenin destroyed the parliamentary system and replaced the constitutional state with the political state.

The fact is well known that, after the October Revolution – when the state power structures were being organised – Lenin rejected the principle of bourgeois democracy, of the separation of the legislature, the executive and judicial powers of the state, principle proclaimed by the French philosopher and moralist Montesquieu (1689 – 1755) in his work "The Spirit of the Laws" as the driving force of economical management, a barrier against the revival of whatever form of dictatorship. Thus, Lenin opened the way to the great tragedy of socialism – the establishment of totalitarianism and absolutism, of the dictatorship of one individual and, under the most fortunate circumstances, the dictatorship of a very narrow elite group of the communist party.

This means that, in the end, Lenin replaced the democratic constitutional state with the political state of a total autarchy where the political bureau, that was in fact a group of extremely dedicated revolutionaries, were taking all decisions in the name of the working class, in the name of the people. Rosa Luxemburg criticised the limitation of the democratic principles by Lenin and wrote in her work "The Russian Revolution": "The political life is retreating more and more to the top; some dozens party leaders are directing and ordering with inexhaustible energy and unlimited ideals. The leadership of public life lies, practically, in the hands of about 10 individuals with outstanding intelligence, while the elite of the working class is summoned now and then to gather and applaud the words of the leaders and to simply vote what they are submitted to examine. This is the government of a clan, a true dictatorship of the politicians, and not at all the dictatorship of the proletariat, in other words, the dictatorship in bourgeois sense, in the sense of Jacobinian dictatorship."[10]

Before his death, Lenin admitted that the greatest peril lurking for the evolution of socialism in the Soviet society was the bureaucracy of the political leaders. In Lenin's opinion, "our greatest inner enemy is the communist bureaucrat, who detains a place of responsibility in our Soviet apparatus and who enjoys general respect, just as an upright person ... . He has not learned to fight bureaucracy and, therefore, ignores, it." This is why Lenin began to erect the new principles of socialist democracy, which "would protect the proletariat against the aggression of its own state" and "its own bureaucracy" which was materialising in the form of a "new bourgeoisie".[11]

In his last battle intended to determine the selection of his successor, Lenin realised the danger of the election of Stalin, whom he had supported himself during his time of sickness, in order to take over the leadership of the party, the state and the revolution. In the post-script to his letter dated December 23-24, 1922, Lenin was expressing his doubts on the selection of Stalin. "Stalin is too rough, and this flaw, acceptable in our mutual relations among the communists, becomes unbearable in his position as the Secretary General. Therefore, I would suggest the candidates to ponder on Stalin's displacement from this position and on the designation instead of a person superior to him in every respect, more patient, more sincere, more polite, and showing more respect to his comrades, less impulsive, etc."[12]

But it was already too late. Lenin died after a severe illness, at the age of 53, in January 1924, not later than four years after the end of the civil war and the victory of the Revolution, just when he would have been needed the most. Shakespeare was right when he wrote in his "Hamlet": "There are more things in heaven and earth, Horatio, than are dreamt of in your philosophy." We can say that Lenin was not completely innocent and flawless in the creation of an economical system which did not justify by all its components the expectations of the Great Socialist October Revolution.

Contrary to the Marxist theory of gradual dismembering of the state, of administration decentralisation and of social self-management of associated producers, Lenin saw in the aggregation of state ownership, in the excessive centralisation of accumulation in the hands of the State, the only way to lay down the economic basis of socialism. The rejection of the postulate of the Russian working class opposition regarding the management of industries by the unions and the implementation of Marx concept, relating to the self-management of the associated producers, had dire effects on the future condition of socialism.

Therefore, when we try to point out to our readers certain practical and ideological failures of Leninism, we have by no means the intent to diminish Vladimir Ilyich Lenin's crucial historical role as a pragmatic political leader, architect and theoretician of the great October Revolution, founder of the first and the greatest socialist state in the world. Lenin was the pioneer of the age of socialist revolutions. "Lenin was thus a political genius, the inventor of the means to change a utopia into a State with claims to universality ...", writes Hélène Carrère d'Encausses, member of the French Academy of Science. "He transformed his dream into reality and his success, which does not motivate any of the tragedies inherent in Leninistic activity, is nevertheless worth of an exceptional place in the history of this century."[13]

However, although they acknowledge the historical merits of certain outstanding personalities, the researchers of the evolution of social progress should know – and undoubtedly know very well – that, in their attempt to discover the objective historical truth, they have to apply the universal law of evaluating the role of personalities in history, according to which the merits for social progress depend on the type and amount of their mistakes and the failures are proportional to the achievement or failure of their actions.

(b) Stalinism, the Gory Jacobinian Dictatorship

As a political and ideological leader, Stalin did by far not equal Lenin's quality and subtleness and even less the latter's capacity as a dialectician to understand the course of history in due time. He was an able organiser and a great Machiavellian, tyrannical captain, capable to protect his ideas with violent arguments, to secure his power by hypocrisy and physical erasing his opponents. Stalin was not clever enough to understand his errors at the right moment and, particularly, to correct them. In his time, Cicero wrote that all humans may err, but only the stupid would persist in their errors. If he were still alive, he probably would have added: to persist in one's errors and to die with them! Lacking all critical outlook, Stalin embraced some of Lenin's strategic errors or certain concepts bearing for a while the mark of that era, but which had to be altered later on, and so he imprinted in Leninism a dogmatic character and raised it to the level of an ideological screen for the achievement of his own, very simplistic and rudimentary vision of socialism. Stalinism, which altered Marxism-Leninism in accordance with pragmatic needs of a determined historical period of time, represents the political expression of the dictatorship of the bureaucratic elite in power position, as well as the transformation of the dictatorship of the proletariat into a Jacobinian dictatorship, directed, on the one hand, against the overthrown classes, and also against all those who, in their memory, in their ethics and actions, foster great expectations for the liberation from submission and dominance relations.

Stalin's greatest strategic error was his concept of the express transition from capitalism to socialism by means of full nationalisation and forcible collectivisation over a very short period of time, nearly 16 years, and the proclamation of the full and final victory of socialism in 1936. This is a totally wrong interpretation of Marxism, of the methods, forms and stages of emergence and development of socialism.

In the transition age from feudalism to capitalism, in its time of emergence and evolution, the early capitalism needed 350 years to reach the moment when its victory could be announced, namely after the French Revolution of 1789, and some 100 years more to reach the stage of developed capitalism.

In order to achieve the transition from one type of ownership to a completely different type of property, the young socialism under way of emergence. would have required a transition period of some 100 years and probably some 50-70 years more to advance to the stage of developed socialism.

It is true that every new society is developing faster than the old one. However, it is equally true that the erection of a new society by violence, during an express 16 years period, is automatically doomed to disappear. Based on his reading of the proletariat dictatorship as a blood thirsty tyranny, Stalin annihilates economic democracy in industries and political democracy in society.

Later on, under the colours of the theory of class struggle escalation in correspondence to the onslaught of socialism in the process of forcible collectivisation, he sharpened the cutting sword of dictatorship aiming at the democratic and liberal part of civil society.

Consequently, the mark of a class enemy was stamped on part of the citizens, employees, officers, middle-class peasantry, democratic scholars, honest and well meaning people, who, because their thinking was different than that of the party, were thrown in prisons and concentration camps, the horrors of which are beyond the comprehension of normal human mind and the atrocities of which have been revealed to the public by the renowned Russian writer Alexandr Solzhenitsyn.

It will remain always an open question how many innocent victims had to suffer in the period of forcible collectivisation, of the "escalation of class struggle" and "victory of socialism". Some day, history will enlighten us on this issue. The number of victims ranges from several hundred thousand to several million. Western propaganda speaks about a range of up to 20 million people. But history does not measure the numbers of ratio of the fallen victims, but rather the very action of intentional and mass-wise annihilation of an innocent population in the name of Revolution and Socialism. The gruelling truth about Stalin's terrorism and totalitarian tyranny, about the one and single party and dictatorship, was kept hidden for quite a long while both to the citizens of the Soviet Union and to the entire international socialist and communist working-class movement, which had put their faith and hopes in the historical, humanitarian and liberating mission of the first socialist country.

The early truthful messages about the Soviet Union, Stalinism and totalitarian tyranny broke out in 1936, when Leon Trotsky, expelled from the USSR, published abroad his book "The Betrayed Revolution". With a lot of details and theoretical analysis of the core and prospects of totalitarian tyranny, he unveiled to the international socialist and communist working-class movement, to the general public, Stalin's deviation from the road of humanism, from the Marxist thinking line, Stalin's betrayal of the enormous hopes and ideals of the October revolution.

Describing the history of the birth and evolution of totalitarianism as the boundless domination of the Soviet bureaucracy, Trotsky wrote that by means of the merger of the party and the State, Stalin had "created the present totalitarian regime and as such Stalin's victory was ensured by his final service rendered to bureaucracy".[14]

Further, Trotsky goes on: "Disguised by the new judicial norms ... the 'socialist' bureaucracy, this revolting contradiction in objection to this horrendous and ever increasing social outgrowth which, in turn, becomes the cause of pernicious fever of the society, reveals its obvious prevailing in economic life."[15] That is to say that it is rather Leon Trotsky, than Mikhail Gorbachev, the one who discovered the need for a "second revolution against bureaucratic absolutism".[16]

After the 'Trotskyst' deciphering of Stalinism, hundreds of books, essays, criticism were written on Stalinism as a ferocious totalitarian dictatorship of the bureaucratic aristocracy, as a realm of concentration camps and political terror, fact that was objectively justified – instead, no exhaustive survey on Stalinism has yet been published, because the events are still quite near in historical time and therefore not enough far away in the past to allow historical truth to settle. However, the moment of revealing the **complete, not partial truth** is gradually nearing its peak.

In my book with the title "Positive Criticism of Socialism", written and published in Romania by the publishing house Samizdat in 1977, several years after the invasion of Czechoslovakia by the soviet tanks, I tried to render an interpretation of the criticism of Stalinism going beyond the totalitarian terrorism (which is more complex and does not touch the totalitarian superstructure, but particularly the economic foundation shaped in totalitarian moulds).

Then, 30 years later, I could see that my estimate on Stalinism was incomplete, because of my total lack of documentary sources– on the one hand, and – on the other hand – of the short distance in historical time, inadequate for a complete estimation.

At present, time seems ripe enough for a full evaluation of Stalinism. Stalinism resides not only in the tyranny of one individual, and even less only in the smothering of the basic political rights of men, in prisons and concentration camps.

Stalinism is a much more complex phenomenon. We are facing the expression of the smothering of the contradictions between the economic foundation and the social super-structure; the entire political, economic and social system of the Euro-Asian soviet state socialism, which had to pay for the historical benefit of implementing the socialist revolution by discovering new ways designed to compensate the detriments generated by economic decline and geo-political isolation.

Although we condemn the political leaders as bearers of the negative features of totalitarianism and soviet socialism, we should not consider, we are not entitled to condemn the great majority of the members of the Communist Party of the Soviet Union, of the left-wing parties of the other socialist countries around the world, the majority of their citizens who, with much dedication, and with great expectations, erected socialism, forged their future and the that of their children.

Never throughout the history of peoples, nations and states, shall the populations of these smaller or larger countries accept the responsibility for the historical failures, errors and atrocities of their leaders. This is the basic ethics of history.

4. Post-Stalinism, Reformism and Socialist Opportunism

(a) Stalin's Death and the Prelude to the New Look of Socialism, Thanks to Malenkov

After Stalin's demise in March 1953 and thereafter the most pompous funeral ceremony mankind had ever witnessed, since the pharaohic rituals, a ceremony arranged under the supervision of Nikita Khrushchev, member of the political bureau of the party, some of the most rational politicians of the soviet civil society were hoping for a new period of easing from the straightjacket of the state, a period of communication and free circulation of the citizens, a period of great structural social reforms.

The soviet citizens, members of the party and the unions, as well as the members of the left-wing political parties from abroad, and many other individuals with leftist thinking were nurturing great expectations in a new generation of young soviet leaders, who were quite sparsely represented in the Political Bureau of the party.

As in every monarchy or in totalitarian systems, the fate of the soviet society was concentrated at the top of the family clan of the power pyramid, in the hands of the Political Bureau of the party, which consisted of about ten potential heirs, claimers of the marshal baton in one of the most powerful states of the then world.

In his discussions with his assistants, noted by the historical archives, Stalin pondered on his succession a number of times. Exhausted by the civil war, by the violent collectivisation, by the industrialisation, by the Second World War, which he ended as a victor, but sensing his nearing end, it seems that Stalin prepared his heir in the person of the very bright young Malenkov; however, Malenkov was also a very obedient character, who had known a quick rise of his political career. From his position as a private secretary to Stalin in 1932, from a member of the Central Committee in 1939, from a candidate to the position of a member of the Political Bureau in 1941, at the age of 44 Malenkov had risen to the position of a full member of the Political Bureau in 1946. He was the youngest Politbureau member. He was the image of the hopes and expectations of the new generation.

Nevertheless, the concealed ambition of Nikita Khrushchev, ex-miner and secretary of the Central Committee of the Ukraine, member of the Political Bureau of the Communist Party of the Soviet Union, a man of primitive education, but of native intelligence, to become the top leader of the Soviet Union guided the course of this country on a different direction.

After the death of Stalin, under the ideological pretense of the "collective management", very trendy at that time, Khrushchev split the vacant chair in two, one half for Malenkov as President of the Supreme Soviet, and the other half, the most important one, for himself, as General Secretary of the party. After much manipulation inside the Political Bureau of the party, Khrushchev's magic wand had the fast effects of a great deception.

It is true that, after Stalin's death, Malenkov, as President of the Supreme Soviet, started radical economic, social and cultural reforms which, two years later, imparted to the soviet socialism the right to potential new changes. The truth is that the "failure of the agrarian reforms" was nothing more than a subject repeatedly mentioned by Khrushchev in order to push away Malenkov, in view of taking over every position, as the head of the state, of the Supreme Soviet, of the party and the army.

Henry Shapiro is the American journalist and analyst of the soviet transformation who, in his 20 years of newspaper career, became quite familiar with the circumstances of the soviet world, that had survived the New Economic Policy (NEP), the collectivisation and industrialisation, as well as the extensive cleaning of the party and the extermination of the army cadres between 1930 and 1940, until the beginning of the cold war. He was the first to open the black box of post-Stalinism. In his book "The USSR after Stalin", Shapiro states:

"Stalin's death liberated the initiative and energy of the people around him. For many years, these people had been arduously striving for a necessary change."

"In the year following Stalin's death, the regime of Malenkov embarked so deeply in a policy of internal reforms, that any turnaround would have caused a disaster."

"There was no economic, political or cultural area where the 'New Look' policy was not obvious."

"36 years after the Bolshevik revolution, the Soviet Union entered a new age, which could drastically change the character of the country over the following years."[17]

But, unfortunately, Nikita Khrushchev, under the pretense of the "failure of the agrarian reforms", dismissed Malenkov, just to take over all the leading positions as a head of the state, the Supreme Soviet, the party and the army.

(b) The Khrushchev and Brezhnev Cocktail of de-Stalinisation and Lame Reforms

History has not always had a casual course, in the direction desired by the greatest part of the society. Khrushchev's ascension to power caused an important change of the social course of evolution and slowed down the dynamics of the profound social reforms. Certainly, Khrushchev's huge historical merit consists in the fact that, in 1956, at the 20th Congress of the Communist Party of the Soviet Union, in his secret report, he revealed "Stalin's personality cult" and disclosed to the national and international public the overpowering terrorism, the physical annihilation of 70% of the members of the Central Committee of the party, of thousands of military and local political leaders and of several million innocent people in prisons and concentration camps. However, it is equally true that, except for the spoken criticism of Stalinism, of the dissolution of the greatest part of the concentration camps and the easing of the strangling belt of police terror, Khrushchev did not touch the economic, political, sociological and ideological foundations of Stalinism, as would have been desirable.

Considering that Stalinism – just to revert to my thesis – does not mean concentration camps and physical and moral terrorism alone – it is in fact an extended economic system that involves also completely the social and bureaucratic relations, the production, exchange and distribution relations; it is an alienating system that pulls society apart from its own production means, a system of estrangement from social management and self-management. Moreover, we may refer to an entire political and state system aiming at the complete subordination of the society to the decisions and will of a minority, a system of feudal dependence of people from their mentors and from their very own human place and vital space. The mobility of labour and the free circulation of people were frozen in the glaciers of totalitarian tyranny.

After a cocktail of partial de-Stalinisation, of reformism, opportunism and recklessness, Khrushchev was eventually dismissed, without much ado or comments. Upon the decision of the Political Bureau of the Party, not based on free elections, in his place was appointed Brezhnev, marshal of the Soviet Union, President of the Supreme Council of the USSR and member of the Political Bureau of the party at that time. More inclined towards the military, towards practical action, rather than to reformism and de-Stalinisation, this new political leader pursued, by erasing reckless adventurism, a conservatory and neo-Stalinian strategy of his own.

Brezhnev introduced more stability, consistency in the domestic and foreign soviet policy, and much less de-

Stalinisation and less radical economic and social reforms.

The great number of lame economic and social reforms is no more than a sign of the fact that the shadow of Stalinism had been present for more than 30 years in the Khrushchevian memory and actions and, even more so, in the memory of their successor, Leonid Brezhnev.

In my summarising investigation of the past of soviet socialism, I have no intention to linger on a detailed evaluation of an historical period, the explanation of which has not been yet completed by the Marxist historiographers.

Only a unique and objective evaluation of the history of the Soviet Union, of the errors and deviations of its leaders, as well as of its positive components during and after the Stalinist era, would be able to bring socialism on the way to social progress.

Some historians who study the Khrushchev and the Brezhnev times and who want to uphold their reputation as objective scientists, describe the 30 years of the domination period of the two leaders above as the time of dogmatic implementation of Marxism and Leninism in a new economic and social environment. According to certain researchers, dogmatism seemed to be brake for the social system, but it was not as much equal to a deviation from the ideological lines of Marxism, than rather an expression of Marxism being transformed into some kind of undisputable religion. Although it produced an entire structure of constraints for the social progress and of cosmetic adjustments of this system by the replacement of the worn-out components of the social machinery by means of shallow reforms of the system, a certain stage of its assertion, dogmatism changed into reformism and opportunism.

Opportunism, mistaken for an ideological and political trend in the socialist and communist working-class movement, is neither the exclusive privilege, nor the monopoly of certain western social-democratic leaders. In turn, the actual eastern socialism is not exempt from reformism and opportunism. As long as advanced left-wing movements will continue to exist in the world, then in the West, in the East and in the South too there will be certain trends to opportunism – more or less obvious.

It is the task of the historians to find the right place where reformism and opportunism of the Khrushchev and Brezhnev era belong to, as opposed to social progress, as new forms of opportunism – the socialist opportunism.

(c) System Crisis in the USSR

When we analyse the 30 years of reformism, we can not consider this period as an era of total stagnation. We are neither radical opponents, nor fanatic supporters of social development. Despite the more and more difficult circumstances of the older social relations, the Soviet Union marked during that period certain positive results in point of extent in the development of the production forces of society. The GNP multiplied 4.5 times, the industrial production about 6 times, the agricultural production increased by 67%. The number of workers rose from 45 million to 115 million people. And it was just this fast increase of the production forces which asked objectively – mutatis mutandis – for certain appropriate changes in the social relations, in the production, exchange and distribution relations. The partial social and economic reforms were not able to terminate, nor reduce the negative effect of the slowing down economic increase. The soviet economic machinery had already started to break down in the eighties. The yearly increase rate of the industrial production dropped from 8.44% in 1966-1970 to 7.46% in 1971-1975 and to 4.38% in 1976-1980, to sink to 2.4% in 1981-1985.[18]

Over a period of 15 years (1967 – 1982), the yearly expansion of the light industry, the food industry and the farming industry – the foundation of the rising of the living conditions – has known a 2.8% increase and, considering the rising number of population, the yearly rate decreased to 0.53%.[19] From that time on, the symptoms of the nearing social hurricane became obvious.

The Soviet Union was flooded by a deep economic, structural and social system crisis; a total change of system was necessary.

My short analysis of the times of the Khrushchev and Brezhnev regimes allows us to conclude on certain indications of the possible social evolution directions that were not implemented. The political leaders of rudimentary and totalitarian socialism should have taken a completely different direction in view of achieving a social evolution. Besides holding on to certain benefits of the public property system, to the centralisation up to an optimal limit of resource accumulation and allotment, which helped for the maintaining of a high increase rate of production, culture and social safety, they should have also used every advantage of the western liberal economy, of the benefits offered by management, by the rational economic management, by competition and the free action of economic laws, by the partial privatisation and the coexistence with a multi-sector economy, in order to allow new ways of social salvage and evolution to be reopened.

The new evolution directions of socialism, as discovered meanwhile by the Chinese, the Vietnamese, the Yugoslavs, the Poles and Czechs and by many leaders of the left-wing movements, have become parameters of the social evolution, of the potential revival of socialism.

5. Breakdown of Totalitarianism, Metastasis of Imperialism, End of Neo-Colonialism – Launching of New Ways to Social Progress

(a) Gorbachevism and Destruction of Totalitarianism

After the death of Brezhnev in 1982 and the promotion to the peak of the Party and State pyramid of Yuri Vladimirovich Andropov, a more open-minded individual, with more daring views on social progress, the great game of radical reforms of the outdated social system.

Because he was very ill, Andropov did not survive the implementation of his profound reform project.

After Andropov's death in February 1984 and the demise of his successor Konstantin Chernenko in March 1985, Gorbachev pushed on up to the very top of Mount Olympus with the help of the old Stalinist guard. It is true that Gorbachev was endowed with all the attributes of a prospective leader: young, charismatic, excellent speaker and at the same time extremely ambition-driven to take over the relay of the radical reforms emerging from Andropov's "incubator of the perestroika" and to lead socialism on the way of freedom, democracy and humanism.

The new team of young political leaders understood at the right time the full danger of the chaos and violent storm nearing from the depths of soviet society. And precisely for this reason, Gorbachev, who was not lacking the instinct of the compulsory destruction of the ancient obstacles of the system, harboured under the umbrella of the highest ranking party structures, prepared his programme for the radical change and rebuilding of socialism, under the designation of "perestroika".

In his book entitled "Perestroika", published in the United States and in France in 1987, respectively 1988, Mikhail Gorbachev wrote: "The urgent need to proceed to the perestroika derives from the deep development processes under way of preparation in our socialist society. This is ripe and ready for change; for a long time, society has had a great desire for a change. Any delay in the implementation of the perestroika would risk to trigger an aggravated domestic situation in the near future, which, to put it clearly, would be marked by serious crises in the social, economic and political area."[20]

If, for a while, we do ignore Gorbachev's weak spot, namely his idolatry for the USA, for the West, and if we take a look at the main objectives of the domestic reforms, we may think that Gorbachev had the most sincere intentions for the revival of socialism, and that the roads he had chosen for his strategy were opposed to the true demands of society.

Instead of taking on certain features of the Chinese and partially of the Czech, the Polish and the Yugoslav directions regarding the thorough economic reforms of the system, on the success of which depended the political reforms, instead of setting the economy and the economic laws free from totalitarianism and to follow the way of denationalisation of the state property, of partial privatisation of small and medium companies and of returning the non-profitable cooperatives to their owners, instead of developing the light and the food industries that were lagging behind and to supply the market with consumer goods, to revive the living standards of the population and to open new spaces for the social market economy and for the economic democracy, instead of all that, Gorbachev chose to tread towards the reverse direction. He opened prematurely, in the widest way possible, the unlimited spaces of the multiparty democracy. He demolished the important pillars of the state and party system, before establishing the new mechanism of economic democracy. Hence, the social construction began to crumble like a house of cards. The country was quickly overtaken by anarchy, chaos, power struggle, general corruption. The archaic concept of the invisible hands of the market triggered the debacle of the economy. The hurricane announcing the downfall of socialism was lurking over the horizon.

Under such completely novel circumstances – consisting of the nearing catastrophe and the dissolution of the totalitarian tyranny, and also of the achievements of socialism – a new opposition began to rise against the Gorbachevian regime.

The main cadre forces of the party asked for the destitution of hesitant and unpredictable Gorbachev from every position of responsibility. Four hundred and twenty regional party organisations asked for his replacement with a person more energetic in exercising authority and able to save the country out of the precipice and dissolution.

From the rostrum of the Supreme Soviet, Pavlov, the President of the Government, requested from the deputies part of the presidential prerogatives so that he be entitled to take urgent salvage measures of the Soviet Union and of socialism. The Vice-President of the Republic, Ianjev, the Minister of Internal Affairs Pugo, Kryuchkov, head of the powerful KGB, Balkanov – king of the military industrial complex, Gorbachev's cabinet director and many other prominent leaders strongly condemned Gorbachev's deviation from the true track of revival of socialism and, eventually, turned the weapons of verbal criticism into armed criticism. According to official version, on the 18th of August 1991, a group of political and military leaders attempted a military coup d'état to save the positive achievements of socialism.

(b) Yeltsinism and Its Actions for the Destruction of Socialism

According to several qualified analysts, the coup d'état was, in fact, a re-enactment of the Reichstag arson and of the annihilation of the resistance against the restoration of capitalism. The instigators of the coup d'état who fell in the entrapment of treason and were brought to justice and sentenced to forced labour. A thorough cleaning action of the state, military and political apparatus was done. It seemed obvious that the coup d'état was not the best way to rescue socialism, on the contrary, it caused the speeding up of the victory and the strengthening of Yeltsinism, the opening of every gate to the restoration of capitalism, as well as kissing up to the American strategy to subordinate Russia to the interests of multinational oligarchy.

After having been elected and after the coup d'état, Yeltsin's first concern was to go on an official visit to the US, with the aim to convince President Bush of his loyalty to the USA and of his determination to completely annihilate communism.

"Boris Yeltsin explained (to President Bush), wrote Eric Laurent in his book "The Collapse", that he wanted to transform Russia into a 'civilised nation that would find a place in the contemporary world' and that such a project should pass through the 'total removal of communism'. 'I will destroy the communist party in Russia', said he repeatedly. His argument fell somewhat to the ground since, according to one of Bush's aides, 'At his back, the President was thinking that Gorbachev wanted to reach the same goal.' "[21]

After the failure of the coup d'état and with the support of the soviet army generals and the political leaders of the USA and other western countries, Yeltsin, who had obtained the majority in the elections by populist promises to salvage Russia, became the President of the Russian Federation. He disbanded the USSR, forced Gorbachev to capitulate and, two years later, with the help of army tanks and cannons, just as Pinochet had done in Chile in the past, he demolished a part of the parliament and killed or arrested the last remains of the parliamentary opposition. This way, by steel and fire, he shattered the legal resistance against the restoration of the liberal economy.

It was the beginning of the most shameful period in the history of Russian civilisation. Yeltsinism was the time of restoration of capitalism, of moral degradation of Russia and the Russian nation on the international stage, the time of

Russia's total submission to the strategy of the IMF and the World Bank, which were the front for the American oligarchy. Yeltsin's policy favoured the generalised privatisation, the sale of the national riches to multinational companies at ridiculous prices, the time of dependence on foreign credits, of rising of the national bourgeoisie, the time of chaos, decreasing production and increasing unemployment and poverty.

This is how – despite its flaws of totalitarian tyranny, nationalism and rudimentary socialism – Russia, the second world power of that time, the international symbol of socialism, was forced to her knees before the World Bank and the IMF, like any other third-world republic.

The main purpose of the USA, the IMF and the World Bank, at the orders of the American financial oligarchy, after the destruction of the Soviet Union, was to hasten the collapse of the SU Eastern European satellites so as to open an immensely wide market of 400 million people with a financial capacity equalling that of the Latin-American market and, thus, to give a new impulse to the resolution of the domestic issues of the developed capitalist countries with regard to their sliding downwards or merely standing still economies. The then largest industrial complexes, the very pride of the soviet citizens, were sold out at preposterous prices to the foreign capital and the local mafia. The multinational companies bought key industries at laughable prices, destroyed part of them as scrap iron and opened thus a huge relief market for the developed capitalist states. This was the beginning of the extensive spoiling of the national riches, unprecedented in the history of peoples and nations. The Russian mafia exported from the country more than 850 billion US dollars of the national capital. Approximately ten multi-billionaires, in collusion with the authorities, with the underground mafia and the concealed corruption, dominated the social downfall.

The economic background of general looting of the national riches in co-operation with the state structures and the invasion of foreign capital were quite similar to the primitive capital accumulation in England and, a little later, all over Europe, in the late 18th century.

Hundred and fifty years after the above period we can see that, by breaking down the socialist barriers in the former USSR and the Eastern European countries, the contemporary capitalism of the international oligarchy achieved its last violent accumulation of capital.

The methods of the violent capital accumulation are the same, the consequences identical, but the area and means have shifted from the West to the East.

For several years, the production decreased yearly by up-to 7%, and the inflation attained two digit figures. More than 35% of the population lives below the poverty limit. The retired persons were the saddest victims of the ultimate capital accumulation. An army of over 20 million unemployed, homeless, beggars, alienated young people, all those were invading the streets of the great cities.

(c) Downfall of Totalitarian Regimes in the East European Countries

The collapse of totalitarian tyranny, the dissolution of the USSR and the beginning of the destruction of socialism hastened the collapse of totalitarian regimes and the successive annihilation of some of the basic pillars of socialism in most of the East-European countries.

In a two years time span, that is between 1989 and 1991, the popular protests and demonstrations in these countries cleared away the old compromising and unpopular regimes with incredible energy and at an unbelievable rate. The entire system began to crumble, like a sand castle.

In my interview given in December 1989 on the occasion of the collapse of the Ceau°escu regime I stated: "Foreign influences have always but a limited share in furthering a progressive movement or a revolution. No doubt that the Gorbachev effect played an important part in the creation of an entirely favourable environment, but the worsening of the system crisis and the aggravation of the internal contradictions of a certain country are always playing the crucial part. If the internal contradictions in Romania had not been ripe, no outside effect could have triggered the revolution. Fortunately for us, the two favourable elements converged."[22]

After the collapse of the totalitarian regimes in Poland, Romania, Eastern Germany, Czechoslovakia, Hungary, Bulgaria, Albania, and after the dismembering of Yugoslavia into six smaller states, in most of these countries democratic regimes of liberal type were installed by right and extreme right political forces. Only in Romania and Serbia the power was conquered by the leftist forces, via popular rebellion (in Romania) and democratic elections (in Serbia).

In Bosnia and Herzegovina, with a population formed of about 45% Serbs, 45% Muslims and 10% Croatians, and in Kosovo, with a population of 88% Muslims, 10% Serbs and 2% other nationalities, a terrible civil war broke out between Serbs and Muslims; it called for the lives of more than 200,000 people. In both cases, the civil war was ignited by the Serbian and Muslim right and extreme right political parties, which achieved a bloody transition to the liberal market economy.

The transition from totalitarian regime to liberal democracy, from a single party to pluralism, set the collective and individual forces and energies free from the right- and left-wing political forces.

Thus, a new site of democratic battle was opened between the left- and right-wing currents. The fact that the former socialist countries advanced to the transition period from socialism to liberal economy is practically the dispute between the onset of the emerging new capitalism and the declining socialism in the matter of economic system. As for their political orientation, the right-wing political forces in power want to enhance their influence on the voters, while the revived left-wing forces struggle for regaining hold on the civil society and the power. It is a long-lasting battle, extending probably over several decades, and the winner will not be the expectations in our minds, but instead the "reality imposed by the society".

(d) Metastasis of Imperialism, the End of Neo-Colonialism and the Transition to Socialism of the Peoples of Our Planet

Eighteen years have elapsed since the dissolution of totalitarian socialism in the former USSR and the East-European countries. In the time gone by, this small fragment of the contemporary world has changed radically. No politician, no economist, no sociologist, no futurologist were able to foresee the cardinal metamorphosis of the relations between capitalism and socialism in favour of the latter.

After the attempt to restore capitalism, Russia revived from the ruins and ashes and renewed her force and authority on the international stage.

Based on the implementation of essential economic reforms and on the transformation of public property and the reducing of bureaucracy, China and India have become the world's greatest potential economic forces, masters of the new emerging world. The economic community of the 12 independent countries, where Russia plays the part of the driving motor, has revived the area of the former USSR.

In certain countries, the comeback of the left-wing political parties, rejuvenated by the alternation to the power lost in the countries of Eastern Europe, represents another surprise in point of evolution of the world progressive movement.

While the newly emerging countries astonished the world with their high economic increase rates, by the social efficiency, by stability and vigour, the developed industrial countries were shaken by the financial crash and the deepest economic and social crisis since the 1929 disaster. Analysts are talking more and more about the end of capitalism, about the breakdown of liberalism, etc. Imperialism went from the system crisis to its extreme growth, to the end of neo-colonialism.

Under the burden of the increasing neo-colonial exploitation (which reaches unbearable dimensions) and the aggravation of the external contradictions between the parent states and the exploited countries, of the internal contradictions between labour and capital, between monopolistic bourgeoisie and civil society, we are witnessing the escalation of the struggle of the peoples in the underdeveloped countries for their national independence and social emancipation. The collapse of neo-colonialism nears its final stage. The snake is not yet dead, but it is expiring.

In the flames of the national and social revolution 15 years ago, Latin America, except Cuba, was the prey to American imperialism. With very few exceptions, Latin America shook free from the dictate of the Bretton Woods institutions, from economic and social dependence, taking the way of national and social revival. The flags of independence and freedom are flying high in the capitals of the great majority of the Latin-American countries. The turn to the left taken by Mexico and the USA, as well as the transfer of the national and social liberation revolution onto the American continent, represent the strongest symptoms of the end of the American domination generally, and of the imperialistic domination particularly.

In Asia, after China, India, Vietnam and North Korea were freed from colonialism, the extent of neo-colonial domination shrank considerably. The recent liberation of Nepal, the notable victory of the social-democratic party in the Pakistani parliamentary and presidential elections, in the parliamentary elections in Bangladesh and Nicaragua, the partial victory of the progressive forces in the parliamentary elections in Malaysia, as well as the relentless struggle of the Iraqi, Afghan, Palestinian and Indonesian peoples for national independence and social emancipation, all that represent the significant signs of total collapse of neo-colonialism.

While Latin America is aflame in the fire of national and social revolutions, underdeveloped traditional and tribal Africa is igniting the sparks of national and social liberation, the light of African Socialism, which has already traversed the intermediate stages from genesis to the investigation of new ways favourable for its implementation. Algeria, Tunisia, Libya, Angola, Democratic Congo, South Africa, Tanzania, Mozambique, Zimbabwe, Rwanda and Ivory Coast, all of them have started their journey towards independence and social emancipation.

The dismembering of totalitarian regimes, the metastasis of imperialism and the end of neo-colonialism have opened wide the doors to the highway to social progress.

Today, no force on earth will be able to block the no-return road of the emerging united new world.

References

1. Friedrich Engels, Anti-Dühring, Naprijed, Zagreb, 1946, pp. 293-294.
2. Raymond Aron, Introduction à la philosophie de l'histoire, Gallimard, Paris, 1986.

3. Jacques Attali, Karl Marx ou l'esprit du monde, Fayard, Paris, 2005, cover.
4. Petit Robert, Vol. I, Sepret, Paris, 1975, p. 1160.
5. Miladin Korac, Socijalisticki samoupravni nacin proizvodnje, Komunist, Belgrade, Vol. I, 1977, p. 11.
6. Jacques Barros, Marxisme, horizon indépassable, publisher L'Harmattan, Paris, 1992, p. 21.
7. Karl Marx, Manuscrits de 1844, Editions Sociales, Paris, 1972, p. 64.
8. Antonio Gramsci, Gramsci dans le texte, Editions. Sociales, Paris, 1975, p. 215.
9. Vladislav Inozemtsev, Contribution à la théorie de la formation post-économique de la société. Les Éditions du Mécène, Paris, 1996, p. 161.
10. Rosa Luxemburg, La révolution Russe, Spartacus, Paris, 1937, p. 42.
11. V.I. Lenin, Poln. sobr. soch. 5th edition,Vol. 45, Moscow, 1971, p. 21.
12. V.I. Lenin, ditto, p. 346.
13. Hélène Carrère d'Encausse, Lénine, Fayard, Paris, 1998, p. 23
14. Léon Trotski, La révolution trahie, Minuit, 1999, pp. 158, 185, 191.
15. *Ibid.*
16. *Ibid.*
17. Henry Shapiro, L'URSS après Staline, Gallimard, Paris, 1954, p. 7.
18. Jacques Sapir, Les fluctuations économiques en URSS 1941-1945, EHESS, Paris, 1989, pp. 51, 184, 186.
19. *Ibid.*
20. Mikhail Gorbachev, Perestroika, Flammarion, Paris, 1987, p. 18
21. Eric Laurent, L'effondrement, Olivier Orban, Paris, 1992, p. 106
22. Gruicci Constantin, Ivoire Soir, Abidjan, 28/12/1989.

2

Worldwide Revival of Democratic, Liberal and Humanitarian Socialism

1. Worldwide Revival of Democratic, Liberal and Humanitarian Socialism

(a) Global Assault of Socialism

After the decline and dissolution of the soviet totalitarian system and the crystallisation of the causes and consequences detrimental to social progress, a new turn occurs in the development of the world socialism. The progressive leftist movements, formerly weakened by interior conflicts, are more and more adjusting their programmes and actions with the purpose of achieving their common goals of social progress.

The new initiatives of the "socialism of what is possible", the new forms and methods of implementation of the common goals and the new driving belts to motivate the civil society pushed the social machinery along the road to progress. The left-wing movements, born from the disunion and the eternal clash of two lines, weakened after a defeat, are entering now a new stage, namely the reunion of their forces, of the assault actions of the worldwide revival and of their hopes for a new future. The rebirth of the hope for a new future of the united socialist society embraces not only the socialist countries lost in their regeneration process, but develops also new dimensions in the underdeveloped countries and in the developed countries of the West. When considered from worldwide perspective, socialism, in its global aspect and the unity of all its forms under evolution, socialism, I say, has changed from the stage of protecting its moral and historical values to the stage of a general assault of the revolutionary development of the social progress.

So that it is possible to draw a number of conclusions of crucial importance from our contemporary history. The socialist revolutions have not followed the course foreseen by Marx, namely at first in the developed countries, nor did they proceed as predicted by Trotsky, that is by a continuous revolution. They evolve in waves, in different groups of countries, where the internal and external contradictions have created the material, social and political conditions that do not allow the dominant classes to hold on to the power, so that these dominant classes can not face any longer the alienation, poverty, ignorance and denial of human dignity.

After the first wave of socialist revolutions at the end of the First World War in Russia and some European countries, a second wave of democratic-popular revolutions followed after the Second World War in China, India, Vietnam, North Korea, the former Yugoslavia, Albania, Cuba, and this revolution was later on imported in Germany, Poland, Czechoslovakia, Romania, Hungary and Bulgaria.

In the 1960s and 1970s, a third revolutionary wave flooded over Algeria, Tunisia, Libya, Angola, Senegal, Ghana, Benin, Burkina Faso, Mali, Tanzania, Mozambique, Congo Brazzaville and many other countries on the globe.

During the year between 1980s – 1990s, a fourth wave of changes occurred in Europe. Most of the European countries saw the flags of the left-wing political parties flying up high in power.

The first decade of the 21st century brings to us the fifth wave of national and social liberation revolutions in Venezuela, Brazil, Chile, Argentina, Bolivia, Peru, Uruguay, Haiti, Nicaragua, Guatemala, the D.R. Congo and the last African star – the Ivory Coast.

The victory in the parliamentary or presidential elections in Nepal, the United States, Pakistan, Bangladesh, Ghana and Salvador triggered the sixth wave of national and social revolutions. We are expecting the victory of the resistance in Madagascar, Greece, Guinea, Afghanistan, Iraq, followed by a potential leftist victory in Japan, which is on the lookout for her own Obama.

(b) Reversing of the Ways of Emergence and Evolution of Socialism

After the power has been taken over by free democratic elections by the left-wing political party, representative of the oppressed people, the emergence and evolution of socialism as a social and economic system of the lengthy transition period from capitalism to socialism are heading the opposite direction then traced by Marxism.

As well known, with no excess of quotations, it should be pointed out that Marxism traced the outline of the main transition road from capitalism to socialism by nationalisation of the main means of production in industry, transports and communications, by collectivisation of agriculture and establishing of state monopole in the domestic and foreign trade, by proportionally planned economic and social development.

The prior achievement of the above parameters was the main instrument of initiating the great social projects for diminishing poverty, eradicating unemployment, improving the quality of life, developing the education system, the social safety system, as well as culture and art.

In other words, the provision of these prerequisites, pushed to the extreme by Stalinism, was made possible only through utter violence, constituting the "sine qua non" condition for setting up a distorted and totalitarian socialist system. Precisely these are the reasons – based on violence – which caused the failure of the totalitarian society after 70 years of such an experience.

And now it happens that, in practice, the global assault of socialism (when the peoples conquered the power democratically through their left-wing parties in 56 country of our planet) and the implementation of the great ideals of the democratic, liberal and humanitarian socialism have started by reversing the achievement order of the main requirements of the new society.

This means that the leftist movements begin with the most urgent, most necessary tasks, of the "possible socialism". Also, this beginning includes the enhancing of the role of the state in the redistribution of the national income in favour of the civil society, by means of speeding up the economic growth, by the achievement of budget balance and by reducing the inflation, by industrialisation, electrification and intensification of the farming industry, by reducing unemployment and poverty, by expansion and modernising the education system, the public health system, by ensuring a general health safety system, etc.

The order and the extent of achieving the requirements of the "possible socialism" depend upon social, economic and historical circumstances of each country separately.

After meeting the primary requirements, the emerging countries will step on to the secondary ones: gradual partial socialisation of the property of the large private companies, expansion of social programmes, modernising the infrastructure, etc.

Further, the transition society will advance to stage three, the stage of completion of the transition period and of advancing to the developed socialist society.

In the developed countries, the sequence and extent of the deep changes are and will be carried out under observance and meeting of their social, economic, cultural and historical conditions.

Those who do not understand the change of methods, forms and, especially, of the gradual implementation sequence of the basic requirements of the emerging and evolving socialism, those have not been able to understand anything of the theory and practice of the new main roads of the global revival of the democratic, liberal and humanitarian socialism.

It is a lengthy coexistence process of the different forms of property and social classes, a long process of re-moralising the society, of blooming of the human race, a process that could probably extend over 100 years or even more. Why hurry? The clock of history must always be considered with respect. Violence has always been destructive, while patience is always constructive.

My concise reports on the implementation stages and sequence of the various requirements of socialism are not an invention issued from my hypothetical-deductive reasoning. On the contrary, they are based on the reality of the development of socialism in 56 countries on the globe.

In order to substantiate my assertions, I will try to offer an analysis and a confirmation of my compilation through varied experiences of the peoples on our planet.

(c) Revival, Development and Globalisation of Socialism

When we talk and write about the worldwide revival of a new society, we revert to the updating and expediting socialism as an ideology, science, political movement and, at last, as a complex of new social relations, which express the generation, development and assertion of great hopes for rescue.

Ten years after the collapse of the totalitarian system and the display of the globalisation trend of capitalism, ten years after its negative consequences had been rejected, the world shifted obviously to the left. In this respect we can notice here and there, more and more, a new kind of approach on the part of the political leaders and those who explain ideologically the social mutations, a completely different type of globalisation: that of the joining of the common interests and dreams of peoples in their endeavour to set the human race free from alienation, fetishism, social injustice, to make our civilisation return to the human values of social progress.

In his recently published study, Robert Hue, former secretary general of the French Communist Party, wrote with reference to the second face of the effects of the pro-American globalisation: "It would be stupid and dangerous to turn the world back. The future does not lie in retreat. We have to advance towards the future: to a different logic, a different meaning, different values, for a globalisation desired and achieved, this time, by the peoples, for the joint erection of their common future. In a nutshell, there is another purpose which, as far as I can see, stands out: that of a globalisation by participation, for the blooming of mankind."[1]

After their perpetual discords and dissensions, the socialists, communists and other leftist parties begin to speak in almost one voice about the unity of their common goals. One of the best known politicians of the French Socialist Party, Henri Weber, reveals to the French public the summary of the project approved by the Congress at Le Mans in November 2005, pointing out the need "to establish a different globalisation and a better international 'government'".[2]

If, on the one hand, in the resolutions, programmes and summaries of the left-wing political parties and in the analyses of the ideological researchers explaining the social mutations we can sense the components of another globalisation, for the benefit of the people and in the name of the people, almost with no further more extended analysis and no synthesis of this process, with no scientific proof of their inevitable historical character; on the other hand, the research on the worldwide revival of socialism is still in its emerging stage.

(d) Why Revival and Not Development of Socialism?

The revival of socialism – as we explained in the foreword to our book – is the anteroom of globalisation, its authentic and integral genetic component. The globalisation of socialism could not have appeared in the world, nor could it have evolved from the old concepts, from the obsolete ideologies, from antiquated social structures of the Eastern totalitarian socialism, nor from certain outdated ideas of the Western social democracy. The demolition of the old socialism construction was necessary and the establishing in both theory and practice of a new strategy and of new concepts of the social progress.

The revival, as a new social renewal movement, appeared for the first time in the history of our civilisation in Europe in the early 15th and the late 16th century. The development of production forces as a result of the great scientific discoveries of Bacon, Copernicus, da Vinci, the expansion of seafaring, the discovery of gunpowder, of the printing press by Gutenberg, as well as many other discoveries, furthered the revival of the updated ancient values.

It was the result of the birth of the bourgeoisie and the working class, as bearers of the social progress. Consequently, the Renaissance acted as an assertion of the western civilisation and was decisively spaced far out from the parallel civilisations. Under specific identical circumstances, history repeats itself, but it repeats itself each time at a different development level of the society and under a different form and method of its inexorable course. In fact, after seven decades of totalitarian and rudimentary socialism and its decay, the new scientific discoveries, those in the fields of atomic energy, informatics, cybernetics, biotechnology, chemistry, space physics, of robotics and a great many other discoveries, favoured the development of the production forces and the destruction of the old production relations. They attracted willy-nilly the updating, the revival of the positive values of socialism within the old system in the East, the South and the West; or else, as Roger Martelli wrote, we had not to reinvent socialism on our own; we should update it, starting from the old universal ideas, on the new foundation of the social evolution.

And then, why are we talking about the revival of socialism instead of its subsequent development on new foundations? Because its ideological, theoretical, scientific and pragmatic basis, which is the dream of the greatest part of the civil society, is sealed in the historiography of our civilisation, and there is no need for us to imagine it again, but rather draw it from the present practice of social progress. The democratic, liberal and humanitarian socialism streams from the universal values of Marxism, from the values of social democracy and from the positive achievements of the real socialism, which have languished for many years between the totalitarian system, the stifled liberalism and the surviving humanism. This is about reverting to the original foundations of socialism, in the form of the revival of the democratic, liberal and humanitarian socialism.

(e) The Democratic, Liberal and Humanitarian Socialism: What Is It?

In the ideological reading of the three main characteristics of socialism – democratic, liberal and humanitarian – we have to point out to the reader not as much the etymological reading of their linguistic form, than rather the ideological reading of their content. At present, democracy has become the flag of every party and political movement and, at the same time, the front for concealing every possible manipulation on the part of dictatorship, of the dictatorship covered behind the cosmetically arranged mask, or on the part of the phony democracy defended by certain social-democratic leaders, who placed their personal benefits above the interests of the dominant classes.

The word “democracy” comes from ancient Greek. It is formed by two Greek words, “demos”, meaning people, and “kratein”, i.e. government, so that, in the beginning, its meaning was the government of the people. From historical point of view, the scientific socialism was inspired by the ancient traditions of the Greek and Roman democracies, but it did not come to be achieved, so that later on it reverted to the sources of the restrained and curtailed European bourgeois democracy and, in the end, the scientific socialism considered democracy to be the actual government of the working class and its historical allies, by means of the democracy of the citizens, of the reform of the parliamentary system and of the participative democracy.

The democratic socialism takes the road of the general development of the genuine democracy, the road of radical reforms of the parliamentary system and of enlargement of the participative democracy. Besides, it discovers new forms of parliamentary and extra-parliamentary political democracy, by the actual separation of the executive, legislative and judicial powers, by innovative organisation forms of the new supervision authorities and of expansion of the economic power, by means of the citizens’ participation in the social capital and corporate decisions.

Separating the political democracy from the economic democracy may be interpreted as a form of domination of the employers, a form of isolation of the civil society from the management of its own destiny, a form of suppression of the total democracy.

In the ideological explanation of the liberal socialism we have to point out the crucial difference between “liberal capitalism” and “liberal socialism” which, because of their etymological identity, may stir confusion in the understanding of the crucial differences between the two systems.

Traditionally, the liberal socialism does not include in its essence any similarities with the liberal capitalism.

The etymological meaning of the word "liberal" originates in the Latin word "liberalis", which entered the dictionary around the 1160s and which is a mark of freedom of thought, action and movement. Nevertheless, the word "liberalism" acquired an economic and political significance only along with the development of the beginnings of the market economy, as a response of the society to the feudal and the monarchic systems. Since the age of commercialism, certain theories on the liberal democracy were obvious, taking on the forms of individual freedoms of the citizens, of the freedom of press, competition, freedom of exchange, freedom of labour marketing, freedom to associate in joint-stock companies. Freedom and liberalism are not exclusive features of the liberal society. They belong to our entire civilisation, no matter of the form of economic relations.

Man is free, wrote Schiller, even if born in chains and, depending of the social-economic systems, freedom has conquered more or less extended areas of the existence of the human race. The actual freedoms of the civil society are possible only within the democratic socialism systems. Without wider participation of the population in the management of public property and in the social self-management of the companies, it is and will not be possible to speak about freedom.

However, the liberal socialism of the transition period, based on the multi-sector economy (private, state, mixed and cooperative economy), trigger the appearance of certain non-socialist relations: increase of unemployment, of inflation, of the flight of the rural population, of the housing crisis, and other negative effects of the transition. Well, then, socialism can become a source of features of estrangement, fetishism, the effects of which could be limited if the political leaders grant priority to the betterment of social relations as compared to the implementation of enrichment. Therefore, we insert humanism as a component part into the definition of socialism, as a part of the revival programme of socialism.

Humanism is the third important feature of the revival of socialism. The humane socialism, which had once become the wishful dream of the working class masses in the totalitarian systems, is turning now-a days into a wide movement of the civil society in the developed countries of the West, in the eastern countries with a medium development level and, the more so, in the underdeveloped countries of the South, where the global reasoning has caused the mercantile, decadent, loitering relations to relegate humanism to the dust bin, considering it as a rationale of a narrow group of charitable intellectuals, associations and organisations.

Humanism, free and universal development and flourishing of the intellectual and humane values of every individual (as a part of the common existence), are the very marrow, the spine of the scientific socialism, and this is how it can be transferred from the once secondary track of practice onto the main track of social progress. It is precisely due to the anthropological human values of socialism that the present day leftist movements place in the foreground of their programmes the defence of the humane dimensions of the civil society.

In his recently published book "The Political and Economic Bases of the Humane Society System", Blaz Boskovic, the former Director of the Institute of Economic Sciences in the former Yugoslavia, wrote: "If mankind will fight for the exclusion of exploitation, for the fair distribution of incomes, before everything else, and for the establishment of self-management, then the humane society in its three dimensions will appear: liberty, equality, that is more exactly equality of rights, and fraternity, more precisely solidarity. In such a society, the human personality will come to its achievement by the appropriation of its three major values; the capacity to work, the capacity to understand the surrounding world and to think, and the capacity to be the leader of man's own creations. Under such circumstances, humans become more fulfilled, richer intellectually, better prepared in front of the new and permanent intellectual challenges."[3]

By their pushing to the forefront rather the actual human requirements of the civil society, which can be materialised, than those illusions on the still far-away future society, the left-wing political parties and movements have conquered and are still conquering gradually the voters for the way of revival of the democratic, liberal and humanitarian socialism.

(f) The New Western Iron Curtain

Our planet suddenly drifted to the left. Freed from dogmatism, totalitarian system, neo-colonialism, sectarianism and from the anaesthesia of liberalism, the peoples of China, India, Russia, Belarus, Kazakhstan, Cuba, Venezuela, Chile, Brazil, Argentina, Peru, Spain, Switzerland, Sweden, Norway, Denmark, Tunisia, Algeria, Libya, Angola, the Democratic Republic Congo, South Africa, Tanzania, Mozambique, the Ivory Coast, Australia and more other countries, have stepped onto the new way of social progress.

The new amazing successful results of the accelerated economic growth, of the decreasing unemployment and poverty, the achievement of important social programmes by the liberated peoples of our planet, all these are the expression of the opposite of the lost hopes for the globalisation of capitalism and neo-colonialism. The general breakdown of capitalism, the end of neo-colonialism, and the transition of more than two third of the inhabitants of our world onto the road to social progress, the sliding to the left of the political zone of the population in the developed countries, all these have become images of concern for the dominant western classes. The latter are more afraid of the influence of the East and South on the social conscience of their citizens than they used to be in the times of the soviet iron curtain.

The question is how the truth from the East and South could be prevented to penetrate into the West? Such are the new difficult issues for the western media tycoons. Certainly, the significant successes of the majority of the underdeveloped countries on their way to social progress are liable to worry the government circles of the developed countries. This is the reason for the western media to weave the fabric of the new iron curtain, in order to prevent the penetration of the truth. The western countries are publishing thousands of books, surveys, tens of thousands of advertising pamphlets and video clips to show China, India, Russia, Brazil, Venezuela, Tanzania, Angola and other liberated peoples of our planet in a distorted way and concealing the truth.

The greatest publishing houses and magazine issue more and more negative fragments from the recently liberated countries, furnishing very scarce and abridged information with regard to the actual changes on the way of progressive social reforms.

In an interview, Vanessa Stojilkovic declared, in connection with one of her new films about Venezuela, and following the journalist's question about the importance of such an event: "... because extraordinary things are happening here! Every visitor of this country is exited, while we, in Europe, on the contrary, we are facing pessimism, fatalism. There is nothing we can change." "... and, look, in Venezuela, people who are involved in the transformation of their country, people who achieve many things ... and the western media do not say almost anything about these things; on the contrary, they are spreading the image of some kind of a dictatorship. Are we really interested to conceal what is going on over there and even to denigrate what is going on there?"[4]

In fact, the western media ascribe the great social-economic successes of Venezuela and of the other countries freed from colonialism and neo-colonialism to the transition to the liberal market of the economy.

It is true that the market liberalisation is achieved in the major part of these countries, but to the benefit of the progress of socialism, not for the restoring and globalisation of capitalism.

The purpose of the documented analyses of the new events of the revival of socialism comprised of the following chapters of my studies consists in raising the new iron curtain off the planetary scene of the birth of a new world; my survey intends to fill up with a great many materials the vast informational void and to light up the dimensions of the new leftist movement issued from the social progress.

2. Pioneers and Victims of the Revival of Socialism

(a) Pioneers of the Revival of Socialism

The criticism of the "present state" of the deviations towards a totalitarian system in the former USSR and in the countries of Eastern Europe was no longer a carrier of social progress. Conservatism and dogmatism became the prevailing accents of the existence of totalitarian regimes. Consequently, the social and party nomenclature acted in relation to criticism just as the Middle Age Inquisition had done to heretics. In the West, the positive criticism of the totalitarian system became ever more extended dimensions, particularly after the 20th Congress of the Communist Party of the Soviet Union, where Khrushchev disclosed the existence of Stalin's gulags. The paternity of launching and promoting the new ideas of the democratic, liberal and humanitarian socialism is due to the well meaning critics of the Western left.

Nevertheless, criticism expressed from a distance of several thousand kilometres was almost as lacking in precision as the astronomical discovery of our galaxy in the sky. The positive criticism coming from economists, political scientists and sociologists of the East-European countries, such as Varga, Kornaj, Kovalevski, Lukatch, Minc, Koratch, Horvat and more others, who had shared the bread and salt, the good and bad parts of the system, was a more objective, more realistic and more complete criticism of the existing state of affairs.

The objective criticism of the "present state", in the form of a summary of the new social changes, contributed to the discovery of the negative sides of the system and, simultaneously, to a glimpse on the new potential ways of revival of socialism.

The history of all social movements discloses to us the eternal truth that says that only the revolutionary criticism coming from below, the criticism from the revolutionary classes, as the materialisation, reincarnation of the ideas of absolute truth, only this criticism can and must push aside all impurities off the way of social progress.

Consequently, the vanguard movements of the most determined, the most brave and the most dedicated pioneers of the revival of socialism play the same triggering role in connection with mass movements, just as the fusion of atoms in physics.

No important social movement is released by the majority of the most discontented society members. The social movement has always and everywhere in history had its starting point in a more daring minority and then spread like the ripples of a stone thrown in a pool of water, sending concentric circles melting into the infinite ocean of social progress.

(b) The First Victims of Tito's Terrorism in 1948-1965

In our attempt to determine and reconstruct the historical truth, we must admit to our readers and to historical justice that the first critical mass movement against the totalitarian system, against terrorism and the dictatorship of a number of political leaders was initiated in the former Yugoslavia in 1948. In fact, after the Kominform resolution of the communist and workers' parties was published in 1948, parties that considered Tito's regime as a "terrorist Turkish regime", almost half of the members of the former communist party (where I was acting in the students' movement of the opposition) and part of its followers raised against the Titoist distortion and the Stalinist intrusion in the socialist movement, to defend democracy and humanism of socialism in the development process.

The working class aristocracy in power, raised under the high protection of the Stalinist ideology, replied to the sincere and positive deviation criticism by launching the most atrocious dictatorship of those years, spiced with terror, prisons and concentration camps. Together with Rankovic, the then chief of the political police, Tito threw over 150,000 communists and other citizens in jail and prison camps, out of which 15,000 were killed by the most horrible torture methods that the human mind could imagine. The former political deportee Dragoslav Markovic (now-a-days a renowned Serbian writer) states that those appalling tortures went beyond the imagination of people who believe in the human race.

The deserted islands at the Adriatic Sea – Goli Otok and St.Grgur, as well as the famous prisons at Belgrade, Zabela, Sremska Mitrovica and other dozens of prisons established on the territory of Yugoslavia were, in fact, a new version of the Stalinist gulags, prisons and concentration camps. The Tito regime, which enjoyed the blind trust and financial support of the West, had become practically the cruel versions of the Yugoslav Stalinism.

As an editor with the illegal radio station Radio Free Yugoslavia, in September 1954, if I remember well, I received via the Italian Communist Party the manuscript of the diary of one of the prisoners of the concentration camp Goli Otok, which became a new collective Golgatha. For one whole month, with no interruptions, twice a day, I read and broadcast excerpts of this dire diary, later on translated in several languages. Several months later, a delegation of the European Union visited the "Marble Construction Site", embellished for the purpose of this visit. I do not know whether this visit was a consequence of my communications or of any other interventions. What I know for sure is that, in 1990, ten years after Tito had died, and after the borders were opened, while I was trying to return to my country, I discovered at the Embassy of Yugoslavia in Paris that I was still blacklisted and prohibited from entering my country. This interdiction remained in force for 20 years from my last visit in Romania in 1970 on, that is for a total of 40 years. Why? Because I had disclosed to the public audience of Europe and the entire world the truth about the gulags of Tito's regime.

It is with bitterness that I am writing these lines, as one of the opponents who escaped from Goli Otok and fled to Romania, and I do not intend as much to evaluate the historical merits, the errors and the genocide of the Tito regime, than to honour those people who, for the first time in the history of real socialism, raised all together to defend freedom, democracy and humanism.

(c) Revolution and Counter-Revolution in Hungary, in 1956

Eight years later, in 1956, the students of the Petöfi club in Budapest organised demonstrations, claiming for the freedom of press, the freedom of expression, for the establishing of management councils of the working class, as well as for the participation of the people in decision-taking and the control of the bureaucracy. In a few days, Budapest was entirely engulfed in the fire of the revolution. The revolution directed against the totalitarian regime and the distortion of socialism turned into a counter-revolution and an armed intervention of the soviet combat cars.

On the 1st of November, 1956, upon the decision taken by the Political Bureau and by Nikita Khrushchev, acting in Hungary as if in their own colony, the soviet troops surrounded Budapest and, after having defeated the resistance, they occupied Budapest with tens of thousands of soldiers and several hundred armoured cars.

And thus, the Hungarian revolution and counter-revolution were smothered in blood and flames through cruel intervention of the soviet army.

According to a mention made by a group of French authors in the General History of Socialism, the stifled revolution counted 2,700 dead, 15,000 casualties and approximately 20,000 prisoners.

(d) The Victims of the "Cultural Counter-Revolution" in China, 1966-1977

Similarly, to most of the other totalitarian countries, since the late 1960s and early 1970, in China, aspects of a standstill of the economic growth became noticeable, the signs of the decline of the efficiency of industries, of an ever stronger inertia of a part of the population, of the intellectuals and students to the bureaucracy and the totalitarian system. Their hopes came to be directed to the investigation of new roads regarding democratisation, cutting down on bureaucracy and modernisation of socialism. Practically, it was the beginning of a clash between the new arriving generation, which asked for changes, on the one hand, and the seventy and eighty-year old-timers close to conservatism, on the other hand. In China, very shortly before the demise of Mao Zedong, Chu En Lai and Deng Xiaoping, the conflict between generations changed into a power struggle for taking over the leading positions.

In 1966, under the cover of the battle against the penetration of bourgeois ideologies from the West and of soviet revisionism from the East, the four climbers, led by Mao Zedong's wife, initiated because of their fear of a strong opposition on the part of the Chinese officers raised in the spirit of the Chinese revolution, the "cultural revolution" of the urban youth, mostly students organised in "red brigades". For months in a row, the heavy demonstrations, coloured by a terrible excitement of the young people, humiliated the intellectuals, mistreated them, deported them to correction camps, lynched or murdered them.

Drawing the line on this cultural counter-revolution shows a terrifying result: about 400,000 dead, if we choose to believe the sources of the authorised western mass-media; and 3 million people deported to rehabilitation centres.[5]

Eventually, in 1968, after some three years of violence and chaos of internal conflicts of the red brigades, the Chinese army took on the task to annihilate the cultural counter-revolution. In 1969, the 9th Congress of the Communist Party threw light upon the true essence of the Chinese counter-revolution. In 1973, Deng Xiaoping was reinstated in the position of a vice-president of the government, just as hundreds of remarkable leaders of the renewal and updating of the Chinese socialism were reconsidered, too.

It was the starting time of the process of an extended rehabilitation of cadres and of the successive purification of the Party and State apparatus. One month after the death of patriarch Mao Zedong, the initiators of the counter-revolution were thrown in jail, and a little later they received the capital sentence. In 1978, Deng Xiaoping assumed all prerogatives as a leader and moderniser of the Chinese socialism.

(e) The Prague Spring 1968

The 1968 Prague Spring was significantly richer in political requests and had much less human casualties than the 1948 Yugoslav Summer and the 1956 Hungarian Autumn. Contrary to the Hungarian revolution and counter-revolution, the Czech revolution originated at the top of the political structure and was accepted as such by the majority of the population. It did not clash with the opposition of conservatism and the totalitarian system.

When he acceded to party leadership, Alexander Dubcek launched a programme of democratisation, of participation of the citizens in the most important decisions, of abrogating censorship, of freedom of press, of establishing the workers' management councils, of free action of economic laws in the market economy and of a wider opening to the West.

Although almost the entire civil society and the 15th Congress of the Party supported Dubcek's direction, in 1968, the soviet armoured cars occupied Czechoslovakia and replaced by force the political leaders with their own people, thus freezing the turning of the wheel of the revival of socialism.

(f) The 1982 Polish Revolution

In its extent and radical requests, Polish revolution differs from the Yugoslav, Hungarian and Czech revolutions. It had a more radical character, not only in point of objective circumstances of worsening contradictions between the power and civil society, but also considering the historical tradition of the participation of the Polish people in most of the revolutions and wars in Europe, as well as the century-long tradition of the struggle for freedom and national independence, with deep roots in the genetic heritage of many generations of Poles.

So that it is not by chance that in the Declaration of the Solidarity Union, which was the leader of the revolution, it was stated that the Polish revolution was the expression of "the most beautiful traditions of the people, the moral principles of Christianity, the political challenge of democracy and socialist social thinking".

The Polish revolution was a mixture of huge and sudden outbursts, an expression of the discontent of the civil society with the totalitarian socialist policies, which complied neither with the traditions, nor with the interests of the Polish society. In December 1970, the first significant strikes and the workers' revolts at the shipyards in Gdansk and those of the workers in Gdynia, Elblag and Szczecin, against the negative effects of the totalitarian system transposed in Poland and against the distortion of the Polish socialism, were repressed with machine-gun fire. According to the free Polish press, the number of casualties, contrary to the officially declared 45 dead, was much higher.

Poland was doomed to go on with rebellions, strikes and demonstrations, with ever more open and clear requests for the replacement of the compromised regime. Between May and August 1982, the workers' strikes were more and more frequent, like mushrooms after the rain, all over Poland. The crucial role in turning the strikes into a revolution was played by the revolt of the 17,000 workers of the Gdansk shipyard, led by Lech Walesa, a young leader of the Solidarity Union, along with a group of new determined leaders of the same union. Hundred and thirty-four enterprises and 350,000 miners of Upper Silesia joined the general strike of the Gdansk workers. In late August, the flames of the revolution had spread throughout the entire Polish nation. Considering the restricted space I have for the summary description of the goals and directions of the Polish revolution, I have to cut short on the curiosity of the readers for an exhaustive story of the course of the Polish revolution, which was the subject of my book "The Soviet Socialism and the Polish Revolution", that I finished writing in 1983. After two years of painstaking mind efforts to study the Polish language, to read documents and to shuttle between Abidjan, Paris, Warsaw and Gdansk, and of meetings with the leaders of the Polish revolution, my book had not the desired impact in Paris, Rome or Madrid. My vision on the features of this revolution was different from the one of a number of European editors.

In the manuscript of my book I defended the concept that most of the Poles had not risen against socialism, despite its abuses, as in any other great revolution, but rather against its distortions.

Assessing the character of the Polish revolution in its relation with socialism, Lech Walesa confirmed my point of view on the occasion of a meeting on the Nova Huta sports arena:

"We are on the way of preparing the Polish style socialism. We are asking the authorities to serve, not to direct. What is going on in our country is our own business ... ." And, further on: "Most individuals imagine socialism in a different manner than do the ideologists and politicians. Some reject it; others think that it would not be bad if we were proceeding according to the socialist manner, with the benefit of the capitalist finances ... To put it in a nutshell, in order to make "socialism" acceptable, we have stated that whatever had been best in economy and social services was socialist ..."[6]

As can be seen from Walesa's statements, the Polish revolution was not anti-socialist, fact which made Walesa, in his position of leader of the Solidarity Union, to approve in his public appearances the expectations of most Polish citizens for the revival of the free, liberal and democratic socialism and thus to preserve his position as leader of the Polish revolution.

Inherently, Walesa gave in sentimentally to the pressures of the western powers which, by means of their financial, moral and political forces, push extensively the Polish revolution on the way of the restoration of capitalism. Socialism failed in Poland and in the remaining East-European countries, too, not as much due to the pressure of the civil society, as because of the incapacity of the political leaders of the communist and workers' parties to get rid of dogmatism and Stalinism and to choose the new ways of revival of the democratic, liberal and humanitarian socialism.

After the fall of Berlin wall and the dissolution of socialism in East Germany and after the failure of Gorbachev's perestroika, socialism in the East-European countries began collapsing as a house of cards, first of all in Poland, and then in Czechoslovakia, Hungary, Romania, Bulgaria, Albania and, finally, in most of the Yugoslav republics. The dissolution of the Soviet Empire supports the words of Samir Amin, the African socialist, who said that, all along the history of our civilisation, the great empires collapse always evolved from the outskirts to the centre.

3. Regeneration of Russia's Great Power. Sharp Turn to the Left

(a) Putin's Regime, the Great Expectation of Social Progress

The failure of the transition strategy to the market economy, influenced by eight years of crisis and decay, as well as the heart attack and the fear of the storm of a new social revolution, forced Yeltsin to relinquish power and to yield it to Vladimir Putin. Fourth-eight years old, dynamic, officer and head of the KGB, a quite decent character, Vladimir Putin became, in August 1999, the President of the government of the Russian Federation. Yeltsin had understood that Russia, lost in chaos and insolvency, could be saved only by the power of the structure of the omnipresent KGB. Playing the patriotic and nationalistic tune of the Chechen war times, Putin attained the popularity of a leader determined to defend the interest of the Great Russia. In the elections of March 2000 he obtained, together with his patriotic party, 52.2% of the votes; Zyuganov, President of the Communist Party, as a leader of the second greatest and powerful Russian party, got 29.2%, Yavlinsky 5.8%, and other right-wing parties less than 5% each.[7]

And thus, Putin, an almost unknown political character, became the President of the Republic. The power assumption by the men in uniform and the ever-present KGB in one of the once most powerful countries in the world, but at that moment in disarray, crisis, and dissolution, was quite convenient to the majority of the Russian population. They were sure that only the strong iron fist of the men in uniform could save Russia from the catastrophic sequels of corruption, global chaos and sudden decrease of the living standard of the population.

Right after his victory in the elections, Vladimir Putin, master of law, high official and chief of the KGB (a man who studied economy and management and went on with his studies for 8 years, during the period of Yeltsin's weakness and errors), took in his hands the reins of the national salvation.

For the western analysts, Putin became the enigmatic leader of a great country under makeover, holding tight in his hands the hidden cards of the Chinese route.

The western media were not able to unravel the Putin riddle after his success in the elections. Jacques Alaman, the French author of the book "Vladimir Putin and Putinism", wrote: "Vladimir Putin remains however a hard to crack equation ... The most unsettling fact about Putin is, undoubtedly, the time when he keeps his silence. For his Ministers, for the American President George Bush, as well as for his French counterpart Jacques Chirac, there is certainly nothing more embarrassing than a long silence from Putin. Bottom line: the Russian President remains an unapproachable, distant, hard to read character."[8]

What would they have wanted to learn? Whether Russia would or would not continue Yeltsin's work, in point of a continuous restoration of liberalism or of Russia's power, in point of the makeover and strong development of the material conditions requirement for the revival of socialism.

The most likely answer to this question came from Yevgeny Primakov, the last prime-minister during Boris Yeltsin's mandate: "When Putin was elected to follow Yeltsin, the West believed that he would proceed on the same path as signaled by his predecessor. This would have been convenient for a lot of people. But soon, Putin's programme of official visits stirred fear. In fact, besides his European tour, he went to China, North Korea, India, Mongolia and Cuba. He proved independence since his very first meetings with the western leaders."[9]

Assuming the historical responsibility to save Russia from another catastrophe, Vladimir Putin saw what neither Gorbachev, nor Yeltsin, nor their western sponsors had understood. Saving Russia from a national tragedy and her guiding onto the road of economic growth, the road of redistribution of national wealth as fairly as possible and finding the ways to the substantial increase of the living standard of the population, all that were possible only based on modernisation methods following the Chinese, Indian and Vietnamese social progress example. This means: development of the mixed competitive economy, reinforcement of the economic and political role of the state, a more important vertical centralisation of the power of the state and accumulation of capital, the subordination of the new billionaires and the plutocracy to the interests of the entire society, the acceleration of economic growth, the reinforcement of the authoritarian democracy of Euro-Asian inspiration, the gradual accommodation of the social policies to the requirements of the civil society, the use of every national natural resources and, primarily, of gas and oil, in the interest of regeneration of Russia's economic power, the expansion of Russia's authority and prestige as a great power in the international relations.

President Putin always pointed out that "our goals are absolutely clear. They consist in a high living standard, providing the safety of a free and comfortable life; respectively, the mature democracy and the developed society; the reinforcement of Russia's position in the world; but the main goal – I have to repeat it – is a significant raise of the living standard of the citizens."[10]

If we intend to investigate the main purpose of his development programme for Russia from the angle of the Marxist economic theory, we may say with no shadow of a doubt that President Putin made the main economic law roll, the driving power of the economy, of socialism, not of capitalism.

Putin is extremely rational. He never entered into any theoretical dispute by putting a label on his ideological vision. He was aware that socialism had been greatly compromised in the eyes of the civil society. For him it was crucial to meet all the promises he had made with regard to rescue and achieving a new prosperity for Russia.

"When we read his speech with great attention, we can see – wrote Hélène Nouaille – that he protects all the parties with great competence – great circumspection – saving at the same time a third way – of his own – for the case the internal events would require it."[11]

The main strategic direction of Putin and his party, the United Russia, was an accelerated economic development, an achievement of high accumulation level by way of a radical economic, administrative and political reforms.

Over just six years of strategy meant to revive the trust of the Russian people in the genuine forces of their original Euro-Asian civilisation. Russia was completely born again and regained its dynamics in the concert of the world's developed nations.

It was obvious that Vladimir Putin – whose grandfather had been Lenin's and Stalin's cook, and whose father had been a worker, war volunteer in the Red Army – secretary of the party organisation of a workshop of railway wagon factory in Leningrad, who kept in his heart and soul a tiny spark of socialist nostalgia, was preparing non-ostensibly, with few sophisticated words, the material conditions for the revival of socialism.

His new opponent of the liberal right-wing, Gary Kasparov, former chess world-champion, who meanwhile, his leftist opponent, the president of the Communist Party, Gennady Zyuganov, declared on the occasion of Putin's speech addressed to the nation in April 2005: "From this speech it is clear that Putin has strongly slid to the left. He spoke about all the social issues I have mentioned afore."[13]

The economic results of Putin's regime are obviously amazing. The gross domestic product has increased at a yearly average rate of 6%, and in 2007 even of roughly 7.6%. The Gross domestic product calculated in US dollars has increased

6.5 times in eight years. In 2007, according to the Romanian magazine "CAPITAL", the GDP per inhabitant attained 12,178 dollars. The inflation decreased from 36.5% in 1999 to 15.1% in 2002, to settle at about 12% in 2007.

The actual income of the population increased by 58.5% in the span from 1999 – 2002, by 13% in 2004 and by approximately 40% in the time from 2005 – 2007. Poverty rate dropped from 40% in 1999 to 27% in 2003, to keep on dropping to 15% in 2006, according to estimations of the specialists.\14

The external debt, which in 1999 was amounting to 92% of the GDP, sank below 20%. The reserves reached from foreign trade attained 300.8 billion dollars in January 2007, rising to the third place in the world – after the USA and China.

These are the actual reasons that make the majority of the population to trust in Putin's capability, in his associates, in his allies, to advance on the chosen path.

This evolution was facilitated, thanks to a yearly increase by 20% of the investments in the private sector. To further the foreign investments, the Duma, that is the Russian parliament, passed a law meant for the establishment of special sea-port economic zones according to the Chinese model.

The extent of foreign investments grew yearly by 50%. Thus, Russia is almost outrunning China, India and Brazil in a most spectacular way.

Even after Russia's unbelievable, but genuine achievements through its economic force and its international prestige as a great power, certain western analysts voiced their doubts and pessimistic outlook in connection with Russia's capability to maintain such a high international competitive standard. They miss the fact that Russia is the first world producer of natural gas and oil, that is has the richest underground resources, consisting in large deposits of oil, gas, iron, zinc, aluminium, copper and other potential mining resources. It has available millions of highly qualified workers with a priceless expertise in swift industrialisation. During the Russian-German reunion on the 18th of January 2007, the German ex-Chancellor Gerhard Schröder cautioned the said critics to avoid making the "typical errors of the past, made in the evaluation of Russia and its President". "The Russian President – as per Schröder – has succeeded in significantly raising the living standard in his country and to restore the State." He has the "historical merit of having launched Russia on the way of stability and reliability as a partner".

(b) Russia, Where Are You Headed To?

We may rightfully say, with no risk of doubt, that the laconic character Putin set up the material conditions and the super-structures of the new external geo-political trend for the revival of the great and mighty Russia. This country reverted into its place as a major player in the game of the super-powers. The same Putin is the one who worked out a domestic strategy of establishing the material conditions for the revival of democratic, liberal and humanitarian socialism. After eight years of Yeltsinian transition, socialism in Russia was not totally destroyed, the new social relations based on private property, exchange and redistribution had not the capacity to grow deep roots in the economic, political and inter-human social relations, considering the fact that capitalism is not easily and organically incorporated in daily life, in habits and in the psychology of the Slavic Russian society.

To speak and write about the victory of liberal economy after eight years of transition from socialism to capitalism is an absurdity of the media spread by these fanatics who have no knowledge of the elementary laws of history.

Russia is still in its transition period where, as in any other transition period, the old and the new social relations, the old and the new economic laws, the old and the new culture, the old and the new customs are co-existing side by side. During such periods, the remainders of socialist relations keep being dominant more than the budding capitalist relations. Certainly, it is a lengthy historical process of development and implementation of the strategy of the leading elite, in view of setting Russia on the course of social progress.

Yeltsin tried to destroy the economic foundations, but failed to do so till the end. Yeltsin sold the great state enterprises at reasonable prices to foreign, national and multinational companies, but had to keep approximately 40% of the public assets, because he could not find any more foreign buyers (and even less private local investors), nor could he distribute for free the not yet sold shares to the old bureaucracy and to the employees of the businesses. At the end of the year 1994, approximately 40 million Russians were the direct or indirect holders, through the agency of investment funds, of the shares of economic enterprises. It is true that part of the shares of the civil society has passed later on into the hands of the new owners, through sales at knock-out prices, but it is equally true that the public and corporative sector of the civil society still is the keeper of roughly 60% – 65% of the national capital. The state ensures its participation in the strategic sectors of oil (50%), gas (90%), nuclear power, weaponry and banking (almost 100%).

Through the State Decree of August 2004, a total number of 1064 large state enterprises of strategic importance were declared as forbidden from privatisation and also from diminishing their state-owned share packet. By acquiring shares or by means of great investments in strategic businesses, the State takes gradually over the part of a main player not only in guiding the activity of businesses, but especially in the production activity.

So that, besides Lukos, the first world oil producer, the state has taken over the shares in Nortgas, Selkupneftgaz, Sibnert, the greatest petrochemical complex Sibour, the complex of the automotive industry – Autovaz, most of the businesses in the metal working industry, the first titanium producer in the world. The decree provides for the start-up of the third greatest airplanes and helicopter production unit, and for the modernising of the atomic industry.

In other words, Russia does not go back to capitalism, instead it is advancing towards setting up the material foundation of socialism.

It is true that Yeltsin's system opened wide spaces for the development of the Russian billionaires who, according to expert estimates, own approximately 25% of the GDP. However, they never had, as it is usual in the West, the decisive role in working out the strategy and the policies for the development of the society. Vladimir Putin made the new Russian billionaires to serve the interests of regenerating Russia's prosperity and authority on national and international scale.

The attempts of the billionaire Khodorkovsky, whose fortune amounted to about 14 billion US dollars, to sell his multinational oil company to the Americans, against the interests of the mighty Russia, ended in disaster, namely an eight year forced labour conviction for large-scale tax fraud. Other characters, such as Boris Berezovski and Vladimir Gusinsky, escaped prison by fleeing abroad. It was a warning to all those who were trying to escape the innovating political framework of Russia. In fact, the Russian people, by Putin's party, defined by analysts as a center party, and the State, as a driving force, are the ones that establish the development directions of the country, not the billionaires and millionaires.

In response to the question regarding the direction Russia was heading to, V.Z. Balikoev, the prominent Russian university professor, member of the Academy of Social Sciences, wrote: "We want to establish a society based on ethical values, a society where human life would be recognised as being the main and unique value, a society that masters every law. In such a society, social and economic justice will prevail. There will be no room for social and economic iniquity, nor will there be for fighting another iniquity. To stamp this society as being communist, technocratic or post-industrial has no value at all. The important purpose of our evolution is precisely such a society."[16]

Balikoev's ideas, which arise from the very mobility of the Russian reality, are no blank checks.

(c) What Will Be Russia's Future Like?

The roots of the new social order, the Russian society is striving for are not destroyed, just as the striving for social justice and equality and for humanism is still alive. The ethical inter-human relations, as a reflection of the civic ideology and conscience and, particularly, as a reflection of the political changes, could not be destroyed in a country that educated several generations in the spirit of socialist morals, of equality and fraternity, of social justice, patriotism and internationalism.

Vladimir Putin and his center party, the "United Russia", approached gradually the center left wing; this is how they attained huge popularity as saviors of Russia. In the presidential elections of March 2004, Putin obtained with flying colours

71.3% of the votes and confirmed, with two-third of the voters, the ways chosen by the Russian nation. In the parliamentary elections for the Russian Duma, Putin's party obtained 104 deputy seats and, together with the independents and the deputies of the popular party, they had the absolute majority. Moreover, the elections of March 2008 confirmed the strategy continuity of Vladimir Putin's party, the "United Russia".

To observe the Constitution, Putin accepted to put an end to his mandate, proposing a new candidate on behalf of his party, namely Dmitry Medvedev, brilliant owner of the powerful company Gazprom. And so it came that "United Russia" has become the party holding the highest offices in the state: prime minister and president. So it is Medvedev's task to ensure the continuity of the chosen roads and to protect them from potential new surprises.

The elections confirmed the will of the people to support the track designed by Putin, through the election of Dmitry Medvedev – 70.28% of the given votes. Gennady Zyuganov's Communist Party improved its results, obtaining 17.75% of the votes, the extreme right party headed by Vladimir Jirinovsky – 9.36%, and Andrey Bogdanov's right-wing party – 1.29%. The complete failure of the right-wing parties was confirmed in various elections in 2004 and 2008.

A crucial issue is to know where Russia is heading to. The Russian people reject definitely the idea to revert to the liberal economy and society. Putin's policies are sliding more and more to the left. Besides the structures they have established, the popular movement is asking more and more a clear and final turn of Russia to the left. The popular movement is still enjoying the benefit of the deep nationalist feelings of the Russian citizens in the protection of the national interests of Mighty Russia. And Russia is irrevocably implementing the highway of social progress.

4. Geopolitics of Revival and Development of the Commonwealth of Independent States

(a) Geopolitics of the Western Powers, Placing Russia at the Frontiers of the 16th Century

The dissolution of the USSR was the greatest economic

and political catastrophe of the 20th century noticed by Vladimir Putin, one of the most important figures of authority in the world. There is no doubt that the annihilation of the USSR through the military intervention of 14 countries after the 1917 revolution and during and after the Second World War had been the main goal of the world domination strategy of the British and the Americans.

The geopolitics of the USA, which exited the Second World War, in a quite braced condition – because they had suffered no war losses or destructions – had as a main goal the weakening and dissolution of the Soviet Union and, thereby, of the Warsaw Pact as well, the annihilation of the bipolar international policies of a power balance and, consequently, the establishing of the world domination of the American financial empire. According to a survey prepared by Zbigniew Brzezinski, one of the most important presidential counselors, the USSR had to be dismembered and its territories be introduced on the neo-liberal market, under the mentoring of the West.

Due to their internal and external support for the chaos and failure programme of Mikhail Gorbachev's perestroika policies, the western counselors pushed the USSR on the brink of precipice.

Taking advantage of the internal political conflicts between Yeltsin and Gorbachev, in their battle for the marshals baton, in the end, and because the bet on Gorbachev's hand was lost, the USA supported Boris Yeltsin's ambitions to take over Russia's leadership; their purpose was the dissolution of the USSR. The project of the "Union Treaty" devised by Gorbachev in an attempt to save the USSR from being dismembered and, at the same time, to save the president's seat for himself, was simply trampled down. On the 8th of December 1991, at Minsk, on the occasion of the meeting arranged upon the request of Boris Yeltsin, the three presidents of the greatest soviet republics – Russia, Ukraine and Belarus – signed a joint statement of dissolution of the USSR as a geopolitical entity and subject of international law. Because of its geopolitical positions, Russia lost, with the dissolution of the USSR, 20% of its territory, about 40% of its population and almost 40% of the total GDP of the former USSR, leaving in uncertainty 70 million of mixed married couples and 25 million of Russians outside the Federation. "Thus, Russia – wrote Yuri Rubinsky – was brought within the frontiers of the 16th century and was almost cut off its access to the warm seas, this perennial goal of the Russian State. The former super-power is facing today all the hardships in the world to maintain its rank as a regional power."[17]

(b) CIS, New Elements for the Expansion of International Cooperation

In order to abate the doubts of Russia's inhabitants on these last intentions of his, Boris Yeltsin replaced the "Union Treaty" by an organisation of the Commonwealth of Independent States. From the very beginning, Yeltsin's formula had rather the goal to dull the great number of new problems issued from the tearing into pieces of the USSR and the peaceful resolution of this "divorce", as well as the redistribution of the burden of the write-off of the old debts, than the development of the economic, political and military cooperation between the former republics of the USSR.

However, as expected, Yeltsin's capitulation strategy shortly met the opposition of the inner ranks of the Russian elite, especially from the Russian generals who were harbouring the nostalgia for Russia's Euro-Asian and global authority.

On the other hand, the former republics of the USSR saw in the fragmentation of this giant a chance for getting their independence and implementing their autonomous social progress policies, liberated from Russian totalitarian domination. Nevertheless, just like orphans in a broken family, where they had lived for four centuries, they were hoping at the same time to find new integration form in the Euro-Asian space. On the 21st of December 1991, just 13 days before the USSR was scattered, 12 of the 15 former Soviet Republics met in Alma Ata and joined the Commonwealth of Independent States.

Only the Baltic countries – Lithuania, Latvia and Estonia – with roughly 7 million inhabitants, whose inclusion into the USSR has never had the recognition of the western nations, did not join the new commonwealth of peaceful adjoining and cooperation.

Although within the CIS there are different opinions regarding the methods, type and forms of cooperation organising and, also, there are different ideological views on the specific features of the commonwealth, the "CIS is forming from now on (after eight years of conflicts, cooperation and mutual collaboration KGV), wrote Jean Christophe Romer, a perfectly outlined geographic space which, to a certain extent, takes the place of the USSR, even if the nature of the integration differs from one state to another".

Jean Christophe Romer goes on: "It has a double purpose: for Moscow, it is the preservation of a certain right to regard these republics, which were part of its empire. Besides, it concerns to preserve, for all, in as far as possible, the economic and industrial connections woven in the USSR times." (18)

Its organisational structure and its functions make the CIS to be closer to European Union, while its actions make of it a new player on the international stage.

The great number of agreements between the member countries of the CIS constitutes proof of an obvious progress feature on the way of common collaboration and cooperation in the economic, political, military, culture and sports areas.

In December 1991, a treaty was concluded for the implementation of a unique headquarters of the strategic military forces, which could provide Russia with the right to control and to decide upon the use of nuclear weapons. In March 1992, joint military forces were set in place for maintaining the peace (at that time, the Ukraine abstained); in June 1994, the Collective Security Treaty was adopted and the Common Defense Convention against military attacks was signed; in March 1996, a new agreement was signed in Moscow between Russia, Kazakhstan, Belarus and Kyrgyzia, in connection with the creation of the Commonwealth of Integrated States, etc.

However, in the analysis of the development of the CIS, it would be impossible to skip the huge economic, ethic, political difficulties of the countries liberated from the soviet totalitarian regime. The military conflicts between the countries and the civil wars in Azerbaijan, Tajikistan, Georgia and other regions, were a major hurdle in the development of economic, political and cultural cooperations.

After Vladimir Putin's ascension to power in Russia in 2000, after the rapid recovery of the Russian economy and after the various conflicts had been settled, the economic, political and cultural cooperation with the CIS countries attained new dimensions.

(c) Putin's and Zyuganov's Geopolitics and the Potential Creation of the Euro-Asian Union

After Russia's economic rise, which surprised the entire western world with its yearly growth of the GDP by 6%, causing the reduction of the inflation, the substantial increase of the augmentation of the foreign currency reserves, Russia prioritised the reorganisation of the CIS and its come-back as one of the great powers on the international stage.

In 2004, Russia, Kazakhstan, Belarus and the Ukraine signed the first agreements referring to the establishing of the new structures within the CIS, named "unitary economic space" (UES). We are speaking here about the constitution of a free trading zone, about the deregulation in view of the free circulation of citizens, of granting tax conveniences, etc., 29 cooperation documents were prepared for signature.

"Speaking about Russia, the Monroe principles declare the entire structure of the ex-USSR as an influence area of its interests, and the former borders as its minimal security outline", says Claire Mouradian. "It weighs quite a lot in the course of history, by its demographic, economic and military supremacy, by its monopoly on the energy resources, as well as by all for encompassing presence of its troops – by its 25 million citizens to be "protected", because of political tensions and ethnic conflicts, and for as many levers to draw the Republic into its orbit."[19]

In his book "Russia after the year 2000. Geopolitical vision of a new state", Zyuganov, the leader of the Communist Party of Russia, writes: "The final goal of the Russian geopolitics must be the creation of some form of confederation, federation or union, of restoring the unity of the to-date split geopolitical field, encompassing also the territory of the ex-USSR."[20]

Contrary to Zyuganov, Putin was very cautious. In his

declarations and meditations, he never disclosed openly his final intentions, undoubtedly because of strategic reasons or of professional distortion, as a former KGB member of the soviet elite. Thus, in his statements, he has always made enigmatic hints to the restoration of the geopolitics of his predecessors, to the opening of the access to the Black Sea and the Baltic Sea, to the strengthening of the multilateral collaboration and cooperation with the member countries of the CIS and to the restoring of Russia's international authority as one of the great powers.

In an attempt to define Putin's enigmatic hints, Jacques Allaman states: "Winston Churchill liked to say that the USSR was a secret packed within a mistery which was concealing an enigma. This wording seems to apply perfectly to Vladimir Putin. Vladimir Putin remains a character as enigmatic as he is mysterious."[21]

Putin's enigmatic ideas found their appropriate echo in the efforts and declarations of Nazarbayev, the president of Kazakhstan, Putin's most faithful spokesmen, a dedicated apparatchik – an official of the old guard of the soviet times. Nazarbayev gets involved in the concept of reorganising and replacing the CIS with the organising project of the Euro-Asian Union of the ex-USSR states.

Most of the member states of the CIS acted very reservedly even in connection with the idea of a Euro-Asian Union and with regard to the premature and immature definitions of the independence statute Nazarbayev submitted to his neighbours. The desire to expand and to enhance the mutual collaboration and cooperation is an objective requirement of social progress, but which continues to meet the opposition of certain right-wing nationalist leaders of the formers USSR states.

(d) The Great Battle for the Ukraine Between the USA and Russia

The militarist circles in the USA, dissatisfied with Vladimir Putin's strategy with regard to the economic rejuvenation of the mighty Russian power and the Commonwealth of the Independent States (CIS), are making secret diplomatic, financial and media efforts for final separation of the Ukraine from Russia.

During the election campaign in October 2004, the United States and, to a certain extent, a number of the EU countries, took advantage of the transition hardships encountered by the Ukrainian economy under the leadership of president Leonid Kuchma, who had been holding this high office for 10 years already, and also of the pro-Russian government of Viktor Yanukovych, to try spreading disorders, using for this purpose the discontent of the part of civil population.

From the moment Viktor Yanukovych, of pro-Russian inclination, offspring of a poor working people family of Donetsk, won the presidential elections at a small difference; the right-wing pro-western opposition took their inspiration from the African banana-republics and made their voters go out into the streets under the pretense of tampered elections. During the demonstrations of the so-called orange revolution, the opposition – which this way had paralysed almost half of the country's economic activities – requested that either the invalidation of the elections or, as an alternative, a civil war should be accepted. The pacifist thinking of Yanukovych's party chose a new election challenge. In course of the new election process – if we could trust the precision of the election results – Viktor Yushchenko reported the victory. The winners were delirious with satisfaction.

The post-election anti-Russian frenzy forced Vladimir Putin to put a stop to the gas pipeline that was supplying and heating most of the Ukraine. Russia warned the new power of the risk of dissolution of the historical and traditional connections to Russia, of the century-long dreams, hopes and will of the two nations.

As regards history and geopolitics, it is very natural for Russia to be vitally interested in the Ukraine and its main cooperation zone. With its 603,700 km^2 and 52 million inhabitants, that is of the size of France, formerly the Russia's granary, centre of the Donetsk mining industry, with a quite developed iron metallurgical, chemical, heating and military industry, with an important seafaring fleet and access to the Black Sea, with 11.3 million Russians (22% of the total population) and almost one quarter of marriages made of mixed couples, the Ukraine justifies in historical and economic outlook Russia's great interest in keeping her as its second important historical, economic and geopolitical partner.

"Millions of Russians are convinced – wrote the chief editor of the Moscow News – that without the Ukraine it would be impossible to speak not only of a great Russia, but simply about Russia as such."[22]

Most Russians considered that, historically seen, Kiev was Russia's cradle. After the Orange Revolution, the majority of the Ukrainians who had awoken from the neo-liberal numbness directed their hopes again towards Mother Russia. The Ukrainians' enthusiasm for the Orange Revolution decreased significantly. The growing popularity and the almost entirely popular support for Viktor Yanukovych forced the president of the republic to accept the will of the people and to give some signs that new positions were taken facing the pro-Russian and anti-imperialistic forces, by the organisation of the new elections on the way of social progress. The new elections forced Viktor Yushchenko, the president of the republic, leader of the Orange Revolution, to step down. He lost the majority of his voters. He had to enter an alliance with the resigned prime minister in order to confront Viktor Yanukovych and the ever more demanding pro-Russia opposition. The latter were asking Yushchenko to be replaced by the organisation of new elections, in view of opening – in case of a victory – new cooperation relations with Mother Russia, of economic and political stability and prosperity relations.

(e) Belarus, Kazakhstan, Uzbekistan and Moldova on the Road of Transition from the Totalitarian Regime to the Democratic Socialism

After the collapse of the totalitarian socialism in the Soviet Union and in other east European countries, the trend for the restoration of capitalism was not a compulsory track for the failed socialism. In these countries of the old Soviet Union, such as Belarus, Moldova, Kazakhstan and Uzbekistan, where the political party leaders understood at the proper time the objective need of the liberalisation, of the erasing of the totalitarian ideology and the liberalisation of the social conscience. They directed their prospects to the democratisation, liberalisation and humanising of the system by way of fundamental structural changes.

Moldova, Kazakhstan, Uzbekistan and, with a few exceptions, Belarus, were, just like other republics on the borders of the former Soviet Union, either underdeveloped or very underdeveloped countries. In 1991, Moldova had a GDP per inhabitant lower than that of Haiti, Uzbekistan and Kazakhstan and, despite the soil and underground rich in oil, gas and other hardly ever mined ores, its GDP reached per inhabitant an amount of 1800 – 2500 US dollars.

After the dissolution of the USSR, these countries chose the way of national independence and mutually equal cooperation, within a new alliance of 12 Euro-Asian countries of the former Soviet Union. One by one, the old totalitarian structures were abolished.

The gradual democratisation of the political system by the establishing of multi-party system, the setting up of the constitutional state under the law, the privatisation of various businesses, the industrialisation, electrification, modernisation of the infrastructure, the reduction of inflation and public debt, as well as a great number of other radical reforms have sped up the economic growth and the diminishing of poverty.

In spite of the presence of many cracks in the system, which made often the object of oversised criticism in the western media, the success of the economic and social reforms is perfectly obvious.

The economic growth rate of these countries balanced in the last years around 6%– 9%. As a result of a relatively high production rate, the GDP per inhabitant rose in 2004 in Belarus to 7,561 US dollars, in Kazakhstan to 8,700 dollars, in Uzbekistan to 2,000 dollars, and in Moldova to 1,500 dollars. The unemployment dropped in Belarus to 1.9%, and in the other countries to about 4 – 6%. Over a time span of 10 years, the inflation decreased to 15%. In most of the countries, the education rate of the children attained 95%, etc.[23]

The economic relations of these countries are developing successfully within the CIS. Russia is still the main economic partner in the trade exchange and in technical cooperation.

China is the second important partner of these countries. The recent signing of an agreement between China and Kazakhstan for the construction of an oil pipe to China, as well as the increasing merchandise exchange, represents a proof of the establishment and development of new economic relations, based on the principle of observing independence, cooperation and mutual benefit. The repeated attempts of the USA to infiltrate their influence in these countries in order to destroy the CIS failed.

The geo-strategic, political and social-economic cooperations of these countries, which open simultaneously towards Europe and the United States, enjoyed a large support from the voters. The updated ex-communist leaders obtained repeatedly the support of the greatest part of the population in course of democratic elections. President Nazarbayev of Kazakhstan, and Pesident Lukashenko of Belarus, as well as Islom Karimov, President of Uzbekistan, renewed their mandates by referendum and free and democratic elections. They have been ruling their countries for 16 years. Also, in Moldova, the representatives of the Communist Party are dominant in power. In the 2005 elections, the mandate of President Vladimir Voronin – representative of the Communist Party – was renewed to no surprise.

The reelection of the best manager of a country, by referendum and by free elections, raises the question whether such an election is justified or legal. It is a completely new issue of the constitutional law. When a president and a political party, or a political alliance of the parties in power, are leading their peoples successfully – which is confirmed by a referendum or by democratic elections, in this case – then to deprive them of the extension of their mandate is not a democratic solution and contradicts the interests of the voters.

The essence of a country's leadership is not only the alternation by elections, even if in most cases it plays a progressive role, but the capability of the political leaders and parties to successfully lead their peoples to the promised land.

5. Return of the Reinvigorated Left in the East-European Countries

(a) The Hiroshima of the Transition to Capitalism

Along with the demolition of the soviet totalitarian system, which extended over several years in most of the countries of

Eastern Europe, except Yugoslavia (Serbia and Montenegro) and Romania, the road chosen for the destruction of the old relations, the transition road to the restoring of liberalism did not encounter any significant opposition from the civil society. In most of the East-European countries there took place "velvet revolutions", revolutions of the Czech type, which brought to power either the right-wing intellectual elite (Czechoslovakia), or the surviving leaders of the older bourgeois parties (Bulgaria), or the newly established right-wing parties, unions and organisations (Hungary, Albania, Croatia).

Under the pretense of the inclusion of these states in the European Union, the IMF and the World Bank, behind which stand the multinational oligarchies, determined – just as they had once done in the former USSR – the rules of the transition to the liberalism of the western type of market economy.

Thus, neo-liberalism, as a strategy of the IMF and the World Bank, became the guiding creed of the right-wing leading circles and of some left-wing groups in the East-European countries. "Established based on the Keynes-like interventionism – wrote the authors of the book "A New Central Europe", under Marcin's heading – on the rejection of the mixed economy and on the trust in the self-regulating market, they found their expression especially in "understanding with Washington", which provides for the indebted emerging countries the liberalisation, privatisation, structural adjustment and austerity programmes meant to throttle inflation and to restore the budget balance."[24]

The consequences of the western neo-liberal strategy on the ways of transition to the market economy, were catastrophic for the ruined economy, dragging along the mafia, the corruption, the sharp decrease of the living standard, sometimes by 30% below the standard prior to the reform, and also the spreading of begging, vagrancy, material and moral decadence of part of the population.

In the difficult times of transition I traveled to almost each of the former socialist countries in Eastern Europe. I could speak to about one hundred of deceived and morally confused people. I can not remember to have ever felt, nor could I have ever imagined what I felt and recorded on the CDs of the human race tragedy. They were more and more alike a social-economic Hiroshima of Eastern Europe, more than the promised anteroom to the wellbeing on earth.

The yearly GDP growth rate, as a sign of the success or failure of an economy, was negative between the years 1990 – 1997: in Bulgaria – 5.5%, in Hungary – 1.1%, in the Czech Republic – 0.4%, in Romania – 2.2%, in Russia – 7.7%, in Slovakia – 0.3%. After eight years of transition, no other country, except Poland, has attained the figure of the 1989 GDP.

According to the official reports, the unemployment rose from 0% to 10%, and according to the estimations of the experts it exceeded 15% of the active population – the last border of patience and revolt.

The sharp drop of the living standard, by 30% in an average as compared to the values of the time span from 1985 – 1990 and, particularly, the increasing poverty of those who were living with less than 02 dollars a day, were the main evaluation parameter of the tragic effects of the transition. While the prices of the consumers goods, as resulting from the economic integration in Europe, were closing more and more on the price levels practised in Europe, the salaries were getting less and less close to the European standards. At that time, in the East European countries, the average salaries ranged between 180 – 250 Euros.

The worst affected victims of the transition were the retired persons, whose minimum monthly incomes were ranging between 80 and 180 Euros.

For instance, in Romania, 5.6 million retired live on the verge of hunger, cold and lacking of any conveniences of the contemporary civilisation. The great French-Romanian writer Emil Cioran wrote that the greatest enemy of our lives is the disappointment of the people leading difficult lives.

While ever larger groups of the new rich are wallowing in expensive gadgets and spending expensive cars and glamorous houses, making an easy life in western luxury, almost 25-35% of the country's inhabitants live under the poverty limit. The quick rise of the wealth difference between the ever richer rich and the ever poorer poor people only confirm the negative consequences of the transition.

(b) Triumph of Liberalism or Revival of Socialism

Now, when the transition has left behind the straights of general damage and started once again on the way of economic growth, certain western authors analyse the positive and negative aspects of the transition. After the transition has outlived the turmoil and drawback moments and taken decisively to the tracks of normal social progress, dozens of surveys and journalist reports have been published in the West on the great successes of transition, on the economic stabilising and the victory of the liberal market economy.

It is not the place for celebrating a triumph of neo-liberalism. The privatisation of public property is not equal to the success and domination of private property, as more than half of the latter is still detained by the state, by its cadres, by the shareholding workers and employees of the state businesses. The share capital of such businesses, with their state and semi-state sectors, in the fields of energy, transports, banking, finances, post and communication, is the foundation of a potential partial socialisation of the main production means, the main basis of a new social alternative.

Confused by the effects of the transition, the civil society in the East European countries has an ever less passive behaviour to their own destiny and even less passive to the fate of their children and great-children. Stunned by the promises of an easier life on the way of market economy, the wonders of which they are told would be beyond the capacity of their generation's memory, the greater part of the civil society is waking up, shaking down their sleepiness and turning more and more their faces to the Church, to the clergy and to God, but also towards the leftist parties, renewed along the search for a different alternative to their own establishment.

(c) Rise and Come-Back to Power of the Left-Wing Parties

Depending on the GDP and the development stage of the production forces, the cultures and civilisations of the East European countries are classified – according to economic and political assessments – as belonging to the group of average developed countries, with a GDP per inhabitant ranging between 7,000 and 20,000 Euros.

Contrary to the expectations of the international financial oligarchy, the democratisation of the East European countries and the transition to the market economy had the positive effects on regeneration, reform and ideological and political redirection of the former communist and workers' parties. The totalitarian system had failed, but a large number of the party members and supporters kept the nostalgia of the return of the left in their spirits, beliefs and wishes, and also the hope for the revival of a united, social, democratic and humanitarian society.

Confused by the shock of the transition, the leftist political parties resulted out of the incubators of the former communist and workers' parties, raised the flag of liberty, democracy, socialism and internationalism from the ashes and ruins. They raised again the flag of revolutionary reforms on the road to social progress.

A new ascension stage of the left is nearing which, by means of its political programmes, is gradually conquering the voters in the East European countries, who are dissatisfied with the transition. A new stage is coming of the return in power of the socialist and social-democratic left, without Lenin's storming the Winter Palace, without Mao's Long March, without Ernest Galant's Columbian guerrilla and without Che Guevara's revolutionary romanticism or Zapata's revolution.

The Bulgarian political scientist Ivan Krastev, who does not hide his hate for the new socialist and social-democratic left, characterised this new progressive movement as populism. "Central Europe – he says – makes a vital image of the new populism. In power in Poland, the new populism conquered the power in Slovakia, in its leftist vision, and pushed forward in Bulgaria. In fact, the populist style is triumphant in most other post-communist countries."[25]

In Poland, after the failure of Lech Walesa's politics, the united left was the one rising to power in 1993. Five years later, in 1997, the right came again to power. In 2001, it was replaced by the left. At the end of 2005, the democratic left was once again released by the moderate neo-liberal right. The political alternation of the left-wing and right-wing parties is precisely the reflection of the new road to social progress.

In Romania, the left had a longer life than the right. In 17 years of transition, the left held the power for the duration of three mandates, respectively for 10 years, while the right governed for seven years, the office of President Bãsescu coming to an end at the end of 2009. In the 2008 parliamentary elections, President Bãsescu's party was forced to share the power with the social-democratic left.

In Hungary, the right-wing parties won the presidential elections, while the left-wing ones dominated mostly the parliaments, the state structures and the most important ministries. In the latest elections, on the 6th and 7th of July 2005, the President of the Republic, Laszlo Solyom, candidate of the Civic Alliance, a right-wing political structure, was re-elected with the majority of the deputies' votes. The Hungarian socialist party won the office of a prime-minister and some of the ministries.

Prior to 2006, Czechia was under the government of the coalition between social-democrats and Christian-democrats. For the 2006 elections, the left-wing coalition – the social-democratic party and the communist party – obtained 100 seats in the parliament, and the left-wing parties other 100 seats. A great coalition of the two political currents was achieved in the end.

In Serbia and Montenegro, or in the shrunken ex-Yugoslavia, the socialist party of Slobodan Milosevic detained the power for 10 years, under the most difficult conditions of the civil war in Bosnia, and suffered economic sanctions, military occupation in Kosovo, bombing of military facilities and material damages estimated at 200 billion dollars. After four government years of the right-wing liberal party, the power was held by a government of the leftist democratic party of Boris Tadic, member of the Socialist International, in alliance with the moderate right-wing party. In January 2008, the left-wing forces of Boris Tadic won the presidential elections and later on, together with their allies, the parliamentary elections, too.

In Bulgaria, the royalist right-wing political parties dominated at power. In the recent years, the leftist socialist party, renewed as the most powerful party of the opposition, arrived to win the parliamentary elections and took on, along with the Bulgarian Popular Alliance, the parliamentary and governmental majority.

In Croatia, the coalition around the social-democratic party (a leftist party) is under the leadership of Stjepan Mesic, the last president of the former Yugoslavia. After he had won the presidential and parliamentary elections in 2000, in 2003 he lost the advanced parliamentary elections, just to win the next presidential elections in 2005, following the repositioning of his politics.

In Slovenia, this small republic of the former Yugoslavia, which counts two million inhabitants, the political parties of the left-wing coalition dominated the power after the independence of 1991. They were going to be replaced by the centre-right parties in the democratic elections. In December 2007, after the catastrophic failure of the right-wing parties, the leftist political parties returned to power through a stupendous victory – 68% of the cast ballots.

In Macedonia, Boris Crvenkovski, the candidate of the social-democratic alliance, a man with a long experience in the left-wing socialist movement, won the last presidential elections of the 14th and 28th of April 2004 – a convincing victory, with 62.7% of the votes – and at present his party is holding the parliamentary majority and the main state structures.

In the Serbian Republic of Bosnia and Herzegovina, the long-lasting administration of the traditional right-wing parties, which bear their part of responsibility in the civil war and the atrocities done during the civil war, was replaced in the democratic elections by the representatives of the moderate social-democratic party.

In the remaining East European countries, for instance in Albania and in Motenegro, the left-wing socialist and social-democratic parties and alliances are the political parties of the opposition. They occupy one-third or half of the parliament seats in these countries and they are preparing to take political revenge in the next elections.

When we study the encouraging process of the awakening of the socialist left on its way of social progress revival, we may determine, with no risk to go wrong, the first balance sheet of the new track of the social progress. The attempt of liberalism, of the savage capitalism, to integrate these countries in the common space of western globalisation is on the brink of failure.

After the failure of the totalitarian system and of the hurricane of the transition to the savage market liberalism, the people of these countries are on their way to the revival of democratic, liberal and humanitarian socialism.

The road to victory is still long ahead. The mist concealing the roads to progress is receding, making the way for light.

6. Revival and Modernisation of Socialism in China

(a) Confucianism, Marxism and Maoism, the Philosophical Foundation of Chinese Socialism

The People's Republic of China, emerged in 1949 from the Long March of the national and social revolution against imperialism and the pro-Japanese bourgeoisie, grown out of one of the oldest world civilisations and bred by Confucianism, Marxism and Maoism, stepped on its own way of social progress.

For a good understanding of the Chinese way of social progress, we have to introduce our readers from the very beginning to the two circumstances that influenced the course of the Chinese revolution.

On the one hand, the historically traditional character of the understanding of human existence differs from the ancient universal philosophies of the West : "China, as wrote the French author François Julien, forms a different world, which was established independently of our thinking systems and landmarks; it is a world which is debating things that we automatically consider as being universal."[26]

This revolutionary and, at the same time, traditional, philosophical system originates from the ethical and philosophical views of the great thinkers, from Laozi and Confucius to Lu Hxuna and Mao Zedong. It discovers the sources of life and of the future of society in the education and development of the individual, of the family, of the community. The tenacious work, the patience, modesty, harmony the absolute respect for the authorities constitute the components of the birth of a new civilisation, which is behaving towards the western civilisation in perfectly the same way the latter used to act once face to the ancient societies.

On the other hand, as far as the social and economic character is concerned, from the economic point of view China was even less developed than tsarist Russia. In 1940, feudalism was the prevailing form of social relations, and capitalism was still in its very incipient stage. The capitalist private property had not yet grown roots in the minds and traditions of people. Practically, the wind of industrial revolution had not yet blown over the Chinese territory. Every year, over 20 million Chinese dies of starvation, while the birth rate attained fabulous figures.

This is why China had become one of the poorest countries in our world, despite its extremely valuable moral and intellectual traditions, despite its huge natural resources and despite its population – the first as number of inhabitants in the world.

The main goal of the Chinese way in the establishment of a new society was to set up new social relations, to liberate labour from estrangement, and to set the production forces free from standstill, to erase starvation and increased mortality. In addition, there were the increase of the farming production and providing nourishment to the population from domestic resources, and also the turning of China from an under-developed agrarian country into an industrial society of average development rate, by means of accelerated industrialisation.

In spite of the 10 year long sabotage (1966 – 1977) caused by the cultural revolution – which was opposed to modernisation – China made great progress in the diminishing of poverty, illiteracy, and ignorance, throughout 26 years of development.

In the years of the cultural counter-revolution, the Chinese economic machinery exhausted its development potential. The average increase rate of the industrial and agricultural production dropped from 12% to 4.2%, to reach then its lowest figure, namely 1.4%.[27]

The need arose for destroying the ideology and practice of the cultural counter-revolution, for leaving behind the dogmatic political thinking of the Chinese Communist Party and for achieving an actual ideological revolution. Moreover, the reform from the grass-roots up was necessary of the Chinese economic machinery, which grew more and more ineffective and, at the same time, the updating, to comply with the spirit of the times, of the economy, the society and even of the theory of development of socialism.

(b) Ideological revolution and Implementation of Marxism in Chinese Style

In the countries with strong reminiscence of state socialism, of bureaucracy, where the social superstructure, the ideology, the political parties and their leaders determine the social-economic development currents and the economic life framework, the radical track changes of the social progress are possible only starting from the ideological revolution and the revolutionary change of the intrinsic concept of the development of socialism. In this case, the economic basis is not decisive for the social superstructure but, on the contrary, in a certain evolution stage of contradictions, the social superstructure is the one to decide the main directions of economic development. This is the real revolution, in the Marxist vision, of the mutual dynamic relation between the economic basis and the social superstructure.

After the "cultural counter-revolution" had been destroyed, and having these new relations as a starting point, the Chinese Communist Party rejected the idea of class struggle as main force of social progress and completed the implementation of Marxism in Chinese style. Besides, they rejected also the Stalinist idea of the final victory of socialism. Hence, after suppressing the cultural counter-revolution, the Chinese Communist Party initiated the modernisation of the Chinese socialism. The state property was re-organised by the privatisation and transfer of art of the businesses in favour of foreign and local private investors. Giving up the collectivisation of agriculture and returning the land to the individual producers, establishing of capitalist customs-free sea zones according to Deng Xiaoping's new theory of "one state, two systems", the free action of the economic laws of socialism and capitalism and the coexistence of the public and private sectors to the benefit of the erection of socialism, all that set free the creative energies of the society from the chains of the state ...

Hence, the Chinese Communist Party destroyed certain taboos of Marxism-Leninism and opened new ways to liberate the creative energy of the popular masses, the new development ways of socialism.

(c) Modernisation, Transition and Revival of Socialism

In 1976, after the deaths of Mao Zedong and Chu En-Lai, the founders of the new China, Deng Xiaoping and the new generation of young politicians took over the historical mission of modernising the economic and political system.

The reinvigoration of the Chinese socialism embraced four progressive forms: readjustment, reform, reorganisation and optimisation. They include an entire scaffolding of gradual and successive economic and social changes which, one by one, destroy the old relations and establish new, wider spaces for a more efficient function of economy and society.

According to the statements of Joseph Stiglitz, Nobel Prize recipient, ex-councilor to Bill Clinton and knowledgeable in the matter of Chinese circumstances, the mentioned Chinese leaders applied the strategy of "creative destruction", meaning gradual and partial liberalisation, which makes the difference to Mikhail Gorbachev's destructive soviet strategy and to Boris Yeltsin's shock therapy. "Hence – wrote Stiglitz – China laid the basis of a new economy on the pedestal of the already existing institutions, preserving and strengthening the social capital, while Russia eroded it."[28]

According to the official documents of the Chinese Communist Party, the observance of the four principles listed below constitutes the main prerequisite for the successful modernisation and continuous development of socialism, namely: the socialist road to development of the society, the power of the working people, the leading role of the communist party, Marxism-Leninism and Mao Zedong's thinking as ideological foundation of the development of Chinese society.

The great reforms of the functioning mechanisms of the economic machinery were directed both to the maximum enlargement of the financial and administrative autonomy of the businesses and to their management in compliance with the profitability principles and the action of market laws, and also to the free constitution of prices, while the reorganisation of the businesses following the provisions of joint-stock and holding companies statutes and the gradual transition to the "social market economy". In other words, the Chinese economy assimilated critically all positive elements of the western society that might be beneficial to the development of socialism. Deng Xiaoping's famous sentence, by which "no matter if the cat is black or white, all that matters is it catches mice", became the new ideological support of the great fundamental reforms.

The restructuring of the entire system of economic property relations constituted the greatest and most daring modernisation action of the said system. Starting from the concept that capitalism has not exhausted all its positive driving forces and that it could still serve the development of socialism in certain circumstances of the prevailing collective property. The Chinese initiated the new paths of social progress as follows :

- Development of agriculture by giving up the collectivisation of a great part of the farming activities and supporting the cottage-type farming and the private industrial businesses in the rural environment
- Development of the private industrial, trading and transport businesses which in 2004 employed 128 million workers and clerks.
- Opening towards the outer world by establishing of free capitalist economic zones for foreign investments, according to Den Xiaoping's ideological principle "one state, two systems".

Until the end of 2000, the structure of the Chinese economy had changed radically, depending on the type of property: the state enterprises were producing 48.3% of the global production, the private foreign businesses accounted for 27.1%, the cooperatives for 15.2%, and the Chinese private businesses 9.4%.[29]

At the end of 2003, a number of 2514 businesses, that is 45% of the total number of state enterprises had been turned into mixed enterprises, where the state held the majority of shares. The Chinese system of partial privatisation leaves room enough for the perpetuation of the role of society in the economic development.

Speaking about the development of the private sector up to a certain limit and about the establishing of free capitalist zones, Deng Xiaoping stated: "We are certain that, if the first one (the capitalist sector KGV) is allowed to exist in certain small areas, then it will be profitable for the development of the second one (the socialist sector KGV). Similarly, we are practising an opening policy in approximately 20 cities, but only under the condition of a prevailing socialist economy; we do not think that the nature of the socialist economy will undergo changes due to this reason. On the contrary, this kind of policy will further the expansion and development of the socialist economy."[30]

(d) The Western Concept of the Chinese Transition to the Market Economy

Contrary to the positive practical results of the Chinese socialism development, the western analysts of the Chinese changes justified the great achievements of this country by means of the effects of restoring the capitalist market. They write, say and spread everywhere the ideas of the progressive shrinking of the Chinese type socialism, with no great disturbances in the transition to capitalism. A Romanian folk saying goes like this: "Sparrow dreams of grain and corn."

What the right-wing media analysts write and say, to deceive the public, is less interesting for us (since it is no more than their comfortable source to make a living), but it is important to reprimand the association of certain neo-Marxists with the western ideology.

In their studies on the Chinese market socialism, they sustain that the project of the Chinese leading class with regard to the modernisation of society has capitalist roots and that the market socialism turns to be a shortcut for the gradual setting up of the essential structures and institutions of capitalism.

Which is the truth and which is the error made by the various analysts of the changes in the Chinese economy?

It is true that, by restoring the market socialism, by partial privatisation of the state property and by establishing free capitalist zones, the Chinese developed capitalist elements, triggered the appearance of a new bourgeois class, of unemployment, of a mass rural flight, they worsened the housing crisis, the inflation and other components of the liberal economy. Nevertheless, it is equally true that the prevailing socialist ideology, the prevailing collective property and the changes of the state and social structure brought by the Chinese Communist Party determine the main roads of socialism development in China.

(e) The 17th Congress of the Communist Party: "Raise High the Flag of Socialism in Chinese Style"

Contrary to the misinformation spread by the western right-wing media, with regard to true social-economic changes and to opening towards the socialist market economy, to the outer world, which lead – say such media – to the "restoration of capitalism", the 17th Congress of the Chinese Communist Party, organised to take place in October 2007, confirmed in steady and immovable way the rightfulness of the Chinese way of socialism.

The radical reforms of the Chinese socialism are not the expression of a temporary adjustment. They are rather the sign of deep structural changes, of a great revolution which alters the direction and the ways of social progress.

"The flag of socialism, pointed out Hu Jintao, General Secretary of the Central Committee of the Chinese Communist Party and President of the Republic, represents a flag that is guiding contemporary China to development and progress and which spurns the entire party and multi-ethnic people to be dedicated to the same struggle, in perfect union."

"From now on, continued Hu Jintao, our country starts her way on a path that was her own and which is no other than that of the erection of the Chinese socialism."

"Socialism alone can save China, the politics of reforms and opening alone can develop simultaneously China, the socialism and Marxism."

"The reforms and the opening – declared Hu Jintao at the 17th Congress of the Chinese Communist Party – are perfectly encompassed in the great revolution carried on by the people under the leadership of the Party, in a new historical background. Also, this revolution aims at pushing the socialist regime of our country to the search of their own optimisation and evolution, to the revival of socialism and the erection and development of the Chinese socialist society."[31]

I have quoted parts of the speeches at the 17th congress of the Chinese Communist Party, with no comments of MY own, in order to provide the defeatist readers the conviction on the steady decision of the Chinese Communist Party to continue on the way of Chinese socialism.

(f) Stupendous Successes of Chinese Socialism

After the initiation of the great social transformations of 1977-1979, the People's Republic of China achieved not only the fundamental goals of the revival and modernisation of socialism, but also, especially, it reinforced socialism as a vital social system, capable to self-reproduce due to its dynamism, to its great achievements which surprised the entire world.

China has already become the second economic power of the world. According to the remarks of the French journalists Serge Marti and Jean Bejat, she has become the "developing economic giant, which scares at present as much as it seduces". China has become the "industrial workshop of the world", somewhat like England in the late 18th and the early 19th centuries. At present, China accounts for 18% of the world exports.[32]

As per a survey prepared by the Rand Corporation, reproduced by Zyuganov, "Nearing 2015, China will catch up with the USA in point of the Gross Domestic Product (11-12 trillion dollars)."[33] Probably, by 2020. In the Report of the 17th Congress of the Chinese Communist Party, Hu Jintao predicted that the GDP per inhabitant would increase four times and that the general development of the society would be achieved, at an average standard of living.

With her up-to-date technique and technologies, with her workers' impetus, responsibility and modesty, China produces all that the human ingenuity may imagine. She produces all kinds of things, from the most up-to-date industrial equipment, to top technology, computers, robots, up to automobiles, tractors, airplanes, atomic submarines, and further on upto inter-continental missiles.

China meets 90% of the needs of her population from her

domestic industrial production. In agriculture, she covers already 95% of her requirements for cereals.

In the last 20 years, the income of the farmers has tripled. According to a study of the OECD, approximately 400 million peasants have left the poverty area (less than one US dollar a day). There were only 88 million left in 2002 and 20 million in 2007.

In the foreign trade, China has become the terrific competitor of the West. So as noted by the aforesaid journalists: "China is manufacturing and selling everything, everywhere. In all fields and on all markets, China is pushing forward."

In the exchange of goods and commodities, China attains yearly a foreign currency excess of roughly 100 billion dollars and a reserve of 1100 US dollars more. This accounts for China having exceeded Japan, the first champion in matter of foreign currency reserves and the top world investor in the underdeveloped countries.

In 2004, when I visited the USA with an official delegation of the Republic of the Ivory Coast, I was stunned by the ridiculously low prices of the Chinese consumer goods, which were plenty in the uptown shops. I bought sight glasses for 1.5 dollars and a pair of house slippers for the same amount, while the cheapest American glasses were selling for about 20 dollars, and a pair of similar slippers with 7 dollars.

Then I was able to understand the quiet, tenacious and almost invisible Chinese strategy to conquer the West and the South. The Chinese have conquered and undermined the Western economy not by means of atomic bombs, inter-continental missiles and socialist propaganda, but rather by the strategy of sales at very low prices and with less expensive capital.

However, China's role in the revival and globalisation of socialism is marking a completely new phenomenon: we might say, a Chinese demographic phenomenon of exporting to less developed countries the Chinese labour, experts, businessmen and, often, common people. The Chinese civilisation, as Zyuganov was writing, is not limited to continental China.

According to the quotes from Zyuganov, approximately 55 million Chinese are abroad. In Singapore, they are accounting for one fourth of the population and are controlling 70% of the capital. In Thailand, they are 10% with 80% of the capital. In the Philippines, they number 1% of the population and have 35% of the capital. In Indonesia, the percentage of Chinese presence accounts for 3% and 70%. In Malaysia, the Chinese are present at a rate of two-third of the population, controlling the entire economy.[33]

It is hard to estimate how many Chinese will be in 20 years time in the underdeveloped countries–Probably some 100 or 200 million messengers of the revival and globalisation of the new social progress.

In his book "When China Will Wake Up, the World Will Shudder", published in 1973 and dedicated to the Chinese philosophy of the social life and progress strategy, Alain Peyrefitte, French sociologist, was drawing the world's attention upon the intellectual, moral and material forceS which, in several decades' time, will shake our planet. 23 years later, the same author published his second book on the Chinese miracle, under the title "China Has Woken Up". In the early 21st century, quietly, but assuredly, China WILL begins to shake our world.

At the middle of this century, she will be the main pillar and the driving motor of the worldwide revival and globalisation of socialism, a promoter of the cooperation in the conditions of equal rights and mutual help, the messenger of the new human civilisation under way of becoming. "The Asian civilisation, said Jiang Zemin, one of those accountable for the modernisation of China, was for some time the very motive power of history; she will regain her glory through the promotion of the development of mankind throughout the new century to come."[34]

"Certainly, the power of China will be not bound to our lands and our possessions, but her regained splendour can prove to be cruel for our arrogance."[35] Having said all that, there can not be any more intelligent warning for those lacking a clear vision on the Chinese revival.

7. Revival of India on the Road of progress of the Great Nations

(a) Gandhi and Nehru, the Founders of the Indian Way of the Non-Violent Democratic Socialism

After a summary of several crucial changes in great China, with a billion two hundred million inhabitants, which amazed the entire world by her economic and social progresses, our attention is turning now to the second greatest in size and number of people nation in the world, namely great India. The attribute "great" China and "great" India is not so much significant as meaning, as by the demographic, social-economic and geo-strategic position occupied by these two greatest nations of the world.

In this new constellation of the great powers, the acknowledgement by the public of India's track, could help the readers to better understand their own future, since the future of every individual, of every local, regional and national community depends more and more not on their individual, collective and national efforts, as rather on the common efforts of the great powers.

The western industry of forging the public opinion has been for a long time quite scarce in information on the evolution of the Indian socialism and, burdened by its own logic reason, it attributed all the great achievements to India's opening to the western world.

The journalists of the French magazine L'Express published, in a highly professional journalistic style, really refined and attractive, on more than 60 pages, a number of interesting news about the mutation of India, ascribed to the opening towards the liberal economy market, not to the opening to the social economy market.

In fact, all the great Indian economic reforms are a reflection of the continuity of the socialist concepts of the founders of the new India.

Mahatma Gandhi, the great Indian thinker, philosopher, sociologist, pioneer of the Indian movement of the struggle for the liberation from British colonialism and founder of free, independent, non-violent and democratic India, also founder of the greatest party – the Congress Party – of leftist political orientation, was dreaming to achieve the Indian socialist revolution. He wrote that "only the non-violent and pure at soul socialists will know how to erect a genuine socialist society in India and in the entire world".[36]

No doubt at all, Mahatma Gandhi, contemporary with the October Revolution and the soviet totalitarian regime, with the Chinese revolution, drew his inspiration for national and social freedom not only from the experience of all the great revolutions, but also from the traditions of Hinduism and from the Indian concept saying that "we are all brethren"; he sketched the Indian route of the non-violent social evolution.

Unfortunately, Mahatma Gandhi did not survive to the achievement of his ideals. The ideas of the non-violent and democratic socialism, spread by Gandhi, were temporarily cut out by his assassination in 1947. The relay of the Indian revival was taken up by his political combat comrade Jawaharlal Nehru who, along a period of 17 years, was the successful leader of the Indian revival, until he was also assassinated in 1964.

As Gandhi's former closest coworker, as a founding member of the Congress Party, as a supporter of the great movement for national liberation and social freedom, Nehru worked out – after Gandhi's assassination – the programme of the democratic and non-violent path of the Indian socialism, taking into account the national traditions and the local social-economic circumstances.

"Jawaharlal Nehru, wrote the authors of the book *India after the Independence*, may be rightfully considered as the architect of modern India. One of the great Indian thinkers of the 20th century, he was characterised as a democrat, socialist, humanist and visionary, but he was far more than all that. Nehru rejects the capitalist development; in turn and instead, he works at the fundamental transformation of the Indian society in the socialist direction."[37]

(b) The Indian Concept on the Social Progress

After having acquired her national independence in 1947, India had to face almost the same issues of underdevelopment: the important remainders of feudalism, the absolute prevailing peasantry, the illiteracy (which had reached a rate of 80%), the terrible poverty, undernourishment and starvation. Moreover, India had to face the same hardships that confronted both Russia in 1917, after the October Revolution, and China, after the victory of the national democratic revolution of 1950.

India had to face the challenges of particular and specific geographic issues (long-lasting and severe drought episodes), with anthropological and sociologic issues of the ancient Hindu culture and of the philosophy of submission, patience and forgiveness, with the great local diversity of 42 federal states, where 16 languages and 500 dialects were spoken, and with a great number of religious tensions between Hindus (82% of the population), Muslim and Sikh (18%). In the labyrinth of diversity, the Indian social progress reunited all the contradicting trends in one national understanding for the establishment of a democratic multi-party system, where the Congress Party, with its leftist social-democratic orientation, played for a long time and is still playing the dominant role.

The approximately twenty political parties of the Indian society are divided into national parties and regional and local parties: the Congress Party, the Communist Party of India, the Communist Party of the Indian Marxists and a right-wing nationalist party, Bharatiya Janata Party (BJP). The remaining parties have local character, and especially religious character, of nationalist, liberal or social orientation.

The social-democratic evolutionist type Congress Party was in power between 1947 and 1977, 1980-1989, 1991-1999. It got the confidence of the voters also in the 2004 elections. It is the most powerful, leading political force of the country. Founded on the principles of democracy, liberty and non-violence, it has been and is still prevailing for the social progress for the last 57 years.

In the 2004 elections, the Congress Party, under the traditional leadership of Sonia Gandhi, obtained 221 seats of the total 543 of the parliament and, in coalition with the communist parties and other democratic parties, it held the majority in parliament.

Due to its ideology, its principles and strategies for social progress, this party differs from the European social-democracy, from the former soviet totalitarian socialism and from the Chinese path of socialism.

The difference of the Indian socialism offered a new vision on social progress and constituted, no doubt, a contribution to the discovery of various ways, having though similar goals of establishing a new society. It deserves, of course, an exhaustive and special investigation, which exceeds the scope of my research. That is why I shall try in this limited volume to show to my readers in short some of the specific features of the Indian social progress.

Taking on some of the positive features of the bourgeois democracy, of the older semi-feudal democracy, based on the caste system and observing precisely the principles of the separation of the three powers (legislative, executive and judicial), the principles of multi-party system, the parliamentary alternation and democracy, the Congress Party implemented thus the most extensive democracy in the world, as assessed by most analysts.

By socialisation of only the largest businesses and banks and by the implementation of a extensive protectionist mechanism for defending its industries, the State mobilised almost all available means for the economic-social development. The state acted with focused attention in the light industries, for the implementation of the Green Revolution and to erase starvation, to reduce poverty, to develop education, teaching, science and culture, and for the social security of its citizens.

At the time, India was facing a dilemma: either to choose a soviet industrialisation method, to develop the heavy industry and thus to accelerate the economic growth rate to 8-10% but, at the same time, to slow down the increase of the agricultural production and that of the consumer goods or, on the contrary, to take the path of the methods of capitalist industrialisation, forcing first the light industries, the food and farming industries, to start then on the way of the socialist industrialisation methods.

India chose the middle road: rapid reduction of starvation, of the latent massive unemployment and of the indescribable poverty, the accelerated development of the light and food industries, of agriculture and, later on, the creation of the heavy industry and the metal working industry. After the agrarian reform, the Congress Party rejected the Soviet way of violent collectivisation and destruction of private property. True to the traditional principles of the non-violent revolution, India took the way of partial collectivisation of agriculture, by keeping up the rural private property, associated in cooperatives, and by material motivation of both the cooperatives and of the small private farming units.

India succeeded in achieving the Green Revolution, with an average increase of the Gross Domestic Product of 3.7% in the period of the years 1951-1980. The country succeeded to feed her entire population from her own production, to get rid of starvation. With 600 million tons, India became the greatest world producer of food produce, the first milk producer in the world, the second producer of fruit, vegetables and cereals, the second greatest rice exporter in the world. Fighting against drought, India has the widest irrigation system in the world.

The food industry, representing 6% of the total industrial production or 70 billion US dollars in sales, has grown, due to its quality and diversity, to one of the most up-to-date in the world.

India did not underrate the development of heavy metal working and energy production industries. She included them into formula: priority of the agricultural production and of the food industry.

Industrialisation, the Green Revolution and their positive effects of social emancipation were supported by the foreign policy, based on the general cooperation with the former states of the USSR. Erection of the foundations of the Indian industry, of her important energetic system, of the steel industry, of the irrigation system, up to the soviet technical assistance in the building of atomic power plants and of the defensive atomic system, which laid the foundations of Indian independence and of social progress, are the positive results of the Indian-Soviet cooperation.

"Nevertheless, declared Rajiv Gandhi, the traditional alliance with the USSR, now-a-days as in the past, preserves its vital character for India. The USSR is kept today near to us, in difficult times."[38]

The restoration of the historical truth on the positive consequences of the Indian-Soviet friendship is not only a matter of scientific morals, but it is also our moral duty to draw out of the ruins of the Soviet era not only the negative aspects, but also certain healthy matter of the international cooperation between nations.

The decline of the soviet totalitarian regime and the revival of the Chinese socialism had positive effects on the later course of the Indian revolution.

(c) Liberalisation and Opening to the Outer World

Like any other revolution in the world, the Indian social revolution witnessed the negative aspects. The 40 years of social-economic relations under the sign of a predominant state sector, of protectionism and state bureaucracy, triggered – on the one hand–new occurrences of standstill, of the economic ineffectiveness, of the slowdown of social progress, of the poor quality of production, and – on the other hand – they generated the emancipation and the expansion of the social conscience of the Indian citizens, who requested wide economic and social reforms. Rajiv Gandhi, son and successor of Indira Gandhi (murdered in 1984), understood the messages coming from the depths of the civil society – already emancipated at the time, rose against all the putrid faults of the state bureaucracy and promised great economic reforms. "Something is not working here, declared Rajiv Gandhi, on the second memorial for the death of his mother – October 29, 1986. Something must change. We have to escape this spiral of high costs and inefficiency, where we are stuck."[39]

Rajiv Gandhi initiated some kind of an Indian style "perestroika", that is an economic liberalisation process, which brought again to life the confidence of the voters in the capability of the Congress Party to pull the country out of the latent inefficiency crisis. As easy to understand, this was not quite to the liking of the extremist national bourgeoisie and of the foreign agents. After Mahatma Gandhi's, Nehru's and Indira Gandhi's assassinations, the enemies of the Indian reforms organised the assassination of Rajiv Gandhi, the fourth on the list of assassinations of the descendents of the Gandhi dynasty. This is how the access ways to the power were opened for the right-wing parties. The left-wing and right-wing political parties built their programmes based on the objective social relations and, with some dissimilarities, they undertook to operate the liberalisation of the economy, India's opening to the outer world and her setting on the track of globalisation.

Therefore, India inaugurated the second generation of much deeper and efficient economic reforms.

As expected, the deep economic and social reforms proved their efficiency not only with respect to the economic growth in point of quantity, but also with regard to the economic and social diversification, to the forging of a free and multilateral economy and the drastic reduction of poverty.

(d) Influence of the Communist Parties of India on the Emancipation of the Country

In a summary of the successes marked by India on the way of social progress, it is not allowed to ignore the contribution of the Communist Party of India and of the Marxist Communist Party and also of other leftist parties of the United Front to the emancipation of the country.

The Indian communists have their own tradition of 80 years of struggle for the great ideals of socialism. On this road of the Indian democracy of the castes, of peace and tolerance among the classes, of coexistence of the two parties and of cooperation with the Indian Congress Party, they found their place in the structure of state power, in the structure of left-wing political parties. These two Indian communist parties conquered the voters in the states of Kerala and West Bengal, with roughly 120 million inhabitants and thus gained an ever greater influence in the political and public life, in the emancipation of India.

Although the communists in Kerala and West Bengal kept, for a long time after the collapse of the totalitarian system, Lenin's and Stalin's portraits on the walls of their offices. But the wind of the perestroika, of reconstruction, of the Chinese modernisation and of the Indian emancipation brought a change of scenery.

Having as a strategy basis their support for the Congress Party in power, in the latter's endeavour for the erection of a modern India, the two communist parties accepted the principles of erasing the bureaucracy, of de-socialisation of the property and of a wider opening of the Indian market to the outer world. At the same time, having the supremacy of the state power in Kerala and West Bengal for several decades, these parties successfully adjusted their programmes to the new requirements of implementing the main principles of the Indian socialism.

However, the great burden of the heritage of colonialism left it to the powers in Kerala and West Bengal to face the challenge of not yet settled issues of poverty, unemployment, lacking health insurance and of the still too low standard of living.

To settle these issues, the 60 people's representatives of the communist left-wing parties in the Delhi parliament, who have the parliamentary majority in conjunction with the Congress Party in power, are making consistent efforts to accelerate the finding of solutions for the very many contradictions of the system. Under the reservation of their veto right in the matter of a number of strategic issues, the communist parliamentary fraction is fighting a fierce battle for defining decisions in favour of India's development and independence.

The question is, will the development of socialism in India speed up the influence of the communist coalition on the way of social progress? Time is the only can bring us the true answer.

(e) On the Way of Becoming One of the World's Great Industrial Powers

A second generation of great economic reforms had positive effects on the acceleration of economic growth.

The yearly rate of growth of the gross domestic product doubled. While the yearly rate of growth of the GDP was 3.7% in the span of the period between 1951-1981, in the next ten years it raised to 5.3% and between the years 1993-2006 it attained almost 7%.[40]

India conquered the second place in the world, after China, in point of the yearly growth rate, and the fourth place in the world in point of the exchange power rate, then it came to rank sixth in the production of electric power, second in the area of roads and railroads, first in her number of yearly educated engineers, etc. Huge steps were made in the energetic development, as the basis of the development of heavy industry, metal working industry, the machine building industry, production of trucks, tractors, building equipment, automobiles, up to airplanes, atomic power plants and atomic submarines, space satellites and, of course, bio-technology and informatics.

Who could have imagined 50 years ago that India might produce yearly eight million automobiles, that it could produce airplanes, helicopters, space shuttles, that it would build the longest highway in the world, of 7,000 km and with 6 lanes and that, eventually, India could win the daring bet to reduce the poverty rate from 80% in 1950 to 25.9% in 2002 and 20% in 2007?

Who could have predicted that India's currency reserves would attain 91 billion US dollars, exceeding those of the Unites States of America, France, Germany? That in a 20-30 years interval India could leave behind the economic potential of the USA? That India could be in a position to decide, along with China, remodeled Russia and Brazil, the fate of our planet?

No one, neither the greatest brains of futurology, nor the novelists of our future, could have predicted the social progress of the poorest people in the world on their way of national emancipation, of social progress, of drastic reducing of poverty. They were not able to project our future, since this is less seated in the human minds and more in the very reality of the social development.

The future is not being invented, it is born from the social foundations of our planet.

8. Vietnam, at the Crossroads of Transition and Revival of Socialism

a. The Vietnamese Hiroshima of American Cruelty

Situated on the 17th parallel in South-East Asia, with 80 million inhabitants, with an area of 328,750 km^2 and extraordinary natural riches, bathed in the West by the Atlantic Ocean along 1,600 km and bordered at North by the high Laos mountain chain, the Socialist Republic Vietnam deserves special attention. It also deserves special respect, not as much to the victims of the 20 years of liberation war against the rightful French and American invaders, than to these living war heroes, who replaced the Kalashnikov machine-guns with the ox cart, the sickle and the hammer, just to rehabilitate their completely shattered country.

From October 1944, when the French general Leclerc landed in Vietnam with his troops, and December 1946, when the conquest war against Ho Chi Minh's republic began, and up to the shameful defeat of the French army at Dien Bien Phu in May 1954, and then to the catastrophic defeat of the American soldiers in 1975, some 32 years elapsed.

The Vietnamese people and their political leader Ho Chi Minh deserve a special attention in the post-war history of our civilisation. They gave proof of an important historical truth. Any united people, that enjoy the solidarity of the progressive mankind, are impossible to be beaten. The great world movements of the leftist parties, of the unions and of other organisations against the aggression on Vietnam, as well as the support in weaponry extended by the Soviet Union joined into an anti-American and anti-imperialist hurricane, which crushed the greatest military force of our planet. More than half a million American soldiers, equipped with the most modern military technique and the ten years of bombings with classic bombs and incendiary bombs of the most powerful military air force in the world were not able to break the will of the Vietnamese people for freedom and national independence, in view of humanising the new society.

After the end of the war in 1975, the American strategy of the "burnt land" left behind, the heritage of a new Hiroshima: that is the Vietnam: 20 million craters, traces of bomb explosions, destroyed roads, demolished bridges, burnt towns and villages, several million dead, one million widows, half a million mutilated invalids and many millions of famished and ruined peasants.

(b) The Success of the Rehabilitation of a Devastated Country

Under the leadership of one of the most reputable political

and military leaders of Asia and founder, in 1930, of the Communist Party, Ho Chi Minh, the leader of the Popular Liberation Front, was facing a new challenge: the need of the makeover of the devastated country. It was necessary to start again from the grassroots, as the saying goes. The Second Five-Year Plan (1976-1980) was a plan of reconstruction, restructuring of the machinery of the centralised economy. The soviet financial and military assistance played an important part in the reconstruction of the country.

In the implementation of the third five-year plan (1981-1985), as per the estimations of Carlyle Thayer, Vietnam received foreign support amounting to 6.5 billion dollars and at the end of the fourth five-year plan it attained a total added-up amount of 14.5-18.3 billion dollars[41] Roughly 300 big investment projects were implemented. Nevertheless, the ineffective use of the internal accumulation and the foreign loans did not bring the expected results. In the early 1990s, the economic machinery began to freeze. It was obvious that the significant remnants of the soviet model were the main handicap standing in the way of the future progress. The Vietnamese society was standing at a vital historical crossroads: either it engaged on the road opened by Gorbachev, the way of partial social reforms and of the shock of the therapy of capitalist restoration, or it chose to go the Chinese way of extensive and radical reforms, the path of modernisation and revival of the positive achievements of socialism. To the question: "What kind of a Vietnamese transition?", Christophe Feuché responded: "In the case of Vietnam, the very regime was the one to apply transition. The choice was similar to that made by China and differed fundamentally from the Russian or East-European 'transitions', where a political revolution preceded the reconstruction of the economy. In China, as well as in Vietnam, there is a progressive, experimental and adjusting process."[42]

(c) Transition to the Social Market Economy—Chinese Style

After a critical analysis of the existing situation, the 4th Congress of the Party, in December 1986, took the decision of a necessary economic and political reorganisation of the system. This was a great turn and a break with the past. The Congress passed the law of agriculture restructuring, referring to the autonomy of rural family economies. It put an end to farming collectivisation. In 1987, a law was passed that allowed the participation up to 100% of foreign capital in local enterprises. In 1990, a law was passed with regard to the operation of private companies. In 1992, the new Constitution was voted, which guarantees the private property. In 1994 the law was issued on the liberalisation of state enterprises and in 1997 the law on free trade. In 1999, the tax system was reorganised. The VAT, as an important tool for social accumulation, came into operation.

On the good road to partial privatisation and to social market economy, the Vietnamese society does not let slip away from its grip, the main progress tools on the path of revival of socialism. In the industry, the public sector was holding 60-67% of the added value, and about 65% in the banking system.

The private sector of the small and medium family businesses developed particularly speedy. Today, the private sector employs some 22 million of the active population, and the public sector roughly 14 million.[43]

The main goal of the Vietnamese Communist Party is to pull the country out of the swamp of retardation, misery and poverty, to implement the general social security, the raise of the living standard of the population and the transition from the status of an underdeveloped country to the condition of a country of medium development.

The GDP growth per inhabitant, as a main sign of a country's success or failure, sends the green signal for the new strategy of the Vietnamese society. The GDP per inhabitant has risen from approximately 60 US dollars in 1975 to 300 dollars in 1999, to reach a figure of 2600 dollars in 2007. Should Vietnam keep up a yearly growth rate of 7-8%, as achieved over the last years, it would not be impossible that by the end of 2020, it makes its entrance among the group of the emerging countries with medium developed economy.

Cutting down the inflation to zero, increasing the active

balance of the foreign trade, the significant diminishing of poverty, all these are the strong signs of a steady stabilising of the Vietnamese economy and of the expansion of the savings of its citizens. It is estimated that the Vietnamese citizens save yearly nearly 5 billion US dollars, an amount that exceeds by much the yearly foreign investments.

(d) Global Growth of the Living Standard

The final result of the accelerated growth is directly proportional to the positive effects of the significant improvement of the living conditions of the citizens, reflected in almost every parameter.

As a conclusion to his essays on the consequences of the Vietnamese transition, Christophe Feuché, the author, wrote: "The global growth had a remarkable result: the significant growth of the state resources. This spectacular increase of the budget sources allowed the infrastructure programmes to be continued, with no revenue taxation pressure, followed by a substantial improvement of the purchasing power. However, the improvement of the income and the living conditions was global. It was manifest in the deep changes in consumption and housing and, as to be seen, it meant a genuine revolution for the prospects of the population."[44] Besides, the implementation of the Chinese model in Vietnam shows that the social market economy could have been achieved without giving up the socialist political regime.

9. Nepal, Mongolia, Pakistan, Bangladesh, Malaysia – on the Way of Social Progress

No doubt, Vietnam is the final stop of the planetary progress of the leftist democratic socialist forces in Asia. The world centre of the revolutionary movement, moved long time ago from Europe to the Asian continent, which houses nearly half of the population of our planet. The stupendous success of China, India and Vietnam in the achievement of the great rescue expectations of the way of national and social liberation acted in a domino effect on the development of the liberation movements in the other Asian countries.

Not long after we had ended to prepare the chapter on Vietnam's steady evolution, news arrived on the crushing victory of the Revolutionary Party of the Mongolian people (the reformed ex-communist party) in the legislation elections of June 2008, about the victory in the parliamentary elections of the social-democratic coalition and of other democratic parties in Pakistan, victory of the left-wing party in the parliamentary elections in Bangladesh and on the partial victory of the coalition of progressive parties in Malaysia. Certainly, these results bring new proof for the truth of our idea on the social progress by the main way of worldwide revival of solidarity and socialism.

In Nepal, a former British colony, the Asian victim of violence and poverty, on the northern border of India and South of Tibet, with an area of 141,000 km^2 and about 30 million inhabitants, the national and social liberation movement after the Second World War had begun. Lacking some degree of freedom and democracy, the Maoist Communist Party of Nepal responded to the armed violence of the monarchy and the right-wing political parties, with material support from the USA, as a springboard for the separation of Tibet and China, through the popular war against the local and foreign usurpers.

The year 2001 was that of the great turn of the national liberation movement. The royal family, the main bearer of feudalism and tyranny, was annihilated. On the throne ascended the last monarch, Gyanendra, as heir to the crown. Instead of the promised changes, of the democratisation and constitutional amendments, he restored the new royal dictatorship. After nine years of armed popular battles and 12,000 casualties, the liberation army controlled about 80% of the liberated territory.[45] Prior to the nearing final victory, on February 1, 2005, the Maoist Communist Party formed, with other seven parliamentary parties which turned their back to imperialism and feudalism, the anti-monarchic alliance.[46] On the 22nd of November 2005, the historical agreement was signed with the anti-monarchic allies. This was a new victory of the social progress in Asia.

The implementation of the agrarian reform, the encouragement of the private businesses and the reconstruction of the economic system as per the Chinese model, offer us the certainty of the exactness of the Chinese way of the Nepalese socialism.

Under the strong wind of the Nepalese revolution, Mongolia, with her six million inhabitants, neighbour to the North with progressive Russia, and to the South to socialist China, chose to keep the positive achievements of the reformed socialism.

By the economic liberalisation and the political democratisation, the People's Revolutionary Party kept the power in the interval 1990-1996 and, after the failure of the right-wing parties, which were in power in the span of 1996-2000, it regained the power for the mandate of 2000-2008. In the elections of June 2008, the Mongolian People's Revolutionary Party proved again its fidelity to the traditional party, associated to the Socialist International. Rejecting absolutely the total privatisation and the politics of savage liberalism of the right-wing parties and supporting the industrialisation programme and the reducing of poverty, the Mongolian people carry on the road of social progress.

All these huge changes in China, India, Vietnam, Nepal and Mongolia, whose values resounded strongly, had a decisive influence in Pakistan, located in an important strategic triangle, between three neighbours, India, Afghanistan and Iran, on the anti-imperialist, anti-militarist track of the Pakistani people.

After the killing of Zulfikar Ali Bhutto in April 1979 (the 1967 founder of the Pakistani People's Party, of social-democratic direction with a centre-left trend, member of the Socialist International)[47], his beautiful daughter, the charming and fascinating Benazir Bhutto took on the task of the party management. After ten years of hard-bitten work for organising and expanding the party's influence, Benazir Bhutto won a decisive victory in the elections. In December 1998, she became the first woman governing a Muslim nation with 77% Sunnits and 20% Shi'its.[48]

Discontent with the victory of the left, with the reforms of the economic and political systems of the Pakistan and with the settling of the conflict between Sunnits and Shi'its, the Pakistani right extremists organised in October 1999 a military coup d'état, destroyed democracy and threw the democratic opponents in jails and concentration camps. Defending the

American interests in Afghanistan, the new master of Pakistan, General Musharraf, closed the border to the Afghanistan and barred the access of the Taliban forces to this country, for the price of an approximately 10 billion US dollar credit.

When the popular opposition understood the deep causes of the nation's misery, Benazir Bhutto, after eight years in exile, returned to her country and took an active part in the election campaign. She asked for the resignation of the president of the republic and on the anti-constitutional army head, for the democratisation of the country, for transparency and severe monitoring of the elections. Fearing the victory in the elections of the Pakistani Popular Party, the governing elite organised, on the occasion of a meeting, the atrocious, cowardly assassination of Benazir Bhutto. Her son, already come of age, took her place, with the support of her husband and of ten leaders true to the movement. The Pakistani-American right murdered Benazir Bhutto, but was not able to destroy the national feeling for freedom of the Pakistani. Appalled by the assassination of their historical leader, the Pakistani civil society, with their massive votes, won a clear victory in the parliamentary elections.

The new parliamentary majority elected the new president of the government (264 out of 342 votes) in the person of Yousaf Raza Gilani, leftist candidate of the Pakistani popular party. The new president requested the recalling of General Musharraf, the release of prisoners, the establishment of the national democracy and the initiation of economic reforms to meet the interests of the majority of the population.[49]

One thing is certain: the Pakistani people decided resolutely to take their fate in their own hands. By the will of the people, general Musharraf was removed and replaced in the office of President of the Republic by Benazir Bhutto's legal spouse.

The flood of liberation movements in Nepal, Pakistan, Latin America and Africa flowed over the stormy sea of the Malaysian Peninsula and part of Eastern Malaysia, the island of Borneo, one of the most developed countries of South-Eastern Asia. The social-economic circumstances of the rebellion in Malaysia, with its 30 million inhabitants, out of which one third are Chinese and Hindu and two-thirds Malay belonging to the Muslim religious confession, and with a GDP of approximately 12,000 US dollars, are different from those in Nepal and Pakistan. Against a background of relative development of the bourgeois democracy, of the bourgeoisie and of the already constituted working class, of relative prosperity throughout the 50 years of juvenile capitalism, the contradiction between labour and capital broke finally out on the political stage of Malaysia.

The increase of unemployment, the decrease of the purchasing power of the civil society, the rising corruption and social injustice caused a mass revolt of the population and broached the victory of the right-wing parties in the parliamentary elections held in early 2008.

For the first time in 50 years of government, the right-wing political parties lost a part of their parliamentary majority of two-thirds, hence losing the exclusive possibility to adjust the Constitution and the fundamental laws to the requirements of the local and foreign bourgeoisie. The Barisan Coalition obtained 137 deputy seats and the democratic opposition 82 seats.

In 50 years of right-wing power, the democratic opposition, including its left-wing, too, occupied for the first time the seats of the regional parliaments in the states Penang, Kedah, Perak, Kelantan, the industrial state Selagar, and nearly all the parliamentary seats in the capital Kuala Lumpur.

Now, the progressive anti-imperialist forces recorded half a victory, "tomorrow, declared Anwar Ibrahim, leader of the largest opposition party (31 seats in the parliament), we will begin to build a better future".[50]

At the last moment, when my manuscript was just being printed (it was the original edition in French – n.r.), we received information on the victory in Bangladesh of Ms Sheikh Hasina Wajed and her leftist trend party in the legislative elections. This success of the leftist forces, after two years of military government, is the sign of the return of democracy and the opportunity for Bangladesh to be in route for a new economic and social order.

10. Historical Background of Democratic Socialism in Europe

(a) Democratisation, the New Booster of Social Progress

Democratic socialism in Europe had the longest, stormiest and most contradictory, challenging encounter between Marxism and social-democracy, as far as the roads of social progress were concerned.

The historical dispute, to determine where the truth lies, has lost its meaning at the very moment when history herself passed a verdict on the matter. The historical ways of social progress were and are the best judges of veracity. However, what truth is it? It is the historical and objective truth, which is always defined by the restricted nature of its given era. In the times of Marx, Engels, Bernstein and Kautsky, truth was on the side of Marx and Engels since, until the end of the Second World War, in no country were the socialist ideas implemented peacefully, except the short period of the leftist power in France, Sweden and in Australia. The violent revolutions in Tsarist Russia, China, Vietnam, North Korea, Nepal, Cuba, Yugoslavia, Algeria, Angola, the ex-Zaire, Mozambique, and many other countries, justified, under the predetermined circumstances, the viability of Marxism in connection with the issue of the revolution.

Nevertheless, the trend of social progress in the world of developed countries, of medium or underdeveloped countries, changed radically. The expansion of the informational and biotechnological revolution, the tremendous growth of production forces, the development and evolution of the working class and of the employees, the blooming of culture and the structuring of new morals, the democratisation of the public and political structures, built up a new environment of the social progress. Almost anything does not resemble any more to the far away, obsolete past, and this means that, in order to win over the favours and support of the majority of the society, most of the leftist movements began to redirect their ideologies, their way of thinking and their strategies towards the new requirements of the great changes.

After the failure of the French Socialist Party in the 2002 elections, a group of high political masters of this party announced in a common statement:

"In one century, we have given the Republic her great social reforms; it is time to exit this "reformist complex" and watch to respond to the questions today's society is actually raising. Another world revolution is possible, but it implies deep reforms."[51]

In the circumstances of the new social processes, the democratic socialism of the old Europe and of the Latin American countries, and of certain African countries, too, evolved from the limited democracy to an ever wider democracy, from the democracy that once used to be the result of economic development to the democracy that becomes the cause and sine qua non condition of the economic and social development of the society.

For the social-democracy, the first and most important prerequisite of social progress is, as shown by Pierre Mauroy, the President of the Socialist International, "democracy everywhere and for everyone". Democracy, wrote Pierre Mauroy, must "set free the energy, the creative force it favours, the imagination, the changes and the ingenuity absolutely necessary for the economic development".[52]

Democracy, liberated from the illusion of Bernstein's ancient social-democracy and from Marx' dictatorship of the proletariat, evolves to be the flag of the fight of the workers masses, of the social-democratic, socialist, communist and workers movements, and of other leftist movements as well, the flag of freedom from the moral dumbness and estrangement.

The expectations of the civil society to advance to total democracy became, with ever less exceptions, the flag of the leftist progressive movements. They became the new booster of history.

(b) Gradual Radicalisation of the Socialist and Social-Democratic Parties

The democratic socialism of the industrialised Europe, as a historical successor of the former reformist traditions of Proudhon, Bernstein and Kautsky, developed on the ground of democratisation, which invaded the existence of society.

"The social-democracy is – as Marc Lazare pointed out –

a constantly changing historical and political constitution, throughout the political challenges it had to beat and the ideological disputes it causes. Somewhat sketchy, as noticed in the glamour period of the 1960s, it features four characteristics which, all together, crown a sometimes chaotic evolution:

- a reformist orientation for the gradual change of society
- a gradual peace-making with democracy ... one of the main pillars
- a social democracy centred on the providential state and on the lack of unemployment
- a partial adjustment of the market ... and an active social redistribution of the economic benefits through the state power and by resorting to the compromise between the powerful social partners."[53]

The achievement of the main directions of the social actions or of certain other requirements specific for each country or group of countries developed, similarly to any other social process, in a spiral, with ups and downs, under the mark of internal turmoil and contradictions around the search for efficient ways of social progress.

In this evolution, rise, fall, self-correction and radicalisation of the European social-democracy along the last 50 years, three different periods can be distinguished.

The first period, that of the after-war rise of social-democracy, is defined by more radical reforms in the social system, when in England, France and especially in Germany and the other European countries, the workers, the socialist and the social-democratic parties requested and achieved the partial socialisation of certain strategic economy branches. It was the time of implementation of general social security, of increase in pay, of legalised minimum wages, of equal rights to work for women, etc.; it was the time of influence of the remnants of Marxism and reformism.

The second period, in the 1980s-1990s, was that of the extensive winning over of the voters and of the rise to power of the socialist and social-democratic parties in most European countries. They enjoyed the support of other left-wing parties and movements. It was also the time of apprenticeship in the research of the management ways and methods of state and social affairs; in fact, it was the period of practical proving of electoral programmes.

The third period, in the first half of the 1990s and in the first half of the 2010s, is the time of ebb for the European social-democracy. In the electoral campaigns of 1990-1995, which had to check the quality of the political programmes actually put into practice, the socialist and social-democratic parties in Belgium, Holland, France, Italy, Austria and Finland lost the trust of a part of the voters. The trust crisis among the masses began to wear down the actual political substance of the social-democracy. The failure of the French Socialist Party in the 2002 and 2007 presidential elections, the failure of the German Social-Democratic Party in 2005, of the similar Portuguese party in 2006 and of the Italian left in 2008, all that unveils the deepening of the European social-democracy crisis. It is obvious that the programmes of these parties do not meet any more the new requirements of the great social changes.

"As compared to the transformations of capitalism, wrote the historian Pierre Rosanvallon, in all great industrial countries there must be completely redefined the strategies of political action, but in order that such thing be possible, an exercise of critical understanding of our societies must be conducted."[54] In the evaluation of the general trend, not their not adjusted political programmes are important, but rather the actual impetus of the progressive social movement which makes social revolutions. Not only political programmes are those that push the voters to the left, although they have a decisive mobilising or demobilising role, but also the contrary. The popular masses, dissatisfied by the existing situation, are pushing the political leaders to the left. Each new electoral campaign is a step of social progress to the left, until the final victory becomes steadfast.

Now-a-days, after victories, rises and temporary downs, the European social-democracy is facing the alternative of radicalisation, redefinition and makeover of its programmes, depending on the social-economic and political changes occurred in the last decades. At present, it is facing the alternative of working out a new strategy of "revolutionary evolution" on the way of serious structural reforms, on the road of revival of the great, not yet exploited values of the democratic socialism.

(c) The Liberalisation of the Communist Parties and of Other Extreme-Left Workers Parties

After the Second World War, and also as a result of the brilliant victories of the Soviet Union, together with the Allied Powers, in the demolishing of the fascist military machinery, of the participation of the communist parties in the anti-fascist resistance movements, the prestige and influence of these parties increased in the European civil society. In the first post-war electoral polls, the communist parties exceeded in many countries the 20% margins of the voters.

The energetic opposition of these parties against the French aggression on Vietnam and Algeria and, a little later, America's attack against Vietnam, in the struggle for peace and peaceful coexistence between the East and the West, reinforced their political positions in Europe.

However, in the 1960s and 1970s, when the authority and influence of the communist parties began to slide downhill and be more and more compromised, by the ambiguous, less critical, support for the soviet totalitarian system, a period of diminishing of the power and impact of these parties occurred. Hence, there can be noticed a period of trust breakdown and of decay. After the 20th Congress of the Communist Party of the Soviet Union, held in 1956, and after the disclosure in Khrushchev's speech, of the truth about mass terrorism and physical annihilation whose toll were millions of innocent soviet citizens, after the written evidence recorded by Solzhentsyn with regard to the soviet concentration camps, after the soviet invasion in Hungary in 1956 and after the soviet invasion in Czechoslovakia in 1968, the authority and reputation of the communist parties dropped to a minimum in their lifetime.

The change from top to bottom was necessary of the strategy, politics, ideological outlook and the adjustment to the great new transformation of the society.

Breaking lose from the concept of the violent revolution, of the proletarian dictatorship and the nationalisation, from the idea of all or nothing, the communist parties gave priority to the achievement of the goals that could have been implemented within and without the market economy. From the position as an unbeatable danger to the market economy, the communist movements shifted to the latter's potential tamers.

"This implies, wrote Robert Hue, former Secretary General of the French Communist Party, that a reliable communist alternative be proposed, which should contribute to the mobilising of our people's forces to succeed in a social change that the very people has decided upon in content and shape. Of course, this is easier to say than to do!

And, in order to do this right, it is quite obvious that we can not be content to just say: 'Our communism is not the same as the soviet type', or'The Communist Party has changed: it is no longer Stalinistic, it is no more dogmatic; it is no longer controlling, is no longer political; it is no more productivity- or collectivity-centered, etc.' The list of what we are no longer is of no interest to us."[55]

The times have long gone when excuses were extended for what the communist parties in Europe were no more. For them the time has come to show what they actually are, what their programmes are as compared to the programmes of other social-democratic or socialist parties. Certain communist parties have abandoned their compromising name and made the move over to the European social-democratic side. Some of them got closer to the latter by their programmes. Others, such as the French Communist Party, have worked out the programmes of the contemporary mutations of social progress.

Moreover, the extremist, Trotskyst, as well as other revolutionary parties in Europe, have shown their shifting to a moderate trend, nearer to the new social changes. They reject and blame Stalinism, considering it as the counter-revolution which compromised socialism and replacing the proletarian dictatorship with the democracy of the working class. An ever larger part of the political left accepts the verdict of the general elections as a method to get access to power. They request a new motivation of socialism and its rehabilitation.

"Contemporary history – wrote Olivier Besancenot, one of the leaders of the French communist league – made up of new struggle rounds, new experiences, new breaches, will produce and impose to communism, probably in the coming years, a re-demonstrated and rehabilitated identity."[56]

The new circumstance of populism and anti-liberalism in Europe represents the striking rise of the popular movement against globalisation, ATTAC, which spread in a few years in 51 countries of our planet. In 2001, ATTAC organised in Porto Alegre one the greatest anti-imperialistic demonstrations, which was joined by more than 100,000 people from 180 countries. As Susan George, one of the leaders of this movement put it, all the citizens of this world, with their various requirements, are joined in such international demonstrations, in the one and single belief that a new world is not only desirable, but can also be achieved, by the union of all progressive forces on our planet.

The changes of certain programmes and actions of the European communist, socialist and social-democratic parties reflect the great changes in the social evolution of history.

The divided workers and socialist movements, once weakened by their mutual conflicts, are under way to join their prospects into one wide pluralist movement for the revival of socialism.

(d) New Requirements of the Great Social Movements

The important economic, technical, structural and class changes in the developed Europe caused an according shift in the requirements of the social movements of parties, unions, students organisations, associations, NGOs and other social associations.

The older political claims for partial nationalisation, for total freedom of speech, for de-centralising, for closeness between the management and the managed, for the development of the Providential State, all that fell back into the archives of history.

The new claims of the great social movements arise, spread and aim at the new trends of social progress: decreasing of unemployment and social inequality, protection of social environment, defending the social security, fighting against insecurity, solutions to the habitation issues, integration of foreigners and many other requirements of the civil society.

round, leaving the victory to Kirchner and the other left-wing parties and movements. This was the civil society's first significant victory, as it looked for salvation in the progressive left-wing parties.

During the pre-election campaign, Kirchner has promised Argentina's emergence from its deep economic crisis, by means of a strategy to re-launch the economic growth and to return to stability, by continuing a rigorous policy and the state interventionism, balancing the budget, establishing 600,000 new jobs, stimulating small and medium enterprises, enforcing a more just social policy, and reducing poverty. Kirchner is being considered a progressive leftist Peronist, promising "national capitalism" and "national independence from American domination".

Who is, in fact, Kirchner and why is he overwhelming with leftist speeches?

A lawyer by formation, Kirchner has chosen, early in his life, the leftist wing of Peronism. When he decided entering politics, Kirchner has tried seducing the center-leftist electorate. As a politician, he is considered to be a progressive political leader. He has been, for 12 years, governor of the South Patagonia province, the one in the very few provinces which were nor debt- nor corruption-ridden, a province which has managed reducing unemployment by 3% and solving a number of social problems.

During the election campaign, by feeling the pulse of civil society, Kirchner has promoted his leftist biography and an image of a righteous and rigorous official. The five year-long coalition between leftist Peronists and the leftist parties and political movements have generated astonishing positive results.

Following the catastrophic decrease of the GDP by 11%, in 2002, and after one of the deepest crises in Argentina's history, the average yearly economic growth was a steady 8% for five consecutive years. Poverty has dropped from 50% to around 35%. Unemployment has also dropped from 20% of the Argentinean active population, stabilising somewhere around 12%. Following the Brazilian example, Kirchner has established a 45 Euros monthly subsidy for the poorest families. Education and professional formation have reached the highest levels in

The promise for the significant decrease of unemployment is the object of the new economic politics aiming at making Brazil to exit the crisis and standstill. Such a strategy brought results beyond any hopes. In 2004-2005, the economic growth attained a 5% rate, the highest level reached in the last ten years.

Inflation fell to 8%, and the interest rate for the credits for investments decreased from 21% to approximately 10%. The export of agricultural produce resulted in a surplus of about 30 billion dollars, the highest surplus figure reached in the post-war economy in Brazil.

The economic policy of budget restrictions, of savings and readjustment of the fiscal policies and of establishing a guaranteed minimum wage, brought stability and economic growth. In the last two years, over 2 million jobs were created.

The World Bank and the IMF are willy-nilly satisfied with the Brazilian stabilisation politics. The Americans are watching attentively this economic process. The new left-wing regime makes promises to the ones and the others that it will meet all its obligations towards the suppliers of funds. The Brazilian hopes that the promise for new credits, of roughly 20-30 billion US dollars, will contribute to the consistent stabilisation and the steady economic growth.

One part of Lula's leftist voters voices certain doubts with regard to some compromises and slips of the Labour Party to the centre left. The attempted compromise with part of the local bourgeoisie and particularly with the international financial oligarchy does not mean a betrayal of the final ideals of Lula's social revolution. Under the given historical circumstances, such compromises prove to be beneficial factors of the social progress.

After his second victory in the presidential elections, Lula da Silva promised to keep the leftist direction of his strategy and the speeding up of the economic growth. Should the already initiated trend be continued, then Brazil will be able to become, in the next 25 years, the sixth world power, after China, India, Russia, the USA and Europe. It opens to the third world new ways of social progress.

unpopular reforms of the liberalisation and integration, by the grafting of the social security budgets, of the subsidies against unemployment and exclusion, and by other social benefits more.

The workers, intellectuals, peasants, unemployed, the marginal layers of society, those who live on the brink of life, as well as those social categories which lose the trust in their own future and in the future of their children, are definitely rejecting the concept of the liberal Europe. In the French referendum on the European Constitution in the fall of 2005 they said a final NO.

Although certain leaders of the French Socialist Party sustained, for reasons we can not understand, the will of the right, the majority of the French population votes, with 53%, voted against the project of the liberal Constitution. The Dutch also gave negative replies when the voters gave in the referendum a negative answer to this project of the liberal Constitution.

According to the game rules of 25 countries, France, Holland, England, Spain and Poland should have confirmed or rejected the European Constitution through a referendum, while the other countries should do so by confirmation in their Parliaments.

Disappointed by the reaction of the French and Dutch civil society, the leading elites of the other European countries were trying to promote the liberal Constitution project, shunning the will of the people, through parliamentary lobby, where the agreement of certain social-democratic parties would have a decisive role.

As an expression of the will of the majority, the French ex-prime minister Laurent Fabius declared: "People are for Europe, but not for no matter what Europe, so that they say: Make it stop! We want a social and strong Europe, not a Europe that does not protect us any more."[58]

It is easy to understand that the social reforms can not be implemented all at once. It is easy to understand that the European financial oligarchy has still available enough manoeuvre room for the confirmation, by means of the Parliaments and with the aid of the right wing of social-democracy, a slightly altered liberal European Constitution. Nonetheless, the proposed Constitution is not the end stop of social progress. In ten, twenty years, more or less, the civil society will request the replacement of the liberal Constitution with the constitution of social Europe and, in probably 50 – 70 years from now, with the new Constitution of the socialist Europe. We are not talking here about a utopia, but of an objective view on our future. Such is the reason of the laws of social progress.

(f) The French Socialism at the Crossroads of Social-Democracy, Reformism and "Revolutionary Evolutionism"

The French people, imbued with the spirit of freedom, brotherhood and equality, have a glorious revolutionary past. I read with great interest the stormy history of France, I read the writings of Balzac, Hugo, Montesquieu, Malraux and Sartre, so as to better understand the essence, the soul of rebellion and freedom, the sources of the desire for a continuous change of the existing situation. The spirit of change is just the core of the life of the French nation, and the human condition is the core of its perpetuity.

I do not intend to write in just a few pages a summarised encyclopedia of the French socialism history. This is a matter for the historians and the encyclopedists.

Within the scope of this book I should just like to show my readers, who are not familiar with the French language, as well as to my French readers who are interested in the causes of the third defeat of the French left in the 2007 elections, which is the place of the contemporary French socialist movement at the crossroads of social-democracy, reformism and revolutionary evolutionism on a global scale.

France is one of the countries where socialism was born. We may say that it is the country of revolution, the cradle of the world's great revolutions, the spearhead of social progress in the developed Europe.

After the Second World War, the leftist political parties, the French Socialist Party, the Communist Party and other left-wing parties came to power through the elections in 1946-1950, 1956-1957 and, after the makeover of the socialist party, with François Mitterand as a leader, they took over the power

"Movement towards Socialism", was leading the demonstrations carrying signs reading "The united people will never be defeated". Under the tremendous popular pressure, President Sanchez de Lozada resigned on October 17th.[79]

"The Butcher", as Bolivians have dubbed Sanchez de Lozada, looked for refuge, naturally, in Miami, without any apparent American intention to see him dragged in the court of law for crimes against humanity.[80]

In such circumstances, with social democracy being removed from the popular aspirations and consistent compromises with ultra-liberal parties, the new truly leftist leader has become the symbol of national and social salvation.

Forty-five years old Evo Morales is a self taught Indian ethnic, with roots running to the world's oldest civilisation – the Inca. He is the president of the Union Federation of peasants in the tropical area used by traditional coca farmers and also founder of the new "Movement towards Socialism". A huge admirer of Fidel Castro and Hugo Chavez, he has an anti-imperialist and socialist orientation, making him the new revolutionary star in Latin America.

"All over Latin America and worldwide, too – wrote Ignacio Ramonet. Evo Morales, imposing figure of an indigenous movement acting with tremendous power in Ecuador, Peru, Chile and Paraguay, has become a very popular personality. By overthrowing Sanchez de Lozada, he is rejecting an economic model which has deepened corruption throughout Latin America, ruining populations and multiplying social exclusion."[81]

After his brilliant victory in the presidential election and after establishing the new popular government, Evo Morales issued, on the 1st of May, 2006, a presidential decree for the nationalisation of the entire hydrocarbons industry and also promised to nationalize other economic sectors. At the same time, he nullified restrictions and legalised the growing of the traditional coca bush, and promised to develop a programme for economic growth, eradication of illiteracy and reduction of poverty.

In the Latin-American arena, Evo Morales is a champion in the fight against American imperialism, a defender of strengthening solidarity and economic cooperation based on the new principles and of establishing a continental union of

Latin America. Kirchner's performances have led analysts to proclaiming Argentina an "economic miracle".

This "economic miracle" has not only been determined by the depreciation of the national currency, el peso, and by the increase in the prices of oil, gas, soy and other cereals, which are certain to play a major part in Argentina's emergence from the economic crisis, but mostly by a rigorous economic and financial strategy, to increase exports to record levels, to generate a boom in the constructions industry and to improve the Argentineans' quality of life – especially for middle-class citizens.

According to stories run in the "El Pais de Madrid", the middle class had grown from 7% in 1999 to 20.9% in 2003. "These social categories have been one of the development factors, making Argentina a nearly unique case throughout Latin America". [77]

After his first mandate, Kirchner has decided to propose the Argentinean people – according to the Peronist tradition and the similar case of Evita Peron – his wife, Cristina Fernandez de Kirchner, senator of Buenos Aires and a great public speaker, an awesome "rebel", dubbed by the local media, "the protector of popular masses". During the election campaign, she promised to continue the trajectory initiated by her husband, and to keep overall stability and prosperity. Given her husband's reputation and invincible success, Cristina gathered 45% of the first round votes, and became the second Argentinean woman-president.

Would Kirchner and his wife, who are not, ideologically speaking, socialists and even less so Marxists, choose Chavez's path, or Lula's path of progressive socialist revival? The conclusion is still not yet decided, and it will be given by the Argentinean people themselves.

This is what Argentineans think: "The exhaustion of the historical cycle –wrote Lucretia Escudero Chauvel and Diana Quattoci – which has governed Argentina in the 20th century is, at the same time, an exhaustion of traditional, radical Peronist parties, which are not in a position to play a social role. The conditions have been met for the emergence of a new force, but this new political and social organisation needs

(g) The Swedish Socialism Model, the Potential Beacon of Socialism in Europe

To resume "multum in parvo" ("much in little", in Latin) the rise, failures and comeback of the European social-democracy, what I intended was not as much to make an analysis, be it as concise as may, of the specific conditions of parties and movements, than rather to attempt to generalize the evolution trend of the great structure of the socialist movement in Europe.

However, we have to point out for our readers that there is a third group of countries whose paths, for each group separately, stands out by a great number of likeness. The first group refers to the countries in North Europe, placed in the front row of European socialism; the second group comprises the countries of Southern Europe, of Latin descent, which stand somewhere in the middle of the measure tape of European development; and the third group, of Anglo-Saxon and Germanophile background, of Tony Blair's and Schröder's social-democracy, which is at the back end of the social progress of the European social-democracy.

The Swedish socialism, of the first group of countries, has a special place in the history of European social-democracy. With more than 73 years in power, situated in the foremost row of the European socialism, the Swedish socialism can serve – due to its expansion and the quality of its social values – as a yardstick, as a beacon for the structural changes that are possible, but not mandatory, in Europe.

Based on her number of inhabitants (roughly 10 million people), Sweden ranks as a small country in the North-West of Western Europe, but her area and her natural riches make this country rather closer to France, while the social progress level, the extent of her wealth and gross domestic product per inhabitant place Sweden in the top group of the most developed countries in the world.

When I decided to enter the Swedish experience within my research on the rise of the European social-democracy, I never had in mind a mechanical copy of the Swedish model, copy which ended in the failure of the East-European countries. Not in the least. As so well put by the Romanian sculptor

Brâncu°i, the founder of modern sculpture art, when he decided to leave the workshop of the famous French sculptor Rodin: "In the shadow of great trees no grass can grow." In the shadow of the Swedish experience, no development of the European socialism is possible.

"Contrary to the generally voiced opinion, says Rolf Nordling, I think that we could learn a lot from Sweden's experience, not by copying what is being done today, but rather taking inspiration from the methods that were able to gradually transform a society where the class struggle was extremely violent into a society where the strikes, even the most harmless ones, have become more and more seldom over the last 25 years."60

While the final goals of the European and the Swedish social-democracies are the same, their ways, methods and means to erect socialism are rather different.

The Swedish socialism rejects the Marxism in the interpretation of the actual core of the class struggle, but it does not reject the dialectics of the class struggle and the cooperation between classes. These two entities are an expression of the contradictory unity of the new historical process of social progress. The Swedes are the first in the world to have understood this new dimension of the social progress when, in 1929, they voted the law on the constitutional value of the union shop contracts.

In 1938, the new union shop contract was signed between the ownership and the unions and, a little later, after the end of the Second World War, through a number of reforms, the principle was authenticated of the understanding between the State, the social-democratic party, the ownership and the unions.

As well, the Swedish socialism rejects the Marxist theory of nationalisation, even if but partial, of the productions means, and it accepts the concept of a socialism of redistribution of the national income, of the leveling of the income of the citizens and the wealth of the ownership, thanks to the gradual taxation system as an intervention of the state for the restraining of the economic power, but not for the restriction of the economic competition and the private property.

future, when right-wing parties will be more and more compromised in the eyes of the voters and will lose more and more influence as leading political parties, then the pluralism of the leftist parties will transpose into life the new ways to develop democracy. As a form of social progress, democracy will not and cannot disappear from the social progress scene. It is permanently perfecting itself and is, in itself, an everlasting social category, always changing its shape and contents. The only things to disappear are those political parties which do not promote social progress. The only ones to develop are those political parties which are bearers of social progress. They are the alpha and the omega of the new processes of social progress, and are pioneered by the political parties in Peru, Brazil, and Argentina.

(h) Colombia, a Country of Blood and Fire.

When writing these pages on the last stand of social regress in Latin America, I spent quite some time searching for a title which would be able to suggest to my readers, in a most concise form, the political landscape in modern Colombia. The title I have settled for, "Colombia, a country of blood and fire", came from journalist Sonia Chironi and was published in Le Monde on August 7, 2006, captures and synthesizes the best, the Colombian political and military panorama.

Colombia is one of the Latin-American countries with the bloodiest political and military dictatorships of right- and far-right forces. It is the last stand of the American imperialism and of neocolonialism on this continent; it is the trampoline of American terrorist, paramilitary private companies, whose subversive actions against progressive forces in Colombia and against recently freed neighboring nations are coordinated by the C.I.A. American central.

Why are the American military circles providing more and more military, paramilitary and financial support to corrupt military regimes in Colombia? What are the mysteries behind this American "charitable generosity"?

With a surface of 1,141,148 sq. km., twice the size of France – and more than 44 million inhabitants, Colombia, the second largest Latin-American producer of coffee and cocaine and the site of extensive, yet to be discovered, underground independant Latin-American countries. The first two high-level meetings on the subject of establishing a new structure for economic and political cooperation (the first held in April 2006 in Havana, and attended by Fidel Castro, Hugo Chavez and Evo Morales, the second held in May 2006 on the Brazilian-Argentinean border, and attended by Lula, Chavez, Kirchner and Morales) have opened the new path of Latin-American solidarity.

Once the Castro-Chavez-Morales leftist-socialist triumvirate was established and reinforced, as well as the more liberal social-democratic power of Lula de Silva and Nestor Kirchner, and that of other progressive leaders, the consolidation of their alliance in the fight for national independence and socialism grew into an expression of various means towards the same final objectives.

(g) Peru, at the Crossroads Between Social-Democracy and Revolutionary Romanticism

In the concerto of Latin-American countries, Peru (with 1,285,216 sq. km., nearly half the surface of Western Europe and home to a population of 26 million) is quoted as a poorly-developed country, with a GDP per capita a little over 2,060 US dollars. Around 45% of its inhabitants are descendants of the largest Latin-American empire – the Inca, with 37% crossbred between Latino-Indians, Spanish, and other Europeans, 15% have European, especially Spanish origin, and 3% are the result of Asian immigration.

Over the last 50 years, this country underwent an agitated urbanisation process, ending with 75% of the population now living in cities, of which nearly half in the poor peripheral neighborhoods. Lima, the nation's capital, counting over 8 million inhabitants, Arequipa over one million, and the famous vestiges in Machu Picchu, the prehistoric capital of Latin America's largest empire, are home to around 300,000 inhabitants.

Geographers and geologists hold Peru as one of Latin America's richest countries, in terms of natural resources. Peru is the world's largest producer of coca leaves used for manufacturing cocaine, the world's largest producer of fish flour, the second largest fish and silver producer, the fourth

As a result of the technical and technological progress, the number of the active population in production and services will drop significantly, probably to a half. Some predictions say even to one-third.

These objective consequences of the scientific, informational and biotechnological revolution will speed up the increase of unemployment up to a maximum boiling point and, presumably, even earlier, and then the radical measures will necessarily be initiated for the termination of unemployment, for turning into reality the utopia of the complete use of manpower.

Due to the constant increase of the labour efficiency, the conditions will be prepared for one-third of the active population to produce more goods and products than once two-thirds. What will happen to the redundant population? The question as such is wrong to begin with. Such a question could be raised in case of the former labour division into productive and non-productive and non-productive, unemployed population. Under the new social-economic circumstances, the "redundant population" disappears not only from the social practice, but also from the theory of social sciences. Due to the reasonable distribution of the working time and the free time, where the working time tends to diminish, and the free time to increase, all our older concepts and our living philosophy will change. The free time does not set man free from labour, it just changes the manner of social and individual expression of this work. After the work hours, people will produce in their spare time the riches of the spirit and the mind designed for their multilateral development and blooming of their personalities, for the education of their children and the strengthening of their families, as basic cells of society.

The working time could be reduced down to 35 hours a week, as the French socialists – although distraught by the right-wing power – have already understood, and then, in – let's say – two-three decades, to 28 hours. Three free days and four seven-hour work days in various businesses are not a utopian vision of the French thinkers. The yearly vacations could extend to 60 days, one month in summer and one month in winter. We may expect the legalising of one year sabbatical leave of absence once every 10 years, for the purpose of renewing and refreshing one's extent of knowledge.

The development of the production forces and the increase of the national wealth undermine the old concepts and relations of equality of men and women, resulting actually in objective economic and material conditions, when presumably most women will choose to cut loose their commitments to double work (40 hours in a factory or an office and 30 hours at home) and when there will remain enough spare time for the children's education and for the personal physical and mental enrichment.

Tourism will become one of the most developed branches of economy. If now-a-days roughly 20% of the population spend their yearly vacation abroad, 30-40 years from now on more than half of the population will spend the yearly vacation abroad. And some 20% will travel twice a year.

Once the supersonic planes will start operating, the distances between continents will "shrink". People will have breakfast at 7 in the morning in Paris, and at 11 a.m. they will attend a conference in Beijing. In many cases, the helicopter traffic will increase as much as the underground train in a great megalopolis.

The housing problem will also be resolved, in general. Each family will have their own apartment and, probably, one of two families will have their own summer house. The real estate speculations with high lease prices, which absorb over 30% of the salaries, will vanish from the inventory of the great businesses.

The higher education, which is still the benefit of the rich and middle classses, will become accessible for all young people. The number of high education cadres may reach up to 50%.

Sports and culture will cease to be the exclusive benefit of the high society and the middle class, or a fashionable item needed to exhibit the position of a minority in society; they will be a mass matter, intrinsic naturally to the majority of the population.

The general social security also will cease to be a Chinese mystery alone. The new advances of the medical science for the successful cure of cancer, heart attack and immune deficiency syndrome, for the extension of the life expectancy up to 80 years and, later on, to 90 years, will be the issues of focus. Cracking the genetic code of the human race will trigger a huge revolution in the very existence of humans.

presented its condolences for the victims, rejoicing, at the same time, in a general satisfaction. The public understood that victory cannot be achieved by means of forged election lists, but by force. After the election masquerade, Uribe's popularity dropped by 15%, the lowest percentage in the history of Colombian presidents.

And yet, Uribe has full military, financial and logistic support from the United States. With a debt of 21 billion US dollars –mostly American loans for arming, amounting to 48% of the GDP – Colombia has recently received a 1.7 billion dollars loan for the financing of the "Colombia plan", mostly for arming the Colombian military police and the private American and Colombian paramilitary organisations. Under the pretense of the "anti-drug operation", the American Congress authorised the military activity of 400 mercenaries, who were to train over 140 paramilitary anti-guerrilla units, so as to clear the American oil areas.

According to estimations of the journalist Hernando Calvo Ospina, Americans have equipped the Colombian anti-guerrilla army with fighter jets, troop carriers, 7 powerful espionage radars, modern satellite equipment designed to photograph the movements of the guerrillas, and a lot of other logistic materials.

After September 11, determined to wipe out the Colombian guerrilla, American president Bush classified it among the terrorist organisations with which no compromise is possible. Total military and physical elimination of the Colombian freedom guerrilla is the main strategic line of the United States and of the president Uribe. Apparently, Bush and Uribe have forgotten the lessons taught by history.

When a nation is united in its fight for freedom and national independence, it becomes invincible. This is proven by the Chinese guerrillas in the Chinese liberation war, by the Algerian guerrilla and their fight for freedom, of the guerrillas in Angola, Congo, etc., and their battles for liberation.

In the new historical circumstances of American neocolonialism falling apart in most Latin American countries, of the victories claimed by progressive forces in elections, and of their economic and political consolidation, it is not impossible resources, holds a highly important strategic position – that of being the last citadel of American domination in Latin America. Bordering Venezuela, Brazil and Peru, recently freed from American domination, Colombia has been transformed in a military starting block for espionage and diversion against countries which have recently become free of neocolonial domination.

It is one of the poorest and most debt-ridden countries in Latin America, with a GDP barely reaching the 2,000 dollars threshold. Around 60% of the population is living below poverty line; two out of three Colombians are barely making a living, in a very narrow range of poverty levels. During the economic and financial crisis, which has been lasting for eight years, yearly growth rate has dropped below 0.5%, while unemployment has soared to 20%.[83] Economic failure, matched with the limitation of social rights and liberties and the reinforcing of the totalitarian rule and the amplification of generalised terror are the main features of the Colombian political scene.

Speaking of the military and police state regime, Ivan Cepeda and Claudia Giron Ortiz wrote: since 1985, "a criminal mindset has become obvious, aiming for the disestablishment of the PU (the Patriotic Union, the main opposing party), and also an increase in the number of criminal acts, of persecutions and harassments, meant for total or partial elimination of the opposition."[84]

Besides innumerable selective assassinations of political and union leaders, we present a few examples of action specific to militarised terrorism.

On November 11, 1988, 88 activists were publicly assassinated in the central square of the town of Savoya. In 1987 and 1990, Jaime Pardo Leal and Bernardo Jaramillo Ossa, presidential candidates, were murdered. Similar assassinations targeted eight deputies and Senator Manuel Cepeda Vargas. Over the following years, hundreds of leftist mayors have been liquidated. According to estimates by the above-quoted authors, over 3,000 political, unionist and leftist party activists have been assassinated over this period.

According to the notes by Sonia Chironi, Colombia has

After having lived through a period of military tyrannies that dominated the 1960s and 1980s, emancipated Latin America entered the era of constitutional legal states with bourgeois democracy and free general elections. All these social and political mutations had a decisive influence on the development of socialist ideas and movements in Latin America.

The doctrine of certain Latin American communist parties, inherited from the Third International, relating to the violent revolution, to the socialisation of the main means of production, as the only way to attain socialism, is already outdated. The general conditions for the conquest of power by the leftist parties and movements through general democratic elections became the universal rule of social revolutions.

In the early 21st century, Latin America became the erupting volcano of social revolutions. After the 1959 Cuban revolution, after the Bolivian guerrilla in the years 1965-1967, under the leadership of the legendary, romantic and humanitarian revolutionary Ernesto Che Guevara, after the Chile revolution in 1970-1973, led by Salvador Allende, the next in line was Venezuela with her stormy Chavez, and now comes the social revolution in Brazil, headed by Lula de Silva, and the rebellions in Argentina, Chile, Bolivia, Peru, Uruguay and the remaining countries, too. Now is the time when the entire Latin America took on the new path of social progress. After six decades of struggle against the military and feudal regimes, the pluralist leftist walks of life and the socialist, social-democratic and communist parties conquered the power through free and democratic elections.

The peoples of Latin America decided freely on their future on the way of freedom, democracy and socialism.

In her book "Democracy and Revolution. Latin America and Socialism", Diana L. Raby describes the effects of globalisation which enabled the emergence of a popular, democratic, liberal and humanitarian socialism.[61]

The Latin American socialism, except the Cuban one, is now in its emerging stage and, hence, it will enrich the social theory and practice with new social progress elements.

(a) The Cuban Revolution and the Latin American Socialism

No doubt, Cuba detains a strategic position, as it is the largest island, with its 114,524 square kilometres and approximately 10 million inhabitants of Spanish descent. It is located between the North and the South Americas, at about 100 km from American Florida. Ernest Hemingway, internationally renowned illustrious American writer, who owned a summer residence on Key Island, enjoyed often with nostalgic feelings the beauty of Cuban beaches.

With the excuse of the Cuba's liberation from Spanish domination, the USA landed there in 1898 and turned the island into a protectorate, just as the French had converted Algeria into a colony. From 1925 to 1933, the Americans placed General Madado in power, and then in 1933 General Batista, who governed as a military dictator, as a protection device for the American interests. Thus, Cuba was transformed into an American colony, in a tourist beach and a Cuban sugar cane plantation, while the Cuban factories became important suppliers of Cuban sugar, cigars and alcohol.

The 50 years of American domination, exploitation and alienation condensed the Cuban poverty in a general movement for national and social freedom. This movement smouldered under the ashes and generated a particular boiling up among the students in Havana and the opposition of the farming proletariat on the Sierra Maestra plateaus.

Emerged from the university nursery of the anti-imperialist and anti-American movement, Fidel Castro became in 1948 one of the leaders of the students federation, and later he joined the orthodox social-democrat party of Eduard Cibasa, that was fighting against corruption and for Cuba's national independence. Fidel Castro had studies law and chose to direct his actions to the left-wing of the orthodox party. In March 1956 he left this party and set up in the mountains, with approximately 100 partisans, the armed guerrilla movement M26, aimed at overthrowing the General Batista's dummy government. Together with his brother Raul Castro, member of the communist youth organisation, with Argentin Ernesto

Che Guevara, another leftist, he formed the core of the Marxist current in the organisation of armed struggle for the national and social liberation.

In January 1959, after two dire years of obstinate guerrilla fights in Cuba's mountains, after the successful general strike in Havana, and with the help of the Cuban communists, Castro's guerrilla groups set Havana free. This was the end of the military dictatorship and the American domination.

"The victory of the bearded warriors – wrote the authors of the study 'Socialism and Communism in Latin America' - united around Castro, who entered Havana on the 2nd of January 1959, does not actually mean only the end of the dictatorship of a little bloody tyrant, among others, but, at a distance of less than 100 kilometres from the United States, the emergence of a nation which, after two years armed fighting, rejected the neo-colonialism and started on the road to socialism." (62)

After the power had been conquered, the first stage of the agrarian reform was implemented. The greatest part of the expropriated land was distributed to the villagers, associated in cooperatives, who were holding 70% of the total tillable areas together with the state farms.

In 1961, an extensive campaign was launched for literacy. The illiteracy rate dropped from 23.7% to 1.5% in a few years. The number of grammar and secondary schools increased; the secondary and university educational system was modernised.

When Che Guevara was appointed as Minister of Industries, an industrialisation plan was worked out. At the moment when the local accumulation level was actually very low, the blocking of the American economy was quite severe, and the soviet economic assistance was totally inadequate for the truly humble ambitions of the Cuban people, the forced industrialisation was quite an utopia.

The Soviet Union wanted to make Cuba into their nuclear military base, instead of turning it – with their financial and technologic support – in a socialist showcase of Latin America, as the French had done in the Ivory Coast or the Americans in Taiwan.

Cuba was facing the same issues of Gorbachev's

"perestroika" and of the Chinese upgrading, after the defeat of socialism in the USSR and in the countries of Eastern Europe and after the annual economic growth rate had diminished.

With reference to the search for new efficient ways of economic and social development, Fidel Castro declared on the 28th of July 1995, after a five years delay: "The unbelievable disasters occurred in the countries of the ex-USSR, as compared with the successes of China and Vietnam, shows us clearly what we can do, and what we can not."[63]

Cuba began cautiously to implement its economic reform for the opening to the foreign private capital and partly, local capital. The 5th Congress of the Communist Party of Cuba increased the participation of foreign capital in the Cuban enterprises from 49% to 100%, it decreased the profit tax and introduced into the economic circuit the savings and investments of the Cuban immigration in Florida. The sales of state owned housing was made legal, as well as currency exchange and several other rather limited reforms.

Despite certain liberalisation measures, the centralised, controlling and planned, economic machinery was not able to push Cuba's gross domestic product beyond the maximum level of 2,500 US dollars per inhabitant. So that Cuba lost the race with the liberal and neo-colonial regimes in Brazil, Venezuela and Argentina, and with other medium developed countries in Latin America.

Nonetheless, the efficiency of a social system is not reflected just by its GDP size. Cuba achieved the radical social revolution, erased unemployment, illiteracy, estrangement and fetishism of social relations, reduces drastically the crucial differences between the rich and the poor and rendered the Cuban people their national and social dignity.

As a response to the questions of a journalist of the news magazine Jeune Afrique L'Intelligent relating to what Fidel Castro had brought to the Cuban nation, Hugo Chavez, the new leader of the Venezuelan revolution, declared as follows: "Look at all that he has done for the Cubans: health, education, dignity, this dignity of a David confronting Goliath. For many long years, Latin America had no dignity. Gradually, Fidel rendered it back, up to becoming its very incarnation. And this is the reason why the peoples of Latin America admire Fidel."[64]

During several decades, the Cuban socialism had a positive role, not to say a forerunner role, on the Latin American continent. Nevertheless, the American blockade that lasted many years, the selfishness of the socialist countries which did not extend any substantial economic and financial support, as well as the fear of democratisation, as a driving force of social progress, were the main hurdles in the way of a faster social progress.

After having played a remarkable part in Latin America and after a continued suffering, Fidel Castro, dubbed with the surname El Lider Maximo, handed over the helm of the Cuban ship to his brother, Raul Castro, Minister of Defence, who gave some shy signs of change. Therefore, the vital question here is: how far will Castro's successor go? The future keeps us this answer in store.

(b) The Historical Teachings of the Chilean Revolution

On September 11, 2005, when I started restoring in my mind the journalistic reports dating since the terrible events of the bombing of the presidential palace "La Moneda", of its encircling by the armoured cars and of the discovery of President Salvador Allende's tragic suicide, arranged by General Pinochet, there had already elapsed 32 years.

In these 32 years, many changes have occurred in the world. History has recorded a geat many events. Nonetheless, history has not yet passed her final verdict. In our memories, just as in the thoughts of tens of millions of Chileans, the eternal truth is still present about the coup d'état and the annihilation of a democratic and social revolution in Latin America. History has left to the young generations the evidence of violence and social inequity, the historical proof of the Chilean revolution. The coup d'état of the 11th of September 1973 had overthrown by violence the first regime emerged out of the 1970 free democratic elections, the pedestal of the national unity in Chilean history. This regime congregated the representatives of socialism, of the communists, of the radicals, the social-democrats and of other political groups, too. Salvador Allende, a socialist, former Health Minister, candidate of the National Front in 1958, 1964 and then also in 1970, winning candidate of the National Unity Party that included six groups, was for three years the leader of the Chilean social revolution. He rests in peace with his several thousand associates, vigorous fighters for freedom, national independence, democracy and social justice.

When reading these lines, the sympathisers of democratic and revolutionary movements will ask questions, either by plain curiosity, or for the desire to discover the secrets of the Chilean tragedy. Why was it necessary for the right-wing parties and their neo-colonialist mentors to squash the Chilean revolution by fire and bloodshed? Will the new Chilean democracy be able to save itself from holocaust in due time? What historic lesson can we learn from the blood quenched Chilean revolution?

Making an attempt to word some answers to these questions, I am placing myself in a truly unpleasant position, that of a judge on history. The most qualified analysts of the Chilean tragedy are Chileans themselves. However, as an objective researcher of the path to the revival of socialism, which the Chilean drama has disturbed for a long time, I feel the need to utter my thoughts.

The answer to the first question, namely why did the local bourgeoisie and the foreign neo-colonialists consider it necessary to quench the Chilean revolution in blood and violence, could be sought in the specific strategic and geopolitical circumstances in Chile, Latin America.

Considering its number of inhabitants, Chile is not a large Latin American country. In 1970 it counted just 10 million inhabitants, out of which 70% were concentrated in urban areas. Still, by its geopolitical position, with an area extending over more than 4,500 km from the North to the South of the Cordilleran Andes flanks, to the borders with Peru, Bolivia, Argentina and neighbouring Brazil, with an area almost double than France, Chile had for the American neo-colonialists a prevailing strategic significance in Latin America.

As Saudi Arabia holds oil deposits, just the same Chile owns the largest copper deposit in the world, mined by the American branches Kennecott Copper Corporation, Anaconda and others more. The Chilean copper is part of the American metal industry and without it the present industrial America would cease to exist. The income in currency resulted from mining and processing copper used to be the very spine of the Chilean economy. The exploitation rate of the working class and the farming proletariat, devoid of land, attained dramatic proportions. The contradictions between labour and capital led to an important enhancement of the labour, communist, socialist and social-democratic movement, advancing to the shores of revolution.

The Chilean labour, socialist and communist movement was the strongest movement in Latin America. Its power to influence the masses made the Chilean leftist movement rank third, following the progressive French and Italian movements, in the times before and after the Second World War. The Communist Party, whose candidate in the 1970 elections was Pablo Neruda, recipient of the Nobel Prize for literature, was the second Chilean party in point of power. Although for about 10 years there continues to exist misunderstandings between the Moscow and, later on, Castro lines of the communists, and the socialist and social-democratic influences of the 4th International, the unity of the left-wing parties in the elections brought them nearer to the achievement of the goals of the Chilean revolution. In the 1958 and 1964 elections, the leftist parties were almost on the peak of success. In the 1970 elections, the National Unity Front, headed by Salvador Allende, together with the majority of the left-wing parties, won a glorious victory.

This was the beginning of a period of great changes on the way of social progress, of democratisation, emancipation and humanisation of social relations.

Through the constitutional law nr 17450, the General Assembly nationalised the American copper companies and all other foreign and local companies, under the right to compensation with the value of the socialised goods. On the 20th of September 1971, the Parliament passed a new law, instating the diminishing of the compensation value for all profits exceeding the annual rate of 10%.

Between the years 1971-1972, 3282 agrarians were expropriated of 5.3 million hectares, who represented 60% of the seized Chilean land.

According to a survey of Jean Jacques Jouvin, "The Allende government intended to apply its agrarian politics within a general strategy meant to transform the Chilean society according to socialist criteria, including in this strategy all the groups of villagers and their participation in the reorganisation activity."[65]

Eleven days after Allende's election, on the 4th of September 1970, Richard Nixon, president of the United States, ordered the CIA executives to depose Salvador Allende. As per the meeting minutes of the CIA leaders, Richard Helms, then Director of the CIA, declared: "The President decided that an Allende regime was not acceptable for the United States. He asked the Agency either to prevent Allende to come to power, or to depose him."[66]

Nevertheless, at the start of the revolution, when Allende enjoyed the support of a part of the army and of the wide popular masses, the wheel of history was not easily turned back. It was necessary to mobilize the internal response and that of the dissatisfied part of the middle class, it was necessary to trigger political chaos, inflation and sabotage of the revolutionary measures, it was necessary to organize strikes and street demonstrations against Allende and so an almost perfect "coup d'état" had to be prepared, in a meticulous way, free of any risk.

On the 11th September 1973, General Gustavo Leight, Chief of Staff, José Merimo, Commander of Airforce and Navy, and Augusto Pinochet, Commander of Land Army and, at the same time, chief of police, prepared secretly a coup d'état. The presidential palace was surrounded by armoured cars and bombed. Allende committed suicide with the very gun Fidel Castro had offered him as a gift, as a symbol of the revolution. The important strategic centres were occupied. Belligerence was declared and the government of General Pinochet's military junta was installed, which lasted for 17 years.

In June 1974, following the assassination of Salvador Allende and of the military coup d'état, General Pinochet became the life-long appointed Chief of State and of the military junta. Under the protection of the USA, the goriest military dictatorship of the far right reactionary circles was installed. During the 17 years of illegal domination and under General Pinochet's terror, 30,000 patriots were killed, tortured, or simply vanished. The Chilean democracy dropped back 200 years.

In 1990, under the pressure of the re-emergence of the opposition of the democratic forces of the moderate democratic right, of the revolutionary left from inside, and of the external ban and blame of the genocide of the military dictatorship, the Pinochet regime was overthrown through the return of the democratic constitutional regime.

As Marta Lagos wrote, 17 years of dictatorship had not erased "the historic memory of the parties. Although subject all this time long to misinformation and propaganda against parties and politicians, children vote today like their parents. And the population can be found, as ever, one third in favour of the left, one third for the centre and one third for the radical right".[67]

Chile did not deny its democratic and revolutionary tradition directed to the left. The centre left coalition, which groups socialists, Christian democrats and leftist radicals, has won the presidential elections four times in a row and, in alliance with other democratic parties, it won also in the parliamentary elections.

In January 2006, in the last presidential elections, the centre left candidate and former Health Minister of the centre left coalition, Mrs Michelle Bachelet, obtained 53% of the votes in the second round and became President of Chile. In the parliamentary elections of the 11th December 2005, the leftist coalition, not allied with any other parties, had obtained the majority in the General Assembly and the Senate.

Madame Michelle Bachelet (aged 54 years) is the daughter of a general faithful to Allende, who had been betrayed and killed by torture during Pinochet's dictatorship. Since her childhood she followed a humanitarian socialist trend. She was confined in 1975, next to her mother, and was tortured. Under the pressure of the public, both of them were set free and they migrated first to Australia, then to East Germany, where Mrs Michelle Bachelet completed her medical studies. After having returned to her country, she was appointed Health Minister in the centre left government.

Ricardo Lagos felt the pulse of the civil society, tilting more and more to the left, and so he broke the too narrow boundaries of the centre left republic, and proposed the nomination of Mrs Michelle Bachelet as a centre left candidate, based on her philosophy inclined to more radical reforms of the system. And he proved to be right. Michelle Bachelet, whom journalists call “El Fenomen”, was able to win in the second election round and obtained the president’s office. She took on the great historical task to meet her promises made prior to the elections.

Throughout the four centre left mandates of social democracy, Chile achieved significant political and economic progress. The Constitution was revised, and then the political democracy was extended. The yearly economic growth attained 6%. Exports doubled. The yearly cash flow in foreign currency obtained from the copper exports reached 40 billion US dollars in 2005, almost equal to the Venezuelan oil exports. Poverty decreased from 45% to 19% of the population.[68]

The new president, along with her parliamentary majority, undertook to substantially reduce unemployment, to eradicate every form of discrimination, to introduce the mandatory and free education for all children, to improve the social security and the retirement insurance. Also, they undertook to reduce even more the poverty rate and to implement the full equality of women and men in the public and political administration, as per the 50-50% principle. Bachelet’s ambition is to establish in Chile, for the first time in the history of our civilisation, the perfect equality between men and women.

And still, it is too early, after the recent elections, to await the fulfilment of the electoral promises. And it is also too early to await the appearance of analyses on the typical features of the Chilean path to socialism. However, at the same time with the present day time differences, we can notice the unavoidable and constant shifting to the left of the Chilean social-democracy on its road to social progress.

(c) The New Bolivar of the Revolution in Venezuela

With 22 million inhabitants and an area of 916,455 square

kilometres, as big as France and Germany together, Venezuela is the most developed country in Latin America. In 1998, the GDP per inhabitant was of approximately 9,000 dollars. The foreign debts were amounting to 35 billion dollars. 93.20% of the population lives in urban areas, out of which seven million in Caracas and three million in Maracaibo. Venezuela is the fourth world oil producer, pumping 3 million barrels a day. It is also the third American oil supplier and owns oil deposits of roughly 78 billion barrels, i.e. 80% of Latin America's resources.

Venezuela has an extensive network of roads and highways, amounting to a total of 94,000 kilometres; it has 61 airports, seven of them for international traffic, 15 sea-ports, 5 TV stations, most of them in the hands of the local and foreign capital.

It is one of the few Latin American countries which, next to the emancipation of the economic basis, developed the fundamental prerogatives of bourgeois democracy, in the form of authority of the ruling classes. For more than twenty years, the Venezuelan power was dominated by two leading political parties, as substitutes of the American democracy: the Christian-democratic party for the right one is and the social other is the democratic party for the left: which is in the service of the great capital.

The rushing increase of poverty, the exclusion, the authority excess on the part of the state and the violence of the police were proportional to the increase of the national wealth. The number of the unemployed attained 16% of the active population. More than three quarters of the population lived in pitiful housing conditions, in crammed outskirts of towns, in ramshackle hovels – ranchos – bordering on poverty, starvation and endurance.

In 1989, in the streets of Caracas, the first huge explosion of discontent took place. It was squashed by the army, with the price of several hundred casualties, according to certain sources, or of approximately 4,000 victims as per other sources, and also with the price of thousands of wounded demonstrators.

Under the influence of the revolutionary ideas of Simon Bolivar and of the revolutionary requests of the demonstrators, Hugo Chavez, a young officer of the elite of sky diver troops of Marakaua, not far from Caracas, a lieutenant-colonel, offspring of a simple family of teachers, organised three years later, together with his group – the Movement of Bolivarian Revolutionaries – a coup d'état to overthrow President Perez. The participants in the coup d'état took over the control of several provinces. Unfortunately, they gave in during the assault attempt on the presidential palace. Thus, Hugo Chavez and his associates were thrown in prison, with manacled hands and feet, sentenced to long years of forced labour.

Two years later, under the pressure of the street and the public, Chavez and his associates were pardoned. Free again, under the aura of a national hero and imbued with the feeling of his historical mission, Chavez denied the old concepts of the armed revolution and accepted the democratic challenge and the verdict of the election poll. In the leftist voters, he saw the potential legal means for getting free from neo-colonialism and the local monarchy.

Chavez laid the foundation of the movement of the 5th Republic and he excelled in the 1998 elections. With his convincing victory, he established the first revolutionary government and published a comprehensive programme of constitutional, political, social and economic reforms. In an interview for the news magazine Jeune Afrique L'Intelligent, two years after his acceding to power, Hugo Chavez stated: "The process of changes is under way. At all levels. On domestic level, we have organised six elections in two years. For the first time in our history, we have organised a popular referendum which provided a framework for the 'constituent' power, if I were to take over a phrase of the French revolution. The new power has destroyed what had to be destroyed and created what had to be created. It is a power simultaneously destructive and creative, in democracy."

"We have a new Constitution and new institutions, a President elected for six years, a new National Assembly. We have created a fourth power, the 'power of the citizen', and even a fifth power, the 'electoral power'.[69] For the first time in the history of our civilisation, the power of the citizens and of the voters is made legal by the Constitution. The new constitution offers the voters the right to recall the deputies who do not comply with the will of the voters."

Hugo Chavez gradually replaced the parliamentary representative democracy with the participative democracy.

"With the participative democracy – declared Vanessa Stojilkovic – the people are taking part in the decisions. This way, the people are those who have to decide, every day, how the decisions are going to be used. The government makes available to the people the means for the achievement of actual projects in the communities."[70]

As far as economy is concerned, the popular government passed a new law on the enhancement of the state control in the oil industry – PDV S.A. – nationalised in 1975, that supplied about 50% of the income of the state. There were voted the new regulations regarding the distribution and exploitation of land, a new law on fishing, for the protection of traditional fishing by hand. The unemployment was reduced from 16% to 14.3%. More than one million homeless children were placed in the circuit of the grammar and secondary schools. Seven hundred physicians were made available for the poor districts of the overpopulated cities.

All these radical reforms, and many others more, which exceed the boundaries of my summarised study, have a social character and, so to say, a deeply revolutionary political character, which does not fit in the Marxist layout of social progress. Obviously, Hugo Chavez is no Marxist. "I am no follower of Bolivar, he declared. Being one of Bolivar's supporters includes several concepts. It is not possible to decide on a dogmatic category – 'left' or 'right', as one may say. I see myself both as a revolutionary, and as a social fighter. I am no Marxist. But I understand Marxism, or rather its motivations. I do not blame it."[71] He did not read Marx in the military academy, but Bolivar and his Latin-American revolution seduced him.

The morals of these revolutions, as democratic, national and social revolutions, with much less idealism and romanticism, and with much more pragmatism, are the characteristic features of Chavez' social progress.

The local and foreign oligarchy of America took a poor view on Chavez revolution. The nostalgia of the lost wealth turned into counter-revolution. With the help of the old corrupt bureaucracy and of a part of the middle class, which did not find its place in Chavez revolution, these former masters of Venezuela, who are the owners of four television stations and an important part of the seventh power, organised on April 15th, 2000, a coup d'état by forcible occupying the presidential palace. Pedro Carmona, president of the ownership union of Venezuela and an individual with close ties to the American interests, declared himself as Head of the State. I had the opportunity to see at the French television the film of the counter-revolution, I saw the organisers of the latter and their failure, the entry of Chavez partisans in the Presidential Palace, Chavez arrival by helicopter and the reinstatement of the power of the people. This was a grandiose proof of the victory of Chavez' strategy, inspired from Bolivar's revolution. "When the army joins the people, said Bolivar, the revolution becomes invincible."

If such are the actual circumstances in Venezuela, then we could hope that Bolivar's revolution will hold good against every pressure and that it will conquer in the end. To have the army and the people on one's side, here is one of the great historical lessons of the revolution in Venezuela!

(d) The Brazilian Social Revolution and its International Significance

The Brazilian social revolution is the youngest revolution of the 21st century. On October 2, 2007, it was five years old. It is still in the stage of forming new social structures. In this country, with 220 million inhabitants, which encompasses 40% of the Latin-American continent, that is 17 times greater than France, the revolution – like once the soviet and the Chinese revolutions – is an event with a worldwide historical significance.

The Brazilian way of the social progress and all that which, in political-ideological slang, could be finally named the "social revolution", is by far different from the soviet, Chinese, Vietnamese, Cuban, West-European and, still, from the African way of social revival. The huge expectations, goals and ideals are the same, but the methods, means and paths are different. The latters are different because the economic, geographic, geopolitical circumstances and the traditions are not at the least similar.

Brazil has lived through the lessons of the monarchic, democratic-bourgeois regimes of Latin character, of the military tyranny and the bourgeois democracy, of the first industrial revolution, and it has begun the informational and biotechnological revolution. According to the classification of the United Nations, Brazil ranks among the new industrial countries, next to Couth Korea, China, India and Taiwan. It is rated as the eighth industrial power of the world, capable to producc the top technology of the energy, metal working, military metallurgy, industries, of the automobile and aircraft building industries, let alone the widest range of the light and food industries. Brazil has become a new force of the travel industry.

I have visited twice Brasilia, Sao Paolo, Rio, and several industrial exhibitions. I had the privilege to admire from the Corcovado the beautiful scenery offered by the unique Brazilian landscape. I was awed by the advance of the Brazilian industry, but also by the tremendous poverty in the suburbs.

The industrialisation of the country, attained under the pressure of the military and supported by the huge investments of foreign capital, mainly American, and the debts of over 140 billion US dollars, have entered Brazil into the modern industrial society. The historical mission of industrialisation consisted at the same time in the development and expansion of capitalism, in the fast development of the working class and of the intellectuals, and in the massive growth of unemployment and general poverty.

The Brazilian agriculture is not only a source of national wealth; On the contrary, more than that, it is the source of national poverty. Now-a-days, 1% of the agrarians in the countryside own 44% of the farming areas, while 40% of the villagers detain less than 1.20% of the tillable land areas. Approximately 6 million peasant families are considered as being "proletarians without land" and they live at the brink of starvation, between life and death.[72]

In Brazil, one of the most developed countries in Latin America, 54 million persons live with less than one dollar a day. The flying inflation, the high interest rate on credits, the standstill of the agricultural development, the general corruption, the mafia and the street violence in the city outskirts and the real armed war for keeping under control the cocaine traffic, all these added and joined to the general poverty of the large majority of the population, generating a real desperate roar for finding new salvation ways.

Overburdened with the multiple contradictions of the existing, the huge dissatisfaction of the population and the social revolution smouldered under the ashes for a long time in the Brazilian scenery of the civil society. In 1980, the ex-peanut salesman, shoeshine, metal worker, charismatic union leader Luis Inácio Lula da Silva created the Workers Party and became its leader. A new page of Brazilian history was opened.

From one demonstration to another, from one sector to another, from one conference to another, Lula imposed himself as the new leader of the Brazilian workers, union and social movement, the new leader of the poor Brazilians. With his pragmatism and charm in attracting masses, he became the invincible guide of the Brazilian social revolution. Enjoying the ever larger support of the population, Silva made his way unfailingly up to the top of the political and state power.

In the second poll round of the 1989 elections, Lula obtained 47% of the votes and was just 6% of the votes far from Ferdinand Collora de Mello, who had got 53% of the votes. In 1994 and 1998, Lula ranked again second, and in the elections on the 27th of October 2002 he was elected President of the Republic with a wide majority, with 61.27%.

In the parliamentary elections, the Labour Party, in coalition with the other leftist parties and their supporters, ensured their majority in the parliament. "His election, wrote his biographer Christian Dutilleux, is a symbolic revolution. In the history of Brazil it is for the first time that a man of the people, born in squalor, rises to presidency. His success is that of the poor and of all those who, socialist or supporters, could never climb to the top of the state. Lula put his biography in the service of the electoral campaign, since he knew that this would comply with the state of mind of that moment."[73]

He gained the trust of the greatest part of the voters not only because he was coming from the ranks of the poor walks of life, but also because his electoral programme broke the narrow conventional patterns of the propaganda of the liberal elites and because he was defending the vital rights of the majority of the popular classes.

The pragmatic character of the Labour Party aimed at avoiding the errors of the Latin-American left and at pulling Brazil out of the crisis, onto the way of revival. Without entering the details of all the pre-electoral promises, some of which were actually successfully achieved, we may state that, in five years of government, the new team of leaders, formed of former union leaders, of Marxists, Trotskysts, social-democrats, or of simple technical experts – defenders of the social progress, scored positive popularity points on the road of social and economic emancipation of Brazil, in spite of their lack of expertise in administrative management.

Lula lost not many great words and made no promises in connection with the future social and democratic society. Before and after the electoral campaign, President Lula declared: "If at the end of my office each Brazilian will be able to eat three times a day, then I would have fulfilled the mission of my life." One of his first priorities was to implement the programme for reducing poverty and starvation, for creating the "family allowance". Each family that has a monthly income less than 27 Euros will receive regularly an additional monthly pay of 41 Euros. At the end of 2004, 6.5 million families, or roughly 36 million individuals received monthly assistance. By the late 2006, 11 million homes, respectively 50 million persons, received regularly the state support, which would contribute to the rapid diminishing of poverty.[74]

The agrarian reform, which was envisaging the distribution of lands to 6 million proletarian peasants lacking land, through expropriation of great agrarians, is advancing much slower. Until the year 2006, just 250,000 families enjoyed the benefit of such an allotment. Partisan of the peaceful revolution, the Labour Party in power is looking for a solution of agreement with the great land owners, in view of distributing to peasants with no land at all some plots, including by clearing forests extending over tens of millions hectares.

The promise for the significant decrease of unemployment is the object of the new economic politics aiming at making Brazil to exit the crisis and standstill. Such a strategy brought results beyond any hopes. In 2004-2005, the economic growth attained a 5% rate, the highest level reached in the last ten years.

Inflation fell to 8%, and the interest rate for the credits for investments decreased from 21% to approximately 10%. The export of agricultural produce resulted in a surplus of about 30 billion dollars, the highest surplus figure reached in the post-war economy in Brazil.

The economic policy of budget restrictions, of savings and readjustment of the fiscal policies and of establishing a guaranteed minimum wage, brought stability and economic growth. In the last two years, over 2 million jobs were created.

The World Bank and the IMF are willy-nilly satisfied with the Brazilian stabilisation politics. The Americans are watching attentively this economic process. The new left-wing regime makes promises to the ones and the others that it will meet all its obligations towards the suppliers of funds. The Brazilian hopes that the promise for new credits, of roughly 20-30 billion US dollars, will contribute to the consistent stabilisation and the steady economic growth.

One part of Lula's leftist voters voices certain doubts with regard to some compromises and slips of the Labour Party to the centre left. The attempted compromise with part of the local bourgeoisie and particularly with the international financial oligarchy does not mean a betrayal of the final ideals of Lula's social revolution. Under the given historical circumstances, such compromises prove to be beneficial factors of the social progress.

After his second victory in the presidential elections, Lula da Silva promised to keep the leftist direction of his strategy and the speeding up of the economic growth. Should the already initiated trend be continued, then Brazil will be able to become, in the next 25 years, the sixth world power, after China, India, Russia, the USA and Europe. It opens to the third world new ways of social progress.

(e) Argentina, at a Crossroads of Peronism and Democratic Socialism

Argentina is, in terms of surface, population and natural resources, the second most important Latin-American country, after Brazil. That is precisely why it has a very important strategic position in the confrontation between the old imperialist forces and the new progressive forces of the ample national and social liberation movements occurring in Latin America.

Placed in the southern part of Latin America, Argentina covers 2,780,000 sq. km., being five times larger than France. It neighbours the Atlantic Ocean in the East, with a 3,500 km. shoreline. In the West, it borders Chile, having the rich mining resources of the Andes Cordillera, with a population over 40 million, of which 90% urban, mostly Spanish, some Italians and around 2% crossbred and Indians, Argentina is quoted as a medium-developed industrial country. With an average GDP of 13,244 dollars per capita, in 2007, Argentina comes second to Venezuela in the top most developed countries in Latin America. Argentina has paid a high price for its progress, a price paid in misery and indescribable poverty.

USA sees in Argentina an ample potential market for capital exports and for importing tremendous profits. The American oligarchy is the biggest investor in the Argentinean economy. Argentina's debts to the World Bank and to the IMF have reached a total of 150 billion dollars. At the same time, exports and capital payments to the American cash registers (and, to a lesser extent, to other western partners of neocolonialism) have reached the tremendous amount of 130 billion dollars .[75] Argentina has become one of the most robbed and debt-ridden countries in the world. The price of the over-dimensioned debt has been directly proportional to the amplification of poverty.

According to the authors quoted before, half of the Argentinean population lives below poverty line, and that means 19 million people. Over half of the previous workplaces are now gone, following the establishment of foreign companies. Unemployment reaches a maximal 25%. Every fifth child is malnourished, while child mortality shatters every single Latin-American record. Statistics register 840,000 new poor people every year, dwindling between life and death. There is more and more talk, in Argentina, of the "economic genocide" in an ocean of generalised corruption and enrichment of the leading elites.

The flyers given around by Argentinean immigrants in Paris, on May 1, read: "Argentina faces an unprecedented social and political crisis. Misery has reached a dramatic heights, the manufacturing capabilities have diminished; the State, the financial system, as well as numerous enterprises are under the threat of bankruptcy. The population is living in extremely deteriorated conditions and the salaries –when they exist- have been cut in half or more, while the healthcare and education systems have been deformed. A significant part of the population is being marginalised."[76]

It's obvious that Argentina is, in the words of Rosendo Fraga, in an "extreme conjectural crisis, following a long historical process of decadence." Argentina is yet another proof of the end of the historical cycle of Peronist populism dominance, of other political parties and of military groups of interests serving the American neocolonialism. Indeed, the 30,000 fighters for democracy and for national and social freedom, who have disappeared and have been killed, have imposed, through their sacrifice, the Brazilian way towards social and national liberation and have shaken Argentina from its Peronist anesthesia.

As an effect of these ample social movements, of the demonstrations and protests held in the streets by the "kaserolazos", in the presidential elections held in May 2003, the Peronist part of the rich classes has been divided in the right-wing cosmopolites, represented by former president Carlos Menem, and the left wing of Nestor Kirchner. In the first round of elections, Menem has received 24% of the votes, while Kirchner had 22%. However, according to all the polls conducted, Kirchner seemed to have left Menem way behind, thanks to the support of Elisa Carlo, of the centre-leftist party, of all the other left-wing parties and of the progressive movements of the civil society. The will of the civil society was obviously going to triumph in the second round of elections. Assessing his failure, Menem has withdrawn from the second round, leaving the victory to Kirchner and the other left-wing parties and movements. This was the civil society's first significant victory, as it looked for salvation in the progressive left-wing parties.

During the pre-election campaign, Kirchner has promised Argentina's emergence from its deep economic crisis, by means of a strategy to re-launch the economic growth and to return to stability, by continuing a rigorous policy and the state interventionism, balancing the budget, establishing 600,000 new jobs, stimulating small and medium enterprises, enforcing a more just social policy, and reducing poverty. Kirchner is being considered a progressive leftist Peronist, promising "national capitalism" and "national independence from American domination".

Who is, in fact, Kirchner and why is he overwhelming with leftist speeches?

A lawyer by formation, Kirchner has chosen, early in his life, the leftist wing of Peronism. When he decided entering politics, Kirchner has tried seducing the center-leftist electorate. As a politician, he is considered to be a progressive political leader. He has been, for 12 years, governor of the South Patagonia province, the one in the very few provinces which were nor debt- nor corruption-ridden, a province which has managed reducing unemployment by 3% and solving a number of social problems.

During the election campaign, by feeling the pulse of civil society, Kirchner has promoted his leftist biography and an image of a righteous and rigorous official. The five year-long coalition between leftist Peronists and the leftist parties and political movements have generated astonishing positive results.

Following the catastrophic decrease of the GDP by 11%, in 2002, and after one of the deepest crises in Argentina's history, the average yearly economic growth was a steady 8% for five consecutive years. Poverty has dropped from 50% to around 35%. Unemployment has also dropped from 20% of the Argentinean active population, stabilising somewhere around 12%. Following the Brazilian example, Kirchner has established a 45 Euros monthly subsidy for the poorest families. Education and professional formation have reached the highest levels in

Latin America. Kirchner's performances have led analysts to proclaiming Argentina an "economic miracle".

This "economic miracle" has not only been determined by the depreciation of the national currency, el peso, and by the increase in the prices of oil, gas, soy and other cereals, which are certain to play a major part in Argentina's emergence from the economic crisis, but mostly by a rigorous economic and financial strategy, to increase exports to record levels, to generate a boom in the constructions industry and to improve the Argentineans' quality of life – especially for middle-class citizens.

According to stories run in the "El Pais de Madrid", the middle class had grown from 7% in 1999 to 20.9% in 2003. "These social categories have been one of the development factors, making Argentina a nearly unique case throughout Latin America". [77]

After his first mandate, Kirchner has decided to propose the Argentinean people – according to the Peronist tradition and the similar case of Evita Peron – his wife, Cristina Fernandez de Kirchner, senator of Buenos Aires and a great public speaker, an awesome "rebel", dubbed by the local media, "the protector of popular masses". During the election campaign, she promised to continue the trajectory initiated by her husband, and to keep overall stability and prosperity. Given her husband's reputation and invincible success, Cristina gathered 45% of the first round votes, and became the second Argentinean woman-president.

Would Kirchner and his wife, who are not, ideologically speaking, socialists and even less so Marxists, choose Chavez's path, or Lula's path of progressive socialist revival? The conclusion is still not yet decided, and it will be given by the Argentinean people themselves.

This is what Argentineans think: "The exhaustion of the historical cycle –wrote Lucretia Escudero Chauvel and Diana Quattoci – which has governed Argentina in the 20th century is, at the same time, an exhaustion of traditional, radical Peronist parties, which are not in a position to play a social role. The conditions have been met for the emergence of a new force, but this new political and social organisation needs some time in order to become active. A week ago, the National congress of Argentinean Workers (an opposing organisation of unions) has decided the establishment of a new political and social movement. The project for a workers' party, not unlike Lula's party in Brazil, has begun taking form, but most protagonists are aware that the Argentinean situation is very different from the one in Brazil."[78]

Argentina is not Brazil. Every extensive national progressive movement has its own specific features. And yet, the final objectives are not specific. The final goals are unique and inevitable. In the concerto of Latin-American peoples, Argentina has already made the first steps on the chosen path of social progress. It doesn't matter whether the cat is white or black, said Deng Xiao Ping, what matters, it is to catch mice.

(f) Bolivia on the "Path Towards Socialism"

Following the electoral victory of the leftist parties and political the movements in Venezuela, Chile, Brazil, and Argentina, the poor Bolivians' decision to elect Evo Morales, the leader of the pan-national leftist movement towards socialism, as the head of the national salvation cabinet, has confirmed yet again the determination of Latin-American peoples to irrevocably choose the road towards national independence, social progress and socialism.

Bolivia, with a population of 8.5 million native citizens of which more than half are of Indian origins and with a surface of 1,099,000 sq. km. Which is about double that of France, is trampling, alongside Haiti, all world records relating to poverty. In fact, 60% of the population is living below poverty line. Illiteracy reaches catastrophic proportions. Moreover, 51% of the population lives in the dark, with no access to electric power. Some of the population doesn't have access to running water.

A national investigation carried out in schools, in 1989-1990, has uncovered the nation's biologic catastrophe: 35% of the children in schools are physically retarded. And yet, Bolivia is one of the richest sources of unexploited metalliferous deposits and one of the richest Latin-American natural gas reserves. It is the world's third largest ethane, wolfram, silver, copper, and zinc producer, as well as the world's largest coca producer.

The huge gas reserves are founding the Bolivian people's major hope for salvation, for liberation from its everlasting poverty. That is precisely why Bolivia has a special place in the geopolitics of national liberation movements on this continent.

After the dramatic extinction of the Bolivian revolution in 1952, and after the growth of the national and social liberation movement, the rising national bourgeoisie, supported by American neocolonialists, has governed for more than 30 years by means of tens of military coups.

After the liberal and social democratic coalition's failure during the presidential and parliamentary elections of August 4, 2002, the national revolutionary movement of Gonzalo Sanchez de Lozada, former ultra-liberal president of the republic (1993-1997), has gained presidential majority and, by means of an alliance with Paz Zamora's leftist social-democratic movement, has gained parliamentary majority. As such, the social-democratic party has sunk even deeper in compromise. As was to be expected, the new governing coalition has attempted, according to the counsel of the famous American counselor Jeffrey Sacha, to direct the use of Bolivia's natural resources in a manner consistent with American interests. The main purpose was that of limiting and destroying the small, illegal coca producers, the privatisation of all public enterprises, railroads, mines, of oil, gas, power, water, telephones and airlines, exports of gas and other mined resources.

Instead of the emergence from the crisis, it was the start of persecutions by coalitions against small coca producers, of cutting down budget on social security and education subsidies, of massive lay-offs of mine and enterprise workers.

In such difficult circumstances, the popular opposition in La Plaza has massively taken to the streets, demanding the cabinet's resignation. Their movement was extinguished by gunfire in February 2003 (33 dead) and, during the October 2003 demonstrations, 80 civilians have been killed. The new Indian revolutionary leader Evo Morales, founder of the

"Movement towards Socialism", was leading the demonstrations carrying signs reading "The united people will never be defeated". Under the tremendous popular pressure, President Sanchez de Lozada resigned on October 17th.[79]

"The Butcher", as Bolivians have dubbed Sanchez de Lozada, looked for refuge, naturally, in Miami, without any apparent American intention to see him dragged in the court of law for crimes against humanity.[80]

In such circumstances, with social democracy being removed from the popular aspirations and consistent compromises with ultra-liberal parties, the new truly leftist leader has become the symbol of national and social salvation.

Forty-five years old Evo Morales is a self taught Indian ethnic, with roots running to the world's oldest civilisation – the Inca. He is the president of the Union Federation of peasants in the tropical area used by traditional coca farmers and also founder of the new "Movement towards Socialism". A huge admirer of Fidel Castro and Hugo Chavez, he has an anti-imperialist and socialist orientation, making him the new revolutionary star in Latin America.

"All over Latin America and worldwide, too – wrote Ignacio Ramonet. Evo Morales, imposing figure of an indigenous movement acting with tremendous power in Ecuador, Peru, Chile and Paraguay, has become a very popular personality. By overthrowing Sanchez de Lozada, he is rejecting an economic model which has deepened corruption throughout Latin America, ruining populations and multiplying social exclusion."[81]

After his brilliant victory in the presidential election and after establishing the new popular government, Evo Morales issued, on the 1st of May, 2006, a presidential decree for the nationalisation of the entire hydrocarbons industry and also promised to nationalize other economic sectors. At the same time, he nullified restrictions and legalised the growing of the traditional coca bush, and promised to develop a programme for economic growth, eradication of illiteracy and reduction of poverty.

In the Latin-American arena, Evo Morales is a champion in the fight against American imperialism, a defender of strengthening solidarity and economic cooperation based on the new principles and of establishing a continental union of independant Latin-American countries. The first two high-level meetings on the subject of establishing a new structure for economic and political cooperation (the first held in April 2006 in Havana, and attended by Fidel Castro, Hugo Chavez and Evo Morales, the second held in May 2006 on the Brazilian-Argentinean border, and attended by Lula, Chavez, Kirchner and Morales) have opened the new path of Latin-American solidarity.

Once the Castro-Chavez-Morales leftist-socialist triumvirate was established and reinforced, as well as the more liberal social-democratic power of Lula de Silva and Nestor Kirchner, and that of other progressive leaders, the consolidation of their alliance in the fight for national independence and socialism grew into an expression of various means towards the same final objectives.

(g) Peru, at the Crossroads Between Social-Democracy and Revolutionary Romanticism

In the concerto of Latin-American countries, Peru (with 1,285,216 sq. km., nearly half the surface of Western Europe and home to a population of 26 million) is quoted as a poorly-developed country, with a GDP per capita a little over 2,060 US dollars. Around 45% of its inhabitants are descendants of the largest Latin-American empire – the Inca, with 37% crossbred between Latino-Indians, Spanish, and other Europeans, 15% have European, especially Spanish origin, and 3% are the result of Asian immigration.

Over the last 50 years, this country underwent an agitated urbanisation process, ending with 75% of the population now living in cities, of which nearly half in the poor peripheral neighborhoods. Lima, the nation's capital, counting over 8 million inhabitants, Arequipa over one million, and the famous vestiges in Machu Picchu, the prehistoric capital of Latin America's largest empire, are home to around 300,000 inhabitants.

Geographers and geologists hold Peru as one of Latin America's richest countries, in terms of natural resources. Peru is the world's largest producer of coca leaves used for manufacturing cocaine, the world's largest producer of fish flour, the second largest fish and silver producer, the fourth largest lead producer, the fifth largest the ethane gas producer, the eight the largest copper producer, while having inestimable quantities of hidden mining resources, yet to be discovered in the Andes Cordillera.

In spite of the rich deposits, the very limited development of processing industries, together with the limited national electrification, have Peru being quoted as an underdeveloped farming, herding and mining country, with a very poor population. Over the last years of mostly American colonial domination, the poverty has spread to such an extent that Peru can be considered, as written by Ramon Pajuelo Teves, the Peruvian author quoted below, one of Latin America's poorest and the most unequal countries. Over the last decades, the brutal exacerbation of contradictions between labour and capital has generated the rapid ascension of social movements for national and social liberation.

"Over the last few decades – wrote Ramon Pajuelo Teves – the social movements have once again taken an important spot on the agenda of Latin-American social sciences. Obviously, the reasons of such a "discovery" are not exclusively scholarly. They answer the need to emphasize the political importance. In a scenario defined by the transformations of global power and of neo-liberal capitalism, following the end of the Cold War, the emergence of new social movements seems to prove nothing less than the actuality and renewing of the anti-capitalist struggle."[82]

After the failure of the neo-liberal economic and social policy, in the 1990-2000 decade, enforced by Alberto Fujimori (the son of Japanese immigrants), after the destruction and squashing of social movements, a new stage be-gun, one of democratisation, of emerging national and social movements with an anti-liberal and anti-capitalist trend.

The five-year regime of Alejandro Toledo (2000-2005), who had promised undreamt-of successes, has ended in yet another electoral catastrophe. In the free democratic elections held in July 4, 2006, two leftist candidates and political parties made it to the second round: Alan Garcia Perez, representing the Popular Revolutionary Alliance, who had gathered 55.4% of the votes, and Ollanta Humala, representing the leftist nationalist revolutionary party named "Union for Peru", with 30% of the votes. The two political forces won a cumulated 85.4% of the votes, ensuring their parliamentary majority.

Thus, for the first time in Peruvian and Latin-American history, an overwhelming majority of the leftist electorate has claimed a historical victory. Right from the first round of elections, the people rejected, by a vast majority, the liberal, pro-American model which supported total privatisation, social corruption and increasing poverty.

Ollanta Humala, dubbed by the media "the Peruvians' Chavez", obtained 30% of the votes in the first round, outmatching Alan Garcia and the right-wing candidate Lourdes Flores (who, according to all the polls, was supposed to claim victory in the second round). In the end, the national revolutionary Humala lost the presidential battle. He is ready to contribute, as leader of the opposing party, to his homeland's social and economic progress. According to the specialists' estimations, Humala lost the presidential chair because his project of nationalising all enterprises, an expression of his revolutionary romanticism, had frightened the middle class of the most conservative society, afraid of American punitive actions and of an increased state bureaucracy.

While too early to judge the future cooperation between the two leftist parties, we can expect the newly elected president, leftist social-democrat Alan Garcia, to learn from his failure as President of the Republic between 1985 and 1990, and to choose, according to his promise during the elections, to go the path of cooperation with all the leftist parties and social movements, the path of progressive socialism, of redistribution of revenue, of reinvigorating the economic growth and of cutting down on unemployment and poverty. We can expect him to follow the Brazilian path of gradual reforms, thanks to the instatement of new economic relationships with Latin-American and other co-interested states.

The deal between the leftist political parties and their emergence in the political scene is a new phenomenon of social progress, gaining more and more ground in Latin America and, hence, in the other continents as well. In a not so distant future, when right-wing parties will be more and more compromised in the eyes of the voters and will lose more and more influence as leading political parties, then the pluralism of the leftist parties will transpose into life the new ways to develop democracy. As a form of social progress, democracy will not and cannot disappear from the social progress scene. It is permanently perfecting itself and is, in itself, an everlasting social category, always changing its shape and contents. The only things to disappear are those political parties which do not promote social progress. The only ones to develop are those political parties which are bearers of social progress. They are the alpha and the omega of the new processes of social progress, and are pioneered by the political parties in Peru, Brazil, and Argentina.

(h) Colombia, a Country of Blood and Fire.

When writing these pages on the last stand of social regress in Latin America, I spent quite some time searching for a title which would be able to suggest to my readers, in a most concise form, the political landscape in modern Colombia. The title I have settled for, "Colombia, a country of blood and fire", came from journalist Sonia Chironi and was published in Le Monde on August 7, 2006, captures and synthesizes the best, the Colombian political and military panorama.

Colombia is one of the Latin-American countries with the bloodiest political and military dictatorships of right- and far-right forces. It is the last stand of the American imperialism and of neocolonialism on this continent; it is the trampoline of American terrorist, paramilitary private companies, whose subversive actions against progressive forces in Colombia and against recently freed neighboring nations are coordinated by the C.I.A. American central.

Why are the American military circles providing more and more military, paramilitary and financial support to corrupt military regimes in Colombia? What are the mysteries behind this American "charitable generosity"?

With a surface of 1,141,148 sq. km., twice the size of France – and more than 44 million inhabitants, Colombia, the second largest Latin-American producer of coffee and cocaine and the site of extensive, yet to be discovered, underground resources, holds a highly important strategic position – that of being the last citadel of American domination in Latin America. Bordering Venezuela, Brazil and Peru, recently freed from American domination, Colombia has been transformed in a military starting block for espionage and diversion against countries which have recently become free of neocolonial domination.

It is one of the poorest and most debt-ridden countries in Latin America, with a GDP barely reaching the 2,000 dollars threshold. Around 60% of the population is living below poverty line; two out of three Colombians are barely making a living, in a very narrow range of poverty levels. During the economic and financial crisis, which has been lasting for eight years, yearly growth rate has dropped below 0.5%, while unemployment has soared to 20%.[83] Economic failure, matched with the limitation of social rights and liberties and the reinforcing of the totalitarian rule and the amplification of generalised terror are the main features of the Colombian political scene.

Speaking of the military and police state regime, Ivan Cepeda and Claudia Giron Ortiz wrote: since 1985, "a criminal mindset has become obvious, aiming for the disestablishment of the PU (the Patriotic Union, the main opposing party), and also an increase in the number of criminal acts, of persecutions and harassments, meant for total or partial elimination of the opposition."[84]

Besides innumerable selective assassinations of political and union leaders, we present a few examples of action specific to militarised terrorism.

On November 11, 1988, 88 activists were publicly assassinated in the central square of the town of Savoya. In 1987 and 1990, Jaime Pardo Leal and Bernardo Jaramillo Ossa, presidential candidates, were murdered. Similar assassinations targeted eight deputies and Senator Manuel Cepeda Vargas. Over the following years, hundreds of leftist mayors have been liquidated. According to estimates by the above-quoted authors, over 3,000 political, unionist and leftist party activists have been assassinated over this period.

According to the notes by Sonia Chironi, Colombia has

registered, over the last thirty years, over 200,000 deaths in military raids and in selective assassinations against leftist political leaders. Colombia is the world's last military totalitarian regime, governing with the outdated instruments specific to totalitarianism, militarism and terrorism.

The years of dictatorship, terrorism and massive liquidation of political leaders, as well as a deep deterioration of democracy, has forced militants in the Colombian democratic opposition to answer the extreme violence of the liberal bourgeoisie with the violence of the working class, of the poor peasantry, of the progressive intellectuals. The only way out of the forty-year long civil war and for Colombia to return to social stability, to peace and democracy, is for the civil society to defend itself, to democratically resist and repel attacks on its most basic social rights and liberties.

Even since the distant 1950s, a part of the peasant class has risen against the pillage and violence of the ruling classes, creating "self-defense zones". In 1966, Manuel Marulanda "Tirofijo" organised the guerrilla of Colombian Marxist revolutionary forces (FARC). The new revolutionary army currently counts around 17,000 soldiers, and, together with the activation, in 1970, of the illegal civil guerrilla of the M-19 movement, the National Liberation Army (NLA) probably amounts to some 50,000 activists and fighters for social and national liberation. The liberation forces control a territory, close in size, to Switzerland or Holland. New representatives of the popular demoeraters leaders will have been instated in the free zones, solving, with the very modest means available to the national solidarity movement, all local problems.

One of the main aims of the armed liberation movement is to free political prisoners from the other side of the barricade. The number of political prisoners suffering the most horrible tortures is still a mystery known only to the special police. According to observations by the journalists, it may vary between 600 and 3,000. In order to put pressure on the militarist circles in Bogota, so as to have the prisoners freed, FARC has used the strategy of kidnapping military, political and economic personalities well-known in Bogota and in other Colombian cities. It is estimated that around 3,000 businessmen and right-wing politicians are in the custody of FARC.

Current negotiations on exchanging prisoners have failed, as the leading circles have refused any kind of compromise with the Colombian guerrilla.

Besides military purposes originating from the civil war, FARC has adapted its social and national liberation programme to new developments. Revolutionary forces have demanded the commencement of negotiations towards ending the civil war, which has now lasted for over forty years. They are also demanding a real and complete democratisation of all political structures, free elections throughout Colombia, important structural reforms in the economic environment, the reduction of unemployment and poverty, the resuming of the economic growth. They have asked for Colombia to take to the cups of peace, democracy, national independence and social progress.

All these democratic demands are, however, conflicting the vital interests of the Colombian governing clique; they are opposing the Unites States' vital interests. Should the free parliamentary elections be enforced, the leftist democratic forces would claim a glorious victory, which would bring neocolonialism, wild capitalism, militarism and terrorism to an end.

In the recent electoral pretense of May 26, 2002, 49 year-old politician Alvaro Uribe, of right-wing roots, gained power right from the first round, with 53.17% of the votes, based on insincere false promises to end civil war, and in the absence of a counter-candidate to protect the interests of the civil society (for which the civil society had intensely boycotted the elections). FARC's reaction, in protecting the interests of the poor civil society, was a new warning issued for Uribe and his collaborators.

On the day of Uribe's investment, at the presidential palace in Bogota, in the presence of 600 illustrious guests, including representatives of the USA and of the other imperialist countries, which were guarded by 2,000 policemen, American anti-missiles and an American military espionage aircraft, FARC launched 114 projectiles on the palace, of which 17 hit the building's rear side. The other guided missiles were annihilated by the American anti-rockets. During the attack, 21 people were killed, and 50 injured. The civilian population in Bogota presented its condolences for the victims, rejoicing, at the same time, in a general satisfaction. The public understood that victory cannot be achieved by means of forged election lists, but by force. After the election masquerade, Uribe's popularity dropped by 15%, the lowest percentage in the history of Colombian presidents.

And yet, Uribe has full military, financial and logistic support from the United States. With a debt of 21 billion US dollars –mostly American loans for arming, amounting to 48% of the GDP – Colombia has recently received a 1.7 billion dollars loan for the financing of the "Colombia plan", mostly for arming the Colombian military police and the private American and Colombian paramilitary organisations. Under the pretense of the "anti-drug operation", the American Congress authorised the military activity of 400 mercenaries, who were to train over 140 paramilitary anti-guerrilla units, so as to clear the American oil areas.

According to estimations of the journalist Hernando Calvo Ospina, Americans have equipped the Colombian anti-guerrilla army with fighter jets, troop carriers, 7 powerful espionage radars, modern satellite equipment designed to photograph the movements of the guerrillas, and a lot of other logistic materials.

After September 11, determined to wipe out the Colombian guerrilla, American president Bush classified it among the terrorist organisations with which no compromise is possible. Total military and physical elimination of the Colombian freedom guerrilla is the main strategic line of the United States and of the president Uribe. Apparently, Bush and Uribe have forgotten the lessons taught by history.

When a nation is united in its fight for freedom and national independence, it becomes invincible. This is proven by the Chinese guerrillas in the Chinese liberation war, by the Algerian guerrilla and their fight for freedom, of the guerrillas in Angola, Congo, etc., and their battles for liberation.

In the new historical circumstances of American neocolonialism falling apart in most Latin American countries, of the victories claimed by progressive forces in elections, and of their economic and political consolidation, it is not impossible that these countries might send volunteers to support the final liberation of Colombia.

It is not impossible for Hugo Chavez, Evo Morales, Lula da Silva and other Latin-American leaders to stand not for much longer, the offences and threats of the Colombian reaction to the Latin-American progressive movements. The example of the Democratic Republic of Congo (ex Zaire), who has received military support from Angola, Namibia and Zimbabwe in saving Joseph Kabila's leftist government, proves to the Colombian progressive forces that the time of omnipotent imperialism and neocolonialism has passed.

(i) The Brilliant Victory of the Leftist Coalition "Frente Amplio" in Uruguay

After one hundred and fifty years of domination by the two center-right parties, the "colred's" party and the national party, which have eventually brought the country on the verge of bankruptcy, the catastrophic failure in the presidential and parliamentary elections of October 2004 was imminent. The coalition of the leftist parties "Frente Amplio" claimed an irrevocable victory.

Frederic Dubois, independent journalist, began his comment by depicting the joy of the Uruguayan people:

"Frente, Frente, Frente". Giant flags, trumpets, drums, explosions of joy, dancing, shouting and kissing. In Montevideo, a boiling wave of people charges on the city center, so as to emphasize, in this last week of October, the victory of the Frente Amplio party. Exiting the voting booths, in the balcony of the Presidente hotel, in front of an electrified crowd which was yearning for change, the Frente Ampolio candidate, Tabare Vaquez, took the reins of a 3.5 million people country. "We will start working as soon as tomorrow", he stated, in a brief speech. "Party, Uruguayans, enjoy!"

The coalition of the leftist parties, comprising ecologists, socialists, communists, all the way to the old Tupamaros guerrilla, founded in 1971, came very close to victory in both 1994 and 1998, with 35% to 45% of the votes. In spite of the electoral maneuvers of right-wing parties, which were leading the electorate, in October 2004 the victory of the leftist coalition was inevitable.

The "Frente Amplio" coalition inherited from the right-wing political parties a ruined economy, with a 14 billion dollars debt, unemployment over 20%, 40% illiteracy, catastrophic education and social protection.

After the victory in the elections, the coalition of the leftist parties developed the programme meant to support the country's revival, to end the crisis, to speed up economic growth, to re-establish social and economic structures, to develop and modernize industry, to cut down on unemployment and poverty, to regenerate the education and healthcare systems.

According to the experts' estimations, the GDP growth rate has nearly doubled, nearing the 7% of the neighbouring countries recently freed from colonial domination. A significant part of electoral promises have been kept.

The new government has undertaken repaying the debts to the World Bank and the IMF, provided 2/3 of the debts would be erased, according to the clauses for debt-ridden poor countries, so as to allow the accumulation of internal resources required for development.

As for its external policy, Uruguay has adopted its Brazilian, Argentinean and Chilean neighbours' strategy. The strategy aims at a regional integration of the countries within Mercosur, a source of economic stability and national independence.

(j) Nicaragua, Guatemala, Haiti and Salvador, on the Path to Freedom

With the victory of the leftist political parties and movements, in presidential and parliamentary elections in small countries, rich in history, such as Nicaragua, Guatemala and Haiti, we are getting close to the end of the list of liberation, democratisation and social progress movements of the Latin-American nations.

Nicaragua, with a surface of 129,494 sq. km. and 5.6 million inhabitants; Guatemala, with 108,889 sq. km. and 11 million inhabitants; Haiti with 27,232 sq. km. and 6.6 million inhabitants; and Salvador, with 21,000 sq. km. and 5.8 million inhabitants, are the geographically and demographically small Latin-American countries. They have been the prey to the colonisation campaigns initiated by the Spanish, the British and, later, by the Americans; we might call them martyrs of the bloody military dictatorships, loyal to the Americans.

In spite of the richness of their fertile lands, their mountains holding priceless mining resources and in spite of the fishing grounds, these countries rate, in the United Nations' chart, as some of the world's poorest countries. They are mostly agrarian countries, with GDPs between 835 and 1720 dollars, with poverty rates which shatter all world records. For example, in Nicaragua 60% of the citizens are unemployed, 63% live in poor peripheral neighbourhoods, 40% are illiterate.[85]

Similar poverty can be found in Guatemala and Haiti. In Guatemala, the poorest families sell their children, in order to survive the food holocaust. Also in Guatemala, United Fruit controls most of the farming land and abundantly exploits top-grade fruit and vegetables.

Animated by their multi-century poverty, the social injustice and the enslaving, feudal, colonial and neocolonial exploitation, the peoples in these countries, descendants of the Maya and Nahuti tribes and of the slaves imported from Africa, find their salvation in resistance and in the fight for a minimal quality of life. Their entire history, not very well known in the historiography of our planet, is a history of military coups d'état and of dictatorial regimes, of civil wars and of genocides against those standing up in defense of human dignity and existence.

The leftist political leaders and of other democratic parties have applied the strategy of armed resistance alternating with peaceful revolution, so as to reach their national independence, freedom and social justice aspirations.

After a successful armed Sandinista revolution (of Marxist orientation) in 1979 in Nicaragua, after overthrowing Somoza's pro-American dictatorship and after Daniel Ortega's victory in the 1984 elections (Ortega being the architect and historical leader of the Sandinista revolution), after the accomplishment of the socialist revolutionary reforms, the American armed intervention has forcefully removed the new regime from office.

After three failures in presidential and parliamentary elections, the Sandinistas have claimed victory in the 2006 elections. Daniel Ortega once again, became the President of the Republic.

Venezuelan president Hugo Chavez and Cuban president Fidel Castro have saluted this "major victory" of social justice emancipation.

Forced by the increasing poverty, the peoples in Guatemala have launched, as early as the 1960s, an ample movement against American occupation, with the potential of becoming a guerrilla. The thirty-five years of illegal resistance and legal opposition, which have seen the death of over 100,000 victims, have had positive results.

In 1996, after prolonged negotiations, a peace treaty was eventually signed between the right-wing holding the power and the rebels. Nine years later, in September 9, 2007 elections, the first round has been won by Alvaro Colom – the candidate of the new left-wing party, the National Union of Hope.

Historically, fortune hasn't favovred Haiti any more than it did Guatemala. After countless civil and anti-colonial wars between 1915 and 1934, the United States imposed their dominance in Haiti. The USA established a military dictatorship. After three decades of pro-American dictatorial regime, under François Duvalier and his followers, Pastor J.B. Aristide, an anti-imperialist democrat, won the December 1990 elections. Unhappy with the victory of popular, anti-imperialist democratic forces, general Raoul Cèdres, a follower of "Papa" Duvalier, removed, in September 1992, president Aristide from office. Under the pressure of ever larger manifestations and protests, the United Nations arranged for new elections. René Préval, former collaborator of Aristide, won the presidential elections, in 1995, with a brilliant victory. In the 2000 free elections, Aristide won a second mandate, followed in 2006 by René Préval.

After the victory of democratic and anti-colonial popular political forces in Nicaragua, Guatemala and Haiti, the agenda of the leading parties now includes: the country's renovation, speeding up the economic growth, eradication of corruption and criminality, reducing unemployment, illiteracy and poverty. The final goals of the revolutions in these countries are erasing the catastrophic consequences of neocolonialism, building and strengthening the democratic institutions, so as to mobilize internal resources, in order to increase the use of natural riches for the benefit of all the members of the society.

The Haitian government, much like most of the leading structures throughout Latin America, has accepted the strategy of a mixed development and, without neglecting public sector investments, supports the development of the private sector, the driving force animating economic growth.

"Putting its trust in the LESPWA platform, his Excellency, president René Préval –stated the Haitian prime-minister – wishes to express his determination to fight against all forms of exclusion; his will, expressed with the utmost clarity, is to live in a society in which the rights of each and all of us are recognised and respected."[86] The Haitians, just like the other Latin American peoples, express the need to promote participative democracy, "everyone's participation in the social life in all its dimensions, the indispensable nature of an ongoing concentration and interrelations between all protagonists…"[87]

As I was preparing my manuscript for the press, I received, via e-mail, information on the victory claimed, in the parliamentary elections in Salvador held on January 18, 2009. by the former leftist guerrilla of the Farabundo Marti Front (FMLN). The national liberation movement, the strongest leftist political actor, proposed Mauricio Funes as its candidate for the presidential elections planned for March 15, 2009.

This new left-wing candidate in an Americanised country promised to have the country emerging from the crisis, out of inflation and corruption, as well as fighting poverty and social inequality. In spite of the incertitude concerning the final results, according to the polls and the people's will, revolutionary left will claim, hopefully, a memorable victory in the presidential elections.

The peoples in Latin America, now freed, are in the stage of starting the establishment of the new society, of new free, equal, socially fair relationships. This way, facing numerous obstacles, some countries will have better results; some will have average results and some rather poor results. The world is constantly developing in an environment of equal chances and different results. The new society and the new order are developing in different economic, historic and social circumstances, and it is these circumstances and the subjective perceptions that provide social progress.

12. The Leftist Course of North America

Mexico's leftist course, the victory stolen from the Democratic Revolution Party

(a) Mexico's Sharp Turn to the Left

The last giant of Spanish-Portuguese America, covering a huge surface area of 1,972,456 km^2, south of North America (more than 100 million inhabitants, the world's fifth oil producer and the eleventh economic power of our planet, with a GDP per inhabitant of 12,780 US Dollars) turned its back to liberalism and pro-Americanism.

For the presidential and parliamentary elections (organised on July 2, 2006), there participated the coalition "Wealth for All", led by the Democratic Revolution Party (PDR), of left-wing bearing – the party of Lopez Obrador, the National Action Party (PND), of moderate right-wing bearing – the party of Felipe Calderon, and the Institutional Revolution Party (PRI), a traditionally bourgeois and oligarchic party, represented by the candidate Roberto Madrazo (the compromised party that led Mexico for 60 years).

According to the pre-election polls and the predisposition to the left-wing of the greatest part of the civil society, with high hopes in the leftist electoral victory, the coalition of Lopez Obrador should have won a sure and convincing victory. According to the estimates of all the moderate and objective politicians and of the seventh power, the journalists, the Mexican civil society took a sharp turn to the left.

Mexican voters turning was confirmed during the presidential elections in 1988, when the leftist candidate, M. Cardenas, won 31.12% of the votes cast. However, the people's electoral verdict was quashed by the massive theft of leftist votes. Today, nobody knows who won the elections. The expected turn to the left has its origins in the revolutionary Zapatista movement, which controls Chiapas, the poorest state in the south-eastern part of Mexico. The Zapatista national liberation army was led by Commander Marcos. Thanks to his revolutionary actions, he drew attention not only on Mexico's civil society, but also to the whole of Latin America.

The compelling turn to the left has its roots in the new strategy of Lopez Obrador, the new left-wing leader, a member of the Socialist International Movement; he successfully led his newly created party, the Party of the Democratic Revolution (PRD), to the top of the social and state pyramid. Obrador became the Mayor of the capital city, Mexico, which counts 20 million inhabitants. The Party of the Democratic Revolution (PRD) won dozens of new cities and states of Mexico.[88]

"Mr. Lopez arrives in this election campaign – the Mexican university professor Ersimo Saenz Carreté wrote – with the political capital accumulated through the administration of Mexico city: the austerity of its life style, the reducing of the wages in the main city government positions, the streamlining of the procurement and administration costs, the creation of the University of Mexico City, various actions in the support of the elderly and of single mothers, the firm supporting of culture, the development of routes - the second floor of the peripheral area, the publishing of the balance sheets and the organisation of referendums."[89]

During the elections campaign, Lopez Obrdor presented the Mexicans a programme that exceeded by far his accomplishments as Mayor (President) of Mexico City – a radical programme to reduce poverty and unemployment, to accelerate the economic growth, extensive structural and social reforms. Internally, Obrador approached the Brazilian version of the democratic socialism, and externally, he is against the integration of Mexico into the ALENA free-trade American strategy and closer to the Latin-American "Continental Union" and to the ALBA programme of Chavez.

The more radical programme proposed by Obrador also caused panic among the Mexican and American oligarchy and especially among the extreme right-wing of the traditional Mexico. The Mexican united reaction arranged Obrador's electoral compromising at any price, his referral to court under false charges and the annulment of his presidential mandate. When, under the pressure of huge street demonstrations,

Obrador attended the elections, a massive electoral fraud, already well organised, was put in motion.

(b) The Victory Stolen from the Revolution Parties

As expected, the Federal Electoral Institute, which was in the hands of the right-wing power, proclaimed the victory of Felipe Calderon, the leader of the moderate right-wing. After massive appeals related to the vote-theft in 50,000 electoral units (out of 300,000 - about 3,000,000 stolen votes), the Court of Justice, after the so-called objective counting of the votes, proclaimed the leader of the right-wing as the winner. Felipe Calderon won 35.88% of the votes and the candidate of the left-wing, Lopez Obrador, 35.31%. Thus, with a small majority, but falsified by approximately 240,000 votes, Calderon won the victory.

The biggest loser of the elections of July 2, 2006 was the candidate of PRI, the traditional right-wing, who obtained 11.27% of the votes. In fact, that was the the defeat of the far right-wing and the victory stolen from the left-wing.[90]

The Mexican right-wing, having in their hands the army, the police, the constabulary, the television and the powerful media, able of public opinion formation, as well as the majority of the electoral commissions, and benefiting from a large American support, actually committed an anticonstitutional coup against the poor Mexicans and all those in the medium structures, who harboured the hope in the victory of social justice.

Most of the international election observers expressed their "serious concern" about the honesty of Calderon's victory. The American Senator Richard Lugar, the Chairman of the Senate Foreign Affairs Committee and Special Envoy of President Bush, acknowledged the existence of "a broad and concerted programme of fraud on the elections day", and other personalities, such as MM Colin Powell, Henry Kissinger and Zbigniew Brzezinski, said that the United States of America could not recognize the official results of the Mexican elections.[91]

Despite Calderon's official proclamation, the democratic civil society, oriented towards the left-wing, did not acknowledge the stolen victory. Could it mean that the splitting of the

Mexican society around the elections results and looking for justice would continue in a peaceful way, or violence would undermine the common sense? The Mexicans themselves will choose their path toward the freedom victory.

If the Mexican right-wing forces try to defeat the national resistance by violence, it is clear that the leftists will have only two choices: either to retort to violence with violence, which would probably lead to civil war, which is not satisfactory either for the left-wing, or for the right-wing, or else to apply the strategy of peaceful demonstrations and street pressure, up to the exhaustion of the right-wing and the organisation of new elections.

But, to cancel the elections and to organize new ones, it is necessary to have not only the internal aid of the population, but also-as it was the case of the elections in Ukraine, Serbia and Georgia – the support of the international public opinion and of the UNO, which is less likely in the current ratio of forces and interests on the two American continents.

Given the historical perspectives of the social progress, the powerful left-turn of the civil society gives great expectations in terms of strengthening the unity of the left-wing parties and political movements and Mexico's unity with the Latin American countries, in view of the new world renaissance.

Is it going to happen in December 2011 or in December 2016? For the Mexicans, the most important goal is the inevitable victory of the left-wing parties and forces, on the way of revival of the society progress.

13. The Americans' Shifting to the Left, Obama's Revolutionary Evolution

(a) The Potential End of American Prosperity

The American elections are scheduled for October 2008 (the French edition of this volume was drawn up in the middle of the campaigning for elections in the U.S.— editor's note). Therefore, regardless of the elections outcome, here this testimony on the public opinion shifting to the left-wing will guide readers more easily toward understanding the actual turn of heart and of political bearing of the American public.

Elections will be held in terms of one of the deepest financial scams, of the economic crisis spreading, of the economic slowdown (the lowest level reached within the late 50 years - 1.2%, in 2007), of the bankruptcy of fifty banks, and of millions of economic businesses, of the expulsion of tens of millions of Americans from their houses and flats bought on credit and yet unpaid, and of the the rising unemployment and uncertainty and of the American citizens' fear regarding the probable outbreak of one of of the deepest economic and financial crises (of which the effects no one can foresee).

The years of the American prosperity, the "new deal" years of the big businesses, of the U.S.A. domination and military interventions, the years of great hopes for prosperity for all the citizens of the American society, have been left behind. Now, that period is history, as if it would never come back. Like all other continents of our planet, America has been touched by the new wave of social turmoil, of the rebirth of the new generation of social progress.

On the American political scene, a new leader of the American Renaissance has emerged: the African-American senator of Illinois, Barack Obama, the man of the other America, the man with clairvoyant, innovative and progressive vision.

(b) The Victory of the Half-Blood Barack Obama in the Democratic Party Primary Elections

When I finished analysing the brilliant victory of the Australian Labour Party, the international press announced the beginning of the primary elections for the appointment of the candidate for the presidential office, both in the Democratic and in the Republican Party. At the moment, I could not imagine and I never guessed that, during the sole primary stage of the duel for the appointment of the democrates' candidate, Barack Obama or Hillary Clinton, most of the delegates would press the key to elect Barack Obama, the senator of the State of Illinois.

After a long confrontation, his opponent, Hillary Clinton, abandoned. During the Convention of the Democratic Party, held on August 30, 2008, Barack Obama, supported by Bill and Hillary Clinton, was declared the official candidate of the Democratic Party. It is clear that Barack Obama will face

McCain, the Republican Party candidate, in the presidential elections.

Until the presidential and parliamentary elections in October 2008, during which the two Americas will face each other, the young generation has already manifested against the war in Afghanistan and Iraq, unlike the conservative electorate, specific for the Republican Party of John McCain (the America of the old generation, of the wealthy American plutocracy, supporting the continuing of the war in Afghanistan and in Iraq and the world domination strategy by pressure, blackmail and military force).

According to the polls by RealClearPolitics on February 12, 2008, Barack Obama would gain the victory by 47.4% of the votes, against the 43.7% votes for John McCain. Most public opinion polling companies give Barack Obama the advantage and possible victory. It is risky to launch the idea of Barack Obama's or John McCain's possible victory. There are less than two months until the election. What programmes and electoral surprises will Obama and McCain run? It is hard to predict. However, "spring is known by the first swallows", according to an old saying. Swallows have overwhelmed the American ship. They show the shifting movement of the American society to the left.

"Obama's revolution, wrote Zyad Limare, the manager of Afrique Magazine, whatever the outcome of the race for the White House, he has already made America and the world to move. He is imposing himself, at the right time, as the candidate representing the break between generations, he is the champion of a new America, the glorious candidate of a youth fed up by the ideological and religious conflicts of supporters of the birth surge. He is the candidate of the 21st century."[92]

(c) The First Sketch of Obama's Electoral Programme

Unrelated to the fact that Obama would win the elections – which depends on the electoral programmes and on the will of the civil society – the slipping of the American electorate to the democratic and antiracist left-wing is the most recent phenomenon in terms of global progressive movement which the analysts of social movements must stress through an objective interpretation.

Who actually is Obama, the man who enjoys the sympathy of most Americans?

The black candidate for the seat in the White House is the son of a North African from Kenya, who came to the United States after winning a scholarship in Hawaii (then a U.S.A. territory) and of a Kansas white American of Irish descent (she gave birth to Barack Obama in Honolulu). After the divorce of his parents and his father's leaving for his native Kenya, Obama was raised by his white grandfather and grandmother, who belonged to the middle class. He studied the law at elite schools at Harvard and married an American black woman, descendant of American slaves.

At the end of his university education, Obama started practising law and, most often, he defended the interests of the blacks and of poor Americans against segregation and social injustice.

After that, he engaged himself in politics. As an activist of the Democratic Party, Obama went through all the political echelons, to the position of Senator of the State of Illinois. Obama is the product and reflection of the new less racial America, which is waking up from the decades of the drowsiness of American prosperity; he is a reflection of the state of mind of most Americans. Entering the pre-elections campaign, the Democratic Party candidate said his campaign's main purpose was to "continue the course of our predecessors, a course for a fairer America, for an equal America, with more freedom, more careful and more prosperous". In the primary elections campaign, he has already launched several items of his electoral programme, touching the weak spot of the American society. Thus, he aims at the introduction of the universal health insurance for all Americans (50% of the Americans do not benefit from health insurance), at the substantial reducing of the unemployment, at the increasing of the purchasing power of unfavovred people, at the tax exemption for small and medium enterprises, at the establishment of jobs, at the withdrawal of the American soldiers from Iraq and Afghanistan, at providing renewable energy from domestic production, etc.

However, for the fulfillment of the civil society demands, Obama wrote in his memoirs, published in the United States – it is necessary to make some significant changes: "A change in the White House, where Reagan and his followers are devoting themselves to their unworthy interest, a change in the Congress, where people are indulgent and corrupt, a change in the mood of the nation obsessively focused on itself; the change does not come downward; the change will come only upward, so we have to mobilize it".[93] Obama has firmly decided to mobilize himself and to mobilize the Americans to fight for a new America, more democratic, more just, less racial and more prosperous.

(d) Barack Obama's New Challenge Facing the Financial Collapse and the Amercian and World Economic Crisis

The elections were held after I had sent my manuscript to the publisher. Without leaving out my analyses on the American people's slipping to the left, I feel compelled to make brief references on the first points of the Obama programme after the elections. As expected, the Americans voted for the change promised by Barack Obama, who won the elections with flying colours.

Obama's brilliant victory is not just a victory for the left-wing Americans. It has an international significance. It represents a new hope to the Americans and not just to them. According to a poll, Obama is supported by the the Italian (70%), by the German (67%), by the French (65%) and even by the British people (49%). We believe that most Africans cherish hope in Obama's victory, since only jointly with the Americans, the Chinese, the Indians, the Russians, the members of the European Union, the Brazilians, and with other nations, too, there could be established a new global social and economic order based on equality, fairness and transparency in the international cooperation and on the poverty reduction worldwide.

Obama won the elections in the worst times, in a period of an outburst of financial bankruptcy and economic crisis that has shaken the whole structure and the entire concept of liberal economy. The analysts of the global crisis have begun to sketch a reassessment of the capitalist system. They are talking more and more about the need for the establishing of a new basis for the modern capitalism, about the end of capitalism, about possible disasters and about the need for radical change in the system. This means that the heavy task which awaits the new president is beyond his electoral programmes. It is the deepest crisis since 1929. It will facilitate the clearing of pathways for deep reforms in the American economy and structures, without the fierce opposition of the high finance.

The American banks, which have lost 1700 billion dollars, are experiencing the insolvency risk. According to the financial experts, the nationalisation of the major banks is the only solution for strangling the American banking gambling house and for injecting additional funds to rescue the collapsing American society. The value of the shares of the companies listed with the stock-exchange fell by half. Thousands of companies went bankrupt. The automotive industry is facing bankruptcy. The unemployment rose from 6.5 million in 2007 to 9.1 million in 2008, and, for 2009, we may add other 3-4 million.

This means that, on top of the election promises previous to the crisis, Obama will have to add the most difficult tasks for getting off the collapse. After his installation in the White House, Obama, together with his experienced team, submitted to the Congress the economic recovery programme.

Besides the 1000 billion dollars injected into the saving of the banking system, considered insufficient, Obama will invest other 1000 billion dollars, of which 300 billion dollars to support banks and businesses in difficulty, 275-300 billion dollars in fiscal aid, 100 billion dollars in tax-credit for small and medium companies, 140 billion dollars in subsidies for people whose incomes are below 20,000 dollars per year, 50 billion dollars in renovating schools, 43 billion dollars in the extension of the payment delay of unemployment allowance, 6 billion dollars in social housing.

The new budget has imposed the increase of the extremely high incomes taxation, the wages increase and the granting of the 400-dollar monthly allowance for the poorest employees. The French newspaper Le Monde published an article entitled

"Mr. Obama submits a strongly leftist budget ...", subtitled "Socialism and return to the class struggle". Considering the investments orientation, Barack Obama's new programme is radically different from the programme of George Bush. "It really shows a net break with the policy of George Bush." (Le Monde, February 28, 2009).

To get out of the deep crisis of all American structures, Obama is forced to operate some socialist methods, namely: the nationalisation of the major banks and the full control of their activities, the redemption by the state of part of the shares of the large enterprises in difficulty, the finding of appropriate formulas for increasing the state's economic role in the economic development, and the fairer redistribution of the national income in favour of those who are working.

All these manifestations of the crisis and, to the same extent, of the metastasis of the American imperialism, require deep changes in all structures, in the existence principles and rules specific to the liberal society. It will still take us a long time to give a more precise answer in terms of the extent to which Obama will fulfill the great expectations of the Americans and not only theirs. For now, Barack Obama has guided America to a course of great expectations.

14. Ignition of the Spark of Independence, Democracy and Socialism in Africa

(d) Neocolonialism, the Main Handicap for Social Progress

If Latin American is alight in the fire of social revolutions, the traditional underdeveloped and tribal Africa is igniting the sparks of national and social liberation.

To better understand the genesis and self-achievement of the African socialism, the infiltration of the socialist ideas and their turning into political movements, we should take into consideration, "multum in parvo" (translation from Latin: "much in little" – Pythagoras' precept: "Do not say little in many words, but much in few words"- editor's note), the political, economic, social and traditional circumstances of the emergence and development of the African socialism, in close relation to the African civilisation.

Although our human species originated from the African

cradle and although we have extended ourselves on all the five continents, Africa has been and still is the most underdeveloped continent on our planet.

Exceptions were, in ancient times, the pharaonic Egyptian and Carthaginian civilisations, which left us the architectural ruins heritage of ancient cultures and civilisations long gone, as well as some maritime cities such as Algiers, Cairo, Dakar, Accra, Brazzaville, which the colonists turned into ports for slave trade and African raw materials exports.

In this case, we may say with more certainty and without any doubt that Black Africa, except for South Africa, is delayed for tens of generations by comparison with the modern developed societies. In Africa, the colonialism and neocolonialism of the great imperial powers, established on the grounds of community, tribalism, traditionalism and illiteracy, were the main causes of their emancipation disability.

Despite the slight progresses during the last fifty years, the social and economic development of Black Africa is now below the minimum level required for stronger starting bases for the modern industrialisation. The GDP per inhabitant, as a leading indicator of the social progress, attained in the Ivory Coast, Cameroon and Gabon about 700-1000 dollars; at the same time, most African countries - poor and less productive – keep being at a level between 200 and 400 dollars. With 870 million people (around 15% of the total world population), Africa's participation in the total world trade is 2% only. This is the reason why 25% of the 2 billion people living "in absolute misery", according to the UNDP estimate, are among the African peoples. Africa beats all world-wide records of poverty, mortality, illiteracy, starvation, thirst, epidemics, infant mortality and, more recently, acquired immune deficiency syndrome.

However, Africa has not stood in place. Its cultural, social and political emancipation has been faster than the development of its economic basis. This simply confirms that, always along the history of peoples and nations, the more evolved social superstructure may have and should have the role of a driving force that accelerates the social progress.

The collective social consciousness of the African peoples

for their liberation from neocolonialism, illiteracy, ignorance and poverty is smouldering under ashes. In almost all African areas it has expanded and has turned into national and social liberation movements. After the Second World War, some African countries won their national independence, willingly or by force, by military or peaceful revolutions, and took the road of the faster emancipation and economic development.

However, the social progress, which is always evolving in a spiral, in its own contradictions, has left most African countries at the mercy of neo-colonialism and of globalisation.

The neo-colonialism and the globalisation have become the main deficiencies of the social and economic progress.

(b) The Pioneers and the Victims of the Primitive Community Socialism

The emergence of the national and social liberation ideas and the development of the socialist movement in Africa are directly proportional to the degree of development of the working class and of the intellectuals, as major carriers of the social progress. In most African countries, by far the least developed countries, the share of industrial workers in the modern sector and of intellectuals, taken together, hardly rises to 3-4%.

The workers and intellectuals are soaked in the ocean of the poor people in the unorganised trade and craftsmanship sector.

The traditional peasantry, recently emerged from the natural tribal economy, and constituting the majority of the population, has taken to the market economy.

In other words, except for Maghreb and South Africa, the working class is not constituted as an autonomous independent class "in its own", as the driving force of social progress.

The new, emerging bourgeoisie has not yet evolved beyond the commercial stage of the capitalism development. Its driving force to internal accumulation and concentration of capitals is a critically feeble basis, in terms of capitalism development. The bourgeoisie has not a leading role in the development of the society, so it seeks for rescue in the state structures and in the enrichment through corruption. Most often, it abides to foreign neocolonialist policies and takes the expansion of the foreign capital for its own chance for prosperity. In this way, the African bourgeoisie has not and cannot have the leading role once played by the European and American bourgeoisie in the social progress.

In most of the underdeveloped countries, the young intellectuals originate from the progressive student movements in the West and in the East and, later on, from the student movements in their own countries. They play the role of catalysts of the social progress.

"I had the opportunity of a temporary stay in Great Britain = said Julius Nyerere - during the Second World War. At that time, they talked of socialism everywhere. It was almost impossible to meet a progressive African student who did not think and talk in terms of socialism."[94]

The progressive ideas of socialism were not born and could not be generated on the soil of Africa, featured by its traditional natural economy, a mainly agrarian and semi-literate area. For the genesis of the utopian socialism and, afterwards, of the scientific one, and, after its implementation, of the real socialism, there would have been required a minimum degree of capitalist development, a level determined by the development and by the degree of pragmatism of the working class, as well as a decisive extent of cultural emancipation of the society. However, the social developments philosophy teaches us that all negative phenomena and processes result into positive seeds of social progress. The traditional bases of the community society, related to anthropological social justice, to freedom and equality, were fertile grounds for the introduction of the socialism both in the West and in the Orient, and, thereafter, for the growing of socialism out of its own foundation.

The African countries movement for national liberation (inspired by the breakthrough ideas of African socialism) received a clearer form in Guinea Bissau, Senegal, Guinea, Mali, Ghana, Tanzania and Burkina Faso and in several other African countries. The leaders of these countries – Léopold Sédar Senghor, Sékou Touré, Amilcar Cabral, Modibo Kéïta, Kwamé Nkrumah, Julius Nyerere, Thomas Sankara and others = were the ideological bearers of the community-type socialism, of the society based on tolerance between classes, on the tribal traditional brotherhood and ethics, covered by the mobile force of the State powers.

In its search for its own identity, the African socialism has taken over a mixture of ideas of orthodox Marxism, of primary anthropological rural community, of self-management and of the authoritarian principles based on the single-party system.

About ten parties and socialist movements participated in the joint conference organised in Dakar in 1962, opened by Léopold Sédar Senghor, and where the first joint formula of the path of African socialism was drawn up.

"It has been easy to find an agreement on the goals of socialism: to build a society where power and wealth should not be the monopoly of a minority, so that the persons within a group should find their own creativity. Effort must be guided toward the peasant masses, and the community tradition should be used to substantiate the new society, without classes, where the African culture should revive. The African unity is necessary to protect this initiative. The African Socialism opposes the vulgar Marxism, by refusing atheism, by the absolute rejection of the class struggle (taken for a division factor) and by distrusting the formulas prepared in Europe. The absolute goal is not directed to the increase, but rather to the true development – a development of qaulity: better to produce less than to destroy communities. The dominance of foreign capital in industry is hard to bear."[95]

The African socialism ideas reflect the understanding of the socialism of this time, as a potential way of the social progress.

In most countries where left-wing political parties were in power, the achievement of the primitive, patriarchal socialism, through nationalisation and collectivisation of the agriculture by means of single-party democracy, of the centralised planning and of the excess of authority shown by the state powers at a time when there did not exist yet the minimum economic, political and social conditions necessary for the development of socialism, met an ever increased opposition from the population.

Thereafter, in several countries, the power was dominated by the socialist parties and movements. Socialism in the African countries proved to be a social-economic system of ineffective stagnation and, consequently, it left the main African political scene.

In Mali, Guinea Bissau or Burkina Faso, the neo-colonists and the internal conservatives committed military coups d'état and assassinations against leftist leaders, such as: Medibo Kéita, Amilcar Cabral, Thomas Sankara, etc. In Guinea, Ghana, Bénin, the socialism was smothered by its own contradictions.

Thus, in the states above, the socialism of the 1960s and 1970s, which we may call primitive or community socialism, failed for natural reasons: there were no minimum conditions for the development of the productive forces, of the working class and of intellectuals, or the minimum conditions for the emancipation of the peasantry. In fact, one can say that there was no modern democracy, not even in its least stage.

Julius Nyerere himself had to declare: "We are working to construct the socialism with few socialists, with few people aware of the main issues of the democracy; we are trying to achieve the fundamental transformation of our economy, almost without technicians. Our wish is to create an egalitarian society and educated elite, whose education encourages the individual advancement reasons."[96]

After he retired from the political life in his native village, Nyerere replied to the question posed by David Gakunzi As'Obe Obe, the author of the book "Meetings with Julius Nyerere", if he would change his political offer, in case he returned to power: "With the experience I have gained, I would definitely implement it differently. I would put more emphasis on the establishment of joint ventures, rather than on nationalisation. I would choose to purchase parts of capital in private enterprises, rather than to nationalize everything."[97]

(c) The North-African Arab Socialism

With Algeria (35 million inhabitants), Tunisia (around 10 million inhabitants) and Libya (about 6 million inhabitants), the North-African socialism, or the Arab socialism, as the analysts frequently call it, has totally different social-economic, theological and cultural backgrounds and it is, in many respects, different from the primitive community socialism of the seven African countries already analysed.

In the 1960s and 1970s, the economic and social landscape and the civilisation of the three mentioned countries differed in many ways from the still very low economic development level of the seven countries in Black Africa, which I have already discussed.

The Islamic Arab civilisation, the community philosophy of solidarity, resulting from the old Carthaginian, Egyptian and Roman cultures and the long colonial domination, flooded, on this side of the Mediterranean Sea, by the progressive ideas of economic development, democratisation and socialism, represented the foundation for the implanting of the North-African Arabic socialism.

The Arab socialism is the result of the somehow developed social-economic relations of the working class and of part of the emancipted peasantry, who organised themselves in unions and political parties. The progressive political parties and their intellectual leaders of social-nationalist orientation played a pioneer role in the mobilisation of the citizens to the struggle for national and social liberation from colonialism, from perpetual misery and poverty.

After fighting for 18 years, the Néo Destour Progressive Party (successfully led for over two decades by Habib Bourguiba, of far leftist socialist orientation), proclaimed the independence of Tunisia on May 20, 1956. On July 5, 1962, after six years of military revolution led by Ben Bella and Harri Boumediène, of Islamic-socialist orientation, the total independence of Algeria was proclaimed. Seven years later, the young revolutionary colonel Muammar Khadafi, together with a group of young officers, overthrew the monarchy by a coup d'état and established the Independent Libyan Arab Republic, a republic of "liberty, socialism and Arab unity".

Since their very beginning, the national revolutions of liberation of these countries included features of social revolution and, after the accession to power of the leftist parties and of the progressive forces, these countries chose the path of the socialism as the great highway of their national revival.

After winning the power and the liberation from the colonialist domination, the main means of production were partially nationalised and the agricultural production was partially redistributed, by still tolerating the private sector of the small and medium producers. State control was established over the foreign trade, the central planning and the state intervention in the national income redistribution in the interest of all the people. In the political relations, the limited democracy, with merely one party, grew over the ruins of the colonialism.

During the last decade of the twentieth century, after many years of experiencing the partnership between Islamism, liberalism and socialism and of discarding the remains of the state-power, of control and dogmatism, the turn of course towards the market economy and the wide opening to the outside world have contributed to accelerating the social and economic development, the democratisation, the humanisation of the social progress. There were years of much less socialism in words and far more than socialism in deeds.

It is difficult, almost impossible, to summarize in a few pages the positive effects of the North-African socialism. Some main indicators of the social progress may, however, give the readers an approximate picture of the new social-economic landscape. We may say that the three countries have strong foundations for industrialisation, electrification, modernisation and irrigation of the agriculture. Almost all the towns in these countries are interconnected by modern highways, railways and airlines. Thousands of new industrial, commercial, banking and transport companies sprouted out of the ground like mushrooms after rain. Except for a few years, the annual growth rate ranged between 4% and 6%. The GDP per inhabitant, the main criterion of the progress, increased in Algeria, in 2007, to 7,952 Euros, in Tunisia to 6,600 Euros and in Libya to 9,600 Euros. The North-African countries have surpassed the threshold of the underdeveloped countries and have been approaching the line of the medium developed countries.

When, after 25 years of career as a professor in economics at the University of Oran in Algeria, I visited again those places as a tourist, I was pleasantly surprised (actually, bewitched) by the great economic, cultural and social progress, that deserves special attention in the historiography of the revival and development of socialism.

It is true that the discovery of oil was a heavenly gift for Algeria's and Libya's economic progress; they have entered thus the family of the top world oil and gas producers. However, it is equally true that Tunisia, which has no natural riches, except for the fish out of sea, the sun and few fertile land plots, reached nearly as many social-economic and cultural achievements by developing the economic branches of energy, manufacturing and tourism (6 million tourists annually) and in some areas, it attained more impressive achievements.

While the technical development was the solid basis of social progress, the general flowering of the human potential, the recovery of the standard of living and the reducing of poverty recorded unexpected positive results in the history chronicles of these countries.

In 2004, the rate of primary schooling in all these three countries rose to 85-92%; in the secondary education there were trained, about 70% young people of appropriate age and, in the higher education institutions, about 25%.

About 85% of the population consistently benefit from free medical assistance, which is approaching the European standards. The rural electrification and the radio broadcast coverage are almost complete (80% - 92%). Between one half and one third of the citizens own an apartment. The standard of living of the population increased considerbly.

The Tunisians, the Algerians and the Libyans have understood the philosophy of the effectiveness of the partnership of Islamism, liberalism and democratic socialism on the way to social progress.

(d) The Costly Fruits of the Fourty Years of Civil War in Angola

Angola occupies a place of honour in the post war history of confrontation between the pro-imperialist forces and those supporting the liberation of the African continent, for national and social emancipation; we may say, it has a special place in the world history. Undoubtedly, those 40 years of revolution and civil war for national and social liberation were the longest and bloodiest in the modern history of our civilisation. They cost Angola a million and half martyrs who died in the battles for liberation, four million people displaced and damages exceeding 20 billion dollars. This tragedy left the new generation with a ruined country, of which enormous natural wealth could and ought to be offered another alternative of peaceful development.

However, as history teaches us, every revolution has as many destructive effects as benefic results. On the ruins of the revolution and of the civil war there were born feelings of human dignity, unity, patriotism, hope and faith in the moral and historical legitimacy of the future fruits of Angola's national and social emancipation.

Angola occupies in southern Africa a special place in the geostrategic policy of the Western powers. The huge space of 1,246,700 km^2, namely 13.5 times larger than its metropolis, Portugal, is bathed by the Atlantic Ocean to the West, rich in oil deposits in the extraterritorial area over a length of 1,600 km. Due to high birth rate, the population increased, in spite of loss of lives, from 5 million in 1960 to over 14 million in 2006. Angola's national wealth in gold and diamond deposits, the enormous untapped reserves of oil and gas, along with its semi-tropical climate, favorable for growing maize crops, coffee, cocoa, rice and African fruits, constituted a true Eldorado for the 700,000 Portuguese immigrants. Thus, Angola became the arena of combat between the United States of America and other powers interested in the conflict against the movement for national and social liberation, in which France did not have a neutral attitude at all.

Unlike other colonial powers which, willingly or by need, accepted during the 1960s the claims of the the African peoples for freedom and national independence, Salazar's former colonial fascist regime denied the efforts of the liberation movement MPLA (the Popular Movement for Angola's Liberation) with the purpose of the proclamation of Angola's independence by negotiations.

Where interest, understanding, goodwill are lacking, the dialogue changes, however, and instead weapons begin to speak. Then, Kalashnikov machine-guns remain the only alternative language of resistance and human existence.

Therefore, on behalf of the people's will, the conference of the MPLA leaders held in London, in 1960, made the historic decision concerning the armed insurrection. On February 4, 1975, the Angolan people launched the armed struggle which, after 14 years of attacks and retreats of the liberation armies, would lead to the victory. On November 11, 1975, Angola's independence was proclaimed. A new flag in six colours, of the independent Angola, was waving at the presidential palace, as a symbol of freedom. This was the great defeat not only of the former Portuguese colonisers and of their servants in Angola, but also of those who were dreaming to govern the Angolan ship in neo-colonial waters. The victory of the left-wing socialist forces, of Marxist trend, was accomplished.

The expansion of the liberation movement conducted by the MPLA, led by its historical leader, Agostinho Neto, replaced after his death by José Eduardo dos Santos, threatened the Western powers' interests in the exploitation of the rich oil deposits, and it was also a threat to lose the territorial bases necessary to put down the liberation movements in Namibia, Zambia, the former Zaire. For the Western powers, Angola has a geostrategic importance for their domination in southern Africa.

The Western powers provided material, financial and military aid in favour of the armed forces of UNITA (the National Union for the Total Independence of Angola) and in favour of their historic leader, Joseph Savimbi, installed in south-eastern Angola, rich in diamond mines (which were bringing billions of dollars to finance the civil war). With its 14,000 well-armed soldiers, Joseph Savimbi won the support of the Mobutu regime and, later, of the regime in Congo Brazzaville. With more or less intensity, the ceaseless civil war lasted until 2002, for 27 years. On the background of the new geopolitical circumstances - abolishing of the apartheid and arrival of the power of Nelson Mandela and Thabo Mbeki in South Africa, and fall of the corrupt Mobutu regime in Zaire – through a final attack by MPLA, the UNITA leader, Joseph Savimbi, died (after being wounded). With him, the whole political and military movement UNITA collapsed.

Thus, in Angola's history a new era started, an era of social progress towards rebuilding the ruined country, an era of independence, freedom, democracy and socialism.

The civil war had left a ruined country to the heirs of the Liberation Movement. According to a World Bank report, the national income per inhabitant fell from 940 dollars in 1990 to 410 dollars in 1993 and, in the opinion of the experts, to 330 dollars in 2002. The civil war destroyed most of the schools, clinics, drinking water networks. The country was lacking drinking water, medical and vital food supplies. Almost half of the children suffered the consequences of a very poor diet. Most people were living on less than two dollars per day. Longevity was barely 37 years.

Angola experienced a humanitarian catastrophe. At that moment, the problem was to find ways out of that fateful legacy. Was it by seeking the support of the United Nations, of the World Bank, of the International Monetary Fund and of other financial institutions, by appealing to Western foreign investments? Angola solved its problems in its original style, by that mystery which troubles many underdeveloped nations: by using its natural resources rich in oil. Angola was the one that dictated the terms for foreign investments, according to the principles of cooperation on equal terms.

We are facing one of the few countries recently liberated that have requested the withdrawal of the United Nations peace mission from their territories. Also, Angola is one of the few countries that did not accept the diktat of the World Bank and of the International Monetary Fund. In fact, Angola is also one of the countries that rely on their internal forces, as the foundation of their economic development, and on foreign investments, as a secondary source.

"In Angola, the late Ambassador of Angola in the Ivory Coast, Belli Bello, said – we decide that in our home we take decisions based on the realities of our country. To decide, we do not call Washington, Moscow, Lisbon, Paris or London. We are proud of what we are, with our flaws and qualities. This is why the international community respects Angola."[98]

This state irrevocably joined the group of free, independent African countries, which aspire to the new African way of democratic, liberal and humanitarian socialism.

In determining its own future, Angola could take appropriate measures, counting on the intensive exploitation of its vast deposits of oil, gas, gold and diamonds. From 175,000 barrels in 1975, the year of the proclamation of its independence, and from 700,000 barrels in 1998, when two-third of the country was liberated, the oil production rose to 1,242,000 barrels per day in 2005 and to 1,365,000 barrels in 2006. The government expects to increase the daily production to 2,000,000 barrels in 2007 and to reach 2,200,000 barrels in 2008 and 2,600,000 barrels in 2012.[99]

Thus, as the fourth African oil producer, Angola will leave behind Algeria and Libya, approaching Nigeria, and it will soon become the second African oil producer.

With the important growth in oil prices in 2006, Angola earned from the exploitation of oil over 100 billion dollars, of which 25 billion went into the state's vaults. How many foreign currency revenues will Angola have by selling 700 million cubic metres of gas, a few tons of gold and thousands of carats of diamonds? The Angolans themselves will reap the fruits of their independence and freedom.

By implementation of the reconstruction programme of the ruined country, based on the principles of democracy and of a multi-party political structure, the MPLA disapproves the remains of dogmatism and the concept of the proletariat dictatorship, as opportunities inappropriate for the survivors of social classes.[100]

The popular democracy and the social market economy became the backbone of socialism in Angola.

By achieving the popular participatory democracy and the social market economy, the state succeeded, in a short time, to take steps on the accelerated growth path. The economic reforms undertaken by the popular government in early April 2002; gave unexpected positive results. According to the statement in January 11, 2006, of the Vice-President of the Government, Aguinaldo Jaime, the achieved growth rate rose to 13% in 2003, to 15% in 2004 and 2005, while the growth rate for 2006 is estimated at 21%.

The national income per inhabitant rose from 330 dollars in 1998 to 675 dollars in 2000, to 700 dollars in 2001, to 1,440 dollars in 2004. It could reach about 1,600 dollars in 2008.[101] It is expected that, at the end of the second decade of the 21st century, Angola will enter the group of the medium developed industrial countries.

Undoubtedly, after forty years of revolution and civil war, a new Angola was born in south-western Africa, free, independent and democratic, harvesting the high-priced, but well deserved fruits of its dead. According to the analysts, a new regional economic and military power is born in south-western Africa. Now-a-days, the shifting of the geopolitical axes toward the East and the South-West generates a new Africa. "This other Africa, writes Philippe Meymarie, is embodied by a new generation of Ethiopian, Erythrean, Ugandan, Angolan, Rwandan, Congolese, South-African leaders, often validated by the armed struggle against the foreign occupation or by the struggle against the corrupt regimes. Pragmatic, proving to be more managers than prophets, they often combine the liberal economic policy with the politics of their sole parties and multiply their statements of defiance against foreign models, against conditioning and foreign interference, facing the UNO, as does the President Kabila of the new Republic of Congo."[102]

(e) The Democratic Republic of Congo, from Patrice Lumumba to Laurent Kabila and Joseph Kabila

Following the collapse of the former colonial regime, on June 30, 1960, the rich Belgian colony of 2,345,409 km^2 and the second African country, by population, proclaimed its independence. Thus, Joseph Kasa-Vubu became the President of the Republic. Patrice Lumumba became Prime Minister and Joseph Mobutu became Chief of Defense. After the proclamation of the independence, Patrice Lumumba, in agreement with President Kasa-Vubu, developed an ambitious new programme for renewal and economic empowerment, for the development and strengthening of the national independence. This programme was not agreed by the Belgian colonisers.

By manipulating a part of the political class under the banner of the "independence", the Belgian colonisers and their people in the Mobutu clan organised the atrocious assassination of Patrice Lumumba, on January 17, 1961. Brutally murdered and incinerated in Katanga, the new legendary leader of the National Movement of the Congo, Patrice Lumumba, became the undying symbol of freedom, of the national independence and of the sovereignty of the people, not only in the Republic of Congo, but also throughout the neo-colonial Africa.

After the assassination of Patrice Lumumba and the elimination of his supporters, Congo took the path of neo-colonialism. In 1965, Mobutu neutralised Kasa-Vubu, the President of the Republic, ordered the killing and hanging on the streets of Kinshasa of four leaders of the new opposition, including the former Prime Minister. The Parliament was completely paralysed. The activities of the political parties were banned. Mobutu installed a single party dictatorship, put into the service of the Belgian neo-colonisers and of others. This dictatorship lasted for over three and half decades.

Deprived of all ways and means of political struggle for their national freedom and independence, the followers of Patrice Lumumba, the left-wing inclined nationalist leaders, prepared, in the mountain ranges in the north and east, a military offensive against the illegal installation of the Mobutu regime. The guerrilla allies began their assault. Antoine Gizenga pushed on with his guerrillas to the capital Kinshasa, coming from the North, Pierre Mulele from the center and Laurent Désiré Kabila, with the support of the Cuban volunteers led by the legendary Ernesto Che Guevara, from the East. In record time, two-third of the Congolese territory was liberated. The liberation guerrilla approached the capital. The Belgian-Mobutian regime was over. To extinguish the flame of the revolution, an energic intervention was necessary of the Belgian elite parachutists, of the French mercenaries led by Bob Denard and of Mobutu's elite guard.

According to the specific ambitions of the great revolutioners, Joseph Kabila retreated in the East along with a group of insurgents, in the mountain ranges in the province of Kivu. The sparks of the smothered revolution dragged on for 20 years. The illegal guerrilla resistance turned into the political school of the revolution. In the early 1960s, Kabila trained for a period of six months at the Great Chinese Military Academy. It was a period of standstill and preparation of the revolution, it was the time of boom for the Mobutu regime.

At first, the Mobutu regime had shown superiority through

demagoguery, false promises, foreign loans and foreign investments.

However, the honeymoon between Belgium and the Congolese regime did not last for very long. Since 1980, the Mobutu regime began to wither, pursuing the same savage colonial logic of the market economy and immeasurable corruption, the same old concept of exploiting the national riches and of growing poverty for the majority of the population. By the end of 1987, the GDP and the exports of raw materials had decresed to half the values of 1980. The public debt rose from 4,770 to 12,651 million dollars.

Inflation rose to astronomical figures. In 1993, the exchange rate of a dollar amounted to 6.5 million zaire. The annual growth rate of the production dropped from 1.8% in 1980/1990 to (minus) –6.3% in 1991/1997. The standard of living of the population was deteriorating catastrophically. The GDP per inhabitant fell from 430 dollars in 1980 to 116 in 1997. Mobutu dug his own tomb. The Mobutu regime tumbled down to the starting level in 1960. It was a genuine national disaster. There had been three decades of lost hope. Three decades of stopping the clockwork of history, three decades of quantitative accumulation of patience and revolt.

When the capital of patience was worn out, when the contradictions between labour and capital, between neocolonialism and traditionalism, between nationalism and imperialism, between the rich national bourgeoisie and the entire society had reached intolerable dimensions, this was the beginning of the collapse of Mobutu's regime and of the neo-colonialism. In 1997, the population of Shaba (former Katanga) mutinied and the insurrection was crushed in blood by the machine guns of the Moroccan military elites and by the most state-of-the-art French logistics. A second rebellion broke out in Shaba in 1978. The French Legion and the intervention of the paratroopers saved again the regime from falling.

The years 1983 - 1993 were the years of expansion of strikes, riots and massive street demonstrations. In September 1991, the country's capital erupted in massive street protests, which turned into generalised and uncontrolled looting of stores, restaurants, boutiques and other private properties. For the third time, the intervention of the Belgian and French paratroopers saved the Mobutu regime from its final collapse. In 1993 - 1996, general chaos, degradation, lack of trust and national weariness of the regime reached national dimensions. The economic chaos and a deep economic and financial crisis engulfed the whole country. In 1996, the National Bank vaults were completely empty. Mobutu, who had suffered from prostate cancer surgery, performed in Geneva, was dying. His regime, placed in the service of neocolonialism, experienced a dramatic and scandalous fiasco.

It was clear that a new revolutionary situation was approaching. Thus, when the ruling classes can no longer govern like in the past, and the dominted classes can no longer live like in the past, the social revolution breaks out. In such perfectly corrupt socio-political circumstances, Laurent Kabila, a leftist political and military leader, who used to be Che Guevara's friend and a student of the Chinese Military Academy, formed, in September 1966, a group of democratic Congolese political parties and of insurgents, in the North and East of the country: the ADFL orgnisation – the Alliance of the Democratic Forces for the Liberation of Congo-Zaire. September 28, with the liberation of Uivra, was the start of the great southward offensive of the Congolese liberation army.

In October and November 1996, there were liberated the towns of Bukavu, Goma, Kisangani and Lubumbashi. Missing endowments, equipment and food, Mobutu's army massively turned over to the rebellions' side. On May 17, 1997, after eight months of military offensive, the army triumphantly marched into Kinshasa.

In the end, the long civil war (which made about 4 million victims) was crowned with a crushing victory. (103). No other African or Latin-American country had paid so dearly the price of freedom.

About twenty ministers and managers of the Mobutu regime were imprisoned. On May 29, 1997, at the great stadium in Kinshasa, under the general acclaim of the people, Laurent Désiré Kabila was officially invested in the office of President of the Republic. After several days, they formed the first government of national salvation, a nationalist, revolutionary and democratic left-wing orientation government.

Rejecting the dictatorship of the proletariat, as a principle of the obsolete past, Kabila and his party introduced in their political programme, after two years of stabilisation through presidential and parliamentary elections, the decentralisation of the administration and the expansion of the participatory democracy.

The economic programme of left-wing orientation of Laurent Kabila headed the social progress towards economic, political and social independence. In the center of the social progress was the goal of inserting the Republic of Congo into the international economic system of free trade, the achieving of economic growth, the rational exploitation of the national wealth in the interest of economic progress, industrialisation, electrification and modernisation of agriculture, based on the principles of the social market economy.

On international level, Laurent Kabila insisted on the multilateral political and economic cooperation with the neighbouring African countries, primarily with the countries of socialist orientation. In April 1998, after the presidential inauguration, invoking his revolutionary past, Laurent Désiré Kabila visited Khadafi, showing no inhibition at all. He had devoted his first visit outside the African continent to travel to the People's Republic of China (in December 1997), where he signed a number of economic and military cooperation agreements. Congo is included among the top ten priority countries for the cooperation with China. China granted Congo an initial loan of 30,000,000 dollars, supplied it with 300 trucks for the liberation army, as well as footwear and clothing, and undertook to care for the technical maintenance of the tanks of the new liberation army.

It was expected that the orientation of the political programme ADFL, of Laurent Kabila himself, would not match the neocolonialist ambitions of the old surviving forces that supported the neo-colonialism.

In September 2002, the local right-wing circles, together

with the old neocolonialist forces, proceeded to the cowardly assassination of the great son of the Congolese people. For one week, the entire Congo was in mourning. Obviously, in 2002, the Congolese people's national consciousness was no longer the same as in 1960, during the age of the atrocious assassination of Patrice Lumumba. On the general request of the people and of the army, the commander of the Congolese liberation army and substitute of the chief of staff, who was the son of Laurent Désiré Kabila, the young general Joseph Kabila, was promoted to fill the office of the President of the Republic.

The young Kabila (34), with views somewhat more liberal and more modern, features typical for the new emerging generation, continued essentially in his father's political footsteps. He made great efforts to pull his country out of a long and deep economic, political and military crisis. He prepared the creation of the national unity strategy and the organisation of the first free democratic elections, but, at the same time, he was firmly holding the steering wheel of the revolution, did not yield more radical points to the neocolonialists or to the right-wing political parties. The internal right-wing opposition, together with the neocolonial forces, tried, in every possible way, to stop the course of history, to compromise and remove Joseph Kabila from the power, by activating new military conflicts.

However, it seems that the great powers understood at their expense that the Congolese issue could not be settled without free elections. Therefore, the intervention of the Blue Berets of the United Nations and of the European Union in monitoring the organisation of democratic elections became the only way out of the new humanitarian catastrophe. Joseph Kabila emerged from the elections with a positive balance, easing the tensions of war, driving the country towards peaceful social progress, toward picking up the economic growth which reached the high rate of 6.5%, toward monetary and financial stabilisation, toward the reduction of the inflation to 21.6% and toward the rapid growth of the national income, from 10 billion dollars in 2001 to 29 billion dollars in 2006.[104]

As expected, during the free and democratic elections of July 2006, the Congolese people and their candidate Joseph

Kabila won a brilliant victory. With 45% of the votes in the first round, and the majority in the second round, Joseph Kabila became, through the people's will, the first freely elected President of the Republic. In the parliamentary elections, the left-wing parties, in alliance with the independent candidates, secured a parliamentary majority. To ensure the continuity of his predecessor's policy, Joseph Kabila appointed as Prime Minister Mr. Gizenga, Laurent Kabila's most loyal army comrade.

Kabila's government and party have still to face great challenges: to fulfill their election promises – the total reconstruction of the country, reducing unemployment and poverty and leading the country towards economic and social revival.

(f) The Transition of Tanzania from State Socialism to Democratic Socialism

Tanzania has a special place in the history of revival and expansion of socialism in Africa. This country is a pioneer of the African liberation movements, of the national emancipation and social progress. It holds a special place in the African history by its transition from colonialism to national independence without civil war and it also has a special place by its silent transition from the primeval state socialism to the democratic and liberal socialism.

Three directions for obtaining genuine social progress by Tanzania have resulted in marking new features in the development of socialism in Africa. These are elements of stability, certainty and faith of the 120 ethnic groups in Tanzania in their own future.

The decisive merit of guiding Tanzania on the path of independence and social progress, avoiding civil war, on the way of smooth transition from state socialism to liberal democratic socialism, is the merit of the historical leader and founder of modern Tanzania, Julius Nyerere, and of his heirs, Ali Hassan Mwinyi, Benjamin Mpaka and Jakaya Kikwete.

Tanzania is the fruit of the voluntary unification into a national entity of two colonial states, Tanganyika and Zanzibar.

Tanganyika, a formerly German colony leased to the British

(and, in 1947, placed under the United Nations' mandate), obtained its independence in 1961, thanks to the clairvoyant strategy of Julius Nyerere and of his newly created party, the Tanganyika African National Union (TANU). Nyerere earned the trust of the United Nations and became their privileged mediator for independence and, afterwards, the first President of the independent Tanganyika. Three years later, in 1964, after successful negotiations, Nyerere, along with the President of the neighbouring republic of Zanzibar, Abeid Karume, unified the two countries into one Republic, Tanzania. Nyerere became the President of the new republic, and Karume, the vice-president.

Tanzania covers an area of 945,087 km^2 in South-East Africa, nearly three times the surfce of Germany. With 40 million inhabitants and its natural wealth unexploited, it becomes an important economic and political factor in Southern Africa.

Tanzania is bathed by the Indian Ocean on a length of 1,424 km. Its magnificent and impressive tourist landscape of immense fertile plateaus, where the prodigious Kilimandjaro (5,895 m) rises, the highest mountain peak in Africa, is embellished by three large continental lakes. Tanzania also enjoys the benefits of the tropical, semi-tropical and continental climate.

Despite its heavenly climate, rich in unexploited hydro-energy resources, Tanzania was, after its liberation, one of the poorest countries in Africa. The country is predominantly agrarian. Only 4% of the land is exploitable. Tanzania has no oil resources, but keeps unused resources of gold, diamonds, phosphate, iron, nickel, coal and gas. Without a developed industry, without specialists, with no oil resources and without external assistance, Nyerere and his left-wing party decided, in 1967, during the conference held in Arusha, through the declaration of the National Executive Committee, Tanzania's transition towards socialism. They considered socialism to be the only possible way out of poverty, of colonial exploitation, the only fast road of social progress.

"Tanzania, the Declaration stipulates, is a State of which population consists of peasants and workers, but it is not yet a socialist state. There are still seeds of capitalism and feudal exploitation. These seeds may develop and take roots."

"To implant and maintain the socialism, we must be sure that the peasants and workers themselves possess and control the means of production, through their leadership and their cooperations. We also need to make sure that the party in power be a party of peasants and workers."[105]

With no experience of pluralist socialism erection in Africa, the Tanganyika African National Union followed, more or less, the Soviet model, a model of bureaucratic state socialism, by adjusting it to the new conditions of traditionalism and collectivism.

Within very shortly, Nyerere nationalised the banks, the social insurance companies, the import-export companies, the industrial enterprises and other private companies. He directed the agriculture cooperativisation by grouping the villages, according to the model of the Chinese communes. The centralisation and the accumulation of funds in the state vaults allowed the funding of the infrastructure, the building of schools and hospitals, the development of the education system, the health care and the poverty reduction. Nyerere set up a law on children's free eduction and on free social insurance. Great efforts were made to develop the national culture and to preserve the African traditions.

Nyerere managed the national campaign aimed at mandatory replacement of the English language by a single national language – Kiswahili, a symbol of the liberation from colonialism and of the language unification via the building of a modern Tanzanian nation.

In 1977, through the merger of the Tanganyika African National Union and the Afro-Shirazi Party, the new revolutionary party was created of socialist orientation and wide Pan-African vision. Tanzania took part in the supporting of various African national liberation movements.

The Mozambican fighters for freedom found refuge in Tanzania, where they received substantial help to organize the guerrillas against the Portuguese colonists.

In 1979, the Tanzanian troops entered Uganda and offered aid to the local forces to overthrow the dictatorial regime of

Amin Dada. President Nyerere, at that time a prominent leader of the Pan-African liberation movements, took part in the negotiations to end the white domination in Rhodesia (Zimbabwe).

We do not have space enough here, and we do not have the need to confirm the new altruistic internationalism of Tanzania. We just want to point out for the readers that Tanzania developed relations of good cooperation with the western countries but, in a particularly privileged manner, with China and the former USSR. The Chinese built a Tanzanian railway that facilitated the exploitation of copper. The Chinese built dozens of schools, health-care institutions, cultural centers, partly free-of-charge and against credits at very low interest rates.

After 18 years of practice, the Tanzanian state socialism has shown, socially, some negative effects, besides the positive ones. It was necessary either to adjust the social relations to the new age requirements or to accept failure. With intelligence and by using their forward vision, Nyerere and his successors chose the gradual, non-confrontational path toward the political and economic liberation from the old social-economic relations, practised a policy of democratisation, multi-parties and economic liberalism system of the market socialism.

In 1985, tired and exhausted by the great political upheavals, under the burden of his old age, Nyerere retired from his presidential office. He handed over the flag to Ali Hassan Mwinyi, a Muslim native of Zanzibar, whose orientation was socio-democratic. However, Nyerere remained, until August 1990, in his position as a party chairman, as Tanzania's political leader and distinguished leader of Southern Africa. President Mwinyi assumed responsibility for Tanzania's gently pushing towards the social market economy, the partial privatisation, the revival of the domestic market, the reducing of bureaucracy and poverty.

After the almost ten years of more or less positive reports of President Mwinyi, multi-party elections were initiated. In the free and democratic elections of October 1995, under the surveillance by journalists and foreign observers, the candidate of the revolutionary party, Benjamin M'Kpata, won a brilliant first round victory, winning 61.8% of the votes. At the presidential and parliamentary elections of December 2005, the candidate of the same governing revolutionary party, Jakaya Kikweté, won a crushing victory during the very first round, with 80% of the votes. At the parliamentary elections of 1995 and of 2005, the deputies of the revolutionary party obtained an absolute majority. The maneuvering field of the right-wing political parties increasingly narrowed.

The result of the elections in Tanzania proves that most of the Tanzanian citizens endorsed the efficient policy of the government left-wing party, which responds to the vital interests of society. This result demonstrates that, in the former colonies, where the Western powers have no interest to interfere, the right-wing forces, without any external support, lose more and more their influence on voters.

The free Tanzania is not one of Africa's economic miracles, but it keeps going quietly on the path of social progress.

"After the death of Julius Nyerere, probably Tanzania is nothing more than a poor country, but, in comparison with most countries in Africa, it has achieved a very remarkable civil peace, since its independence"[106] and, we dare to add, a modest but constant improvement of the living standard of the population.

Tanzania's GDP per inhabitant increased from 120 dollars in 1960 to 700 dollars in 2004 and the country got closer to the Ivory Coast, the first world producer of cocoa, which had long carried the label of "African miracle". The annual growth rate of the gross domestic product in the past few years was within the range of 4-6%, the industrial production growth, around 8%, the inflation rate, around 5%. There were built thousands of schools, health-care centres, hundreds of new enterprises, mainly in the agro-industrial branch. The social production structure has changed considerably. The share of the agriculture declined in 2005 to 48%, the industry share rose to 16.7%, the service sector was amounted at 34.9%. Today, Tanzania has around 2.5 million industrial workers and clerks in the tertiary economy sphere. The infrastructure got a new place in the country's development. Tanzania has about 3,569 km of railways and 4,250 km of asphalt coated roads, 12 sea-ports and 18 airports with runways.

However, besides the remarkable progresses, Tanzania continues to record some great problems of the past: the agricultural modernisation, the electrification, the development of the modern industrial society and the reducing of poverty. Convinced of the correctness of the chosen path, the Tanzanian people follows in serenity and much hope their country entering, within about 15 years, the group of the medium developed agro-industrial countries.

(g) Mozambique, 27 Years of National Liberation War, of Civil War, and 15 Years of Reforms

The postwar history of the Mozambican social progress differs from the evolutionary, peaceful history of Tanzania. After 11 years of struggle for national liberation, led by the Marxist left-wing forces FRELIMO (the Mozambique Liberation Front), after other two years of lull and other 14 years of civil war of the RENAMO insurgents, backed by pro-imperialist forces, against FRELIMO, Mozambique finally took, after the 1992 Rome Agreement, the peaceful way of building its own future.

Established on a surface of 799,398 km^2, 9 times larger than Portugal, with its 20 million inhabitants, the population in Mozambique has lived and has "stubbornly" kept on living, for almost five centuries, under one of the most ferocious colonial exploitation and dehumanisation. With a GDP per inhabitant of about 60 dollars after the proclamation of the independence in 1975, with 95% illiterate and only 200 doctors, of which one-third domestic volunteers, Mozambique is ranked among the world's poorest countries. The weapon-in-hand fight for national and social liberation was then the only possible alternative to the Mozambican existence.

After the unification of various factions of the movement for national emancipation, supported by Eduardo Mondlane Marcelin, Eduardo Dos Santos, Kwamé Nkrumah and Julius Nyerere, the first congress of FRELIMO was held on June 20, 1962. Two years later, namely in 1964, the historic decision was made to start the armed struggle for national and social liberation, with 250 soldiers trained in Algeria and Egypt.

Using the experience of the Algerian, Chinese and Vietnamese liberation revolutions, FRELIMO, with the people's support, gradually extended the liberated territory on the Makondé plateau, up Montepuez. The 4,000 soldiers heroically resisted the Portuguese army of 50,000 soldiers.[107] Throughout the two years of military battles, the liberation movement covered almost the whole country.

The rapid expansion of the liberation movement forced the Portuguese colonisers to start the "Gordian knot" offensive, which failed. After multiple attempts to stop the offensive to the south, the army staff of the colonisers was compelled to sit at the negotiations table. Finally, in September 1974, in Lusaka, the peace agreement was signed which provided the cease fire ending the fights, the proclamation of the independence on June 25, 1975, and the transfer of power in the hands of FRELIMO. This was another historic victory of the poor South against the rich West, the victory of the freedom morals over the slavery concept.

Through the proclamation of the independence, the new Constitution came into force; it legitimated the "People's Republic of Mozambique and the building of the new society liberted from the exploitation of man by man, the transfer of power in the hands of the workers and peasants." In 1977, the third congress of the party proclaimed the Marxist-Leninist ideology as its own chosen ideology. When the copying of the Soviet experience attained its limits of inefficiency, the leader of FRELIMO, Samora Machel, acknowledged the error in the following terms: "The truth is that we knew perfectly what we did not want - oppression, exploitation, humiliation. Our ideas were, however, vague on what we wanted. They were born in the field and were adjusted by practice. No doubt, we shall experience failures, but we shall learn from them."[108]

The 4th Congress of the FRELIMO Party, held in April 1983, at the time of the Polish revolution and the beginning of the dissolution of the totalitarian system, under difficult political and economic circumstances, blamed the dogmatism, the deviation to the left, the bureaucracy and the corruption, bringing important measures intended to liberalize the system. Some industrial enterprises were freed off the custody of nationalisation, the private family businesses and farming sector was restored. Trade was liberalised. There were various errors corrected in the management of the economy.

Gates were opened wide to foreign investors. All these measures, taken after the example of the Chinese modernisation, but mismanaged, had a weak effect on the improving of the economic situation of the country.

Despite all the positive corrections brought by the liberalisation, the strengthening and expansion of new social reforms in Mozambique were not in accordance with the interests of the pro-imperialist circles in Smith's Rhodesia and in Botha's South Africa. Taking advantage of the miscontent of a part of the population, caused by the new but insufficient liberalisation measures and by the great strategic errors of FRELIMO, the circles governing Rhodesia and South Africa, in collaboration with the Portuguese colonisers, organised the anti-FRELIMO military movement; first, in the border areas with Rhodesia and South Africa and then throughout the country. The anti-FRELIMO movement, which acted according to the "leopard strategy", won the political, media, logistic and armed support of Rhodesia and South Africa. Thus, just as Angola and once Vietnam, Mozambique became the battlefield for the great powers in the times of the Cold War, aiming at the rescue or demolishing of colonialism, the African military battlefield of the confrontation between the East and the West.

The effect of the 15 years of military confrontation was catastrophic. Over one million people were dead, a million and a half became refugees in the neighbouring countries, the electrical network was almost entirely destroyed, the roads, bridges, schools and hospitals were in ruins. The Government intervention, with all its ups and downs, could not extricate the country from the economic catastrophe. More radical reforms were needed, the liberalisation and the debureaucratisation of the system.

The 4th congress of the party rejected Leninism as the main ideological guidelines and adopted the "scientific socialism", resulting from the contemporary conditions of the social progress. The 7th congress continued restructuring and modernising the society. Fundamental constitutional amendments were introduced. The army was no longer subordinated to the party, but to the government. A separation was made between the party and the state, as well as the separations of the executive, legislative and judicial powers.

There were opened new paths of the social market economy, through local and foreign investments.

Under such new circumstances, RENAMO agreed to initiate negotiations for peace and national reconciliation. These negotiations were quite lengthy and were assisted by international organisations; they ended by the signing of the peace agreement in Rome, on October 4, 1992. President Joachim Chissano, the leader of FRELIMO, remained President of the Republic, and Pascal Mocumbi, the Minister of Foreign Affairs, was appointed Prime Minister. Alfonso Dhalakama, the head of RENAMO, accepted the role of the new opposition leader. The republican and the insurrectional (rebellion) armies were merged into a single army under the command of the chief of staff, appointed by the President of the Republic. The programme for economic liberalisation brought positive results. During the following years, the enforcement of the peace agreement was controlled by 5,000 Blue Berets of the United Nations. The government coalition set in motion a series of new economic and social reforms in order to accelerate the economic growth. The banking system, the taxation, the customs and the financial services were put in the service of the economic growth acceleration.

Success was obvious. Starting from 1992, the economic growth of the GDP evolved within the range of 6.1% - 8.2%. The country got out of crisis and stagnation. The GDP per inhabitant rose from about 100 dollars in 1992 to 400 dollars in 2007. The inflation rate declined to 6.8%, in 2005. Despite the privileges they were granted, the foreign investments continued to be insufficient for the needs of the country. The State budget declined, for the authorities were relying on foreign donations when drafting it (in 2006, donations met 46% of the total state sources). The industrial production (which reached to 32% of the GDP) marked the recovery process of the industrialisation.[109]

However, the colonial underdevelopment inheritance kept being the main disability for the speedy industrialisation and electrification of the country. The Mozambicans needed much larger investments than those offered by the developed countries. On the occasion of his solemn visit to Mozambique, the Chinese President, Hu Jintao, released 154,900,000 dollars for an aid in the agriculture, health-care and education. In fact, he cancelled the old debts, China advancing a new strategic plan for Africa's development. The Chinese government provided a fund of 15 billion dollars for the development of Southern Africa.

As for South Africa, besides the continued financial help, there was an amount of 1.2 billion dollars for the natural gas operation and for the laying of a 965 km long pipeline to South Africa. The period of colonialism and neo-colonialism ended, as well as the period of development decline of the African countries, awaiting modest Western loans. A new process emerged, the process of socialism revival and globalisation, involving the great China, India, Russia, Brazil, South Africa and other countries liberated from colonialism and neocolonialism, on the basis of their mutual benefits.

(h) South Africa on the Way of Social Progress

South Africa is the most developed country, from the economic point of view, on the African continent, qualified by the journalists as the "Africa's locomotive". It has an area of 1,212,912 km^2, about 50 million inhabitants, of whom 79.5% black people, 9.2% white people, 8.8% half-blood people and 2.5% Asian people; it covers 40% of the total African GDP. On the planetary map of the free countries, already on their way to social progress, South Africa is an undeniable exception. Is the way of liberty, of equality of races, democracy and social progress, the way of revival of South Africa, is this road bearing the print of this country's own originality in the world history?

Four hundred years elapsed since the era when navigators Bartolomeu Dias and Vasco da Gama landed at the Cape of Good Hope (in 1488), at Natal (in 1489), when the first white settlers, departed from Ireland and The Netherlands, began to populate the wide areas of South Africa and chased the black population off their lands, until the British colonisation, the establishment of ghettos for the black people and the proclamation of the independence on May 31, 1910. These were the years of countless wars of the black people against the white occupants, the years of the white population concentration in large cities, the years of the first industrial revolution in Africa.

It was the period of incessant revolts of the local black population (around 80%) against the British colonists, for social liberation from explotation, exclusion and racial segregation, as well as against political discrimination.

The proclamation of national independence was not able to solve the basic contradiction between the whites and the blacks, totally excluded from the political life. Gathered round their political parties, in the White Union of South Africa, founded in 1910, and Herzog's Nationalist Party, exclusively for Boers (colonists - note of the translator), the parties, the feudal classes ruthlessly suppressed the national opposition and the social sense of the black population, united round the political Bantu party African National Congress (ANC), founded in 1912 and, a little later, round the Communist Party. The common goals of these two left-wing political parties, despite the different methods applied for liberation - the Communist Party had chosen the strategy of revolutions, while the ANC preferred the strategy of the temperate democratic evolution, led to a merger of the two left-wing progressive forces in the battle for the liberation of the black population from racial segregation.

The establishment of racist terror against the leftist progressive parties and the ban on their activities, similarly to the time of the Nazis in Germany, of Mussolini in Italy, of Franco in Spain and Salazar in Portugal, was the worst alternative of the regime in South Africa in its attempt to escape the fury and will of the rebelling black population.

After the ban on the African National Congress (ANC) and on the Communist Party, the racist leaders organised a lawsuit against Nelson Mandela, the political leader of the ANC, and against his eight companions. During the mentioned process, Nelson Mandela, Walter Sisulu, Govan Mbeki - Thabo Mbeki's father - and Denis Goldberg were sentenced to perpetual hard labour, and the others to 15-20 years of prison. The general racial terror, instituted against the black population, was one of the bloodiest postwar racial dictatorial regimes but, this time, against the black population.

During this period, some South African and Western media justified the terror, accusing Nelson Mandela of communism and violent revolution. What is true and what is not true in it? How and which are the political directions of Nelson Mandela and of his companion, Thabo Mbeki? What political ideal were they ready to sacrifice their lives for?

The answers to these questions may help the readers to better penetrate and understand where South Africa is going to: on the way of the liberal capitalism or on the way of transition to a new solidary non-capitalist society.

We may say for sure that Nelson Mandela's ideological vision on the ways to establish the new society is opposed to that of the communist parties and of Moscow.

"I do not know whether I was a communist, said Mandela. If being a Communist means to be a member of the Communist Party, one of those persons who embrace the ideas of Marx, Engels, Lenin and Stalin, and who bend to the party discipline, then I have not been a communist."[110]

In the same book (Alfred Bosch - note of the translator), the author quoted the statement of Nelson Mandela for the newspaper Sunday Mail in London: "I, myself, am a socialist and I believe in a society without classes", "it is true, as I have already said, that I have been influenced by the Marxist thinking, but this also applies to most of the new leaders of the independent states. We all accept the need for some form of socialism, to give our people the opportunity to catch up with the developed countries and to get over their miserable inheritance. This does not mean, however, that we are Marxists."[111]

Thabo Mbéki, the student, the comrade and the successor of Nelson Mandela's great work, is the son of a militant of the Communist Party and the editor of the communist newspaper "The Guardian", and also a militant of the African National Congress (ANC). He grew up with his father's ideas, with his father's Marxist library. Mbéki formed his ideas at the university, then spent many years in emigration and in rebuilding the split African National Congress, adjusting his democratic, humanitarian and socialist beliefs. When I am writing these lines, Mbéki is the President of South Africa, a member of the Socialist International and the inflexible and logical successor of the beliefs assumed by his mentor.

Starting from the more realistic political positions of the

period when the anti-apartheid liberation movement, under the slogan "Freedom for Mandela", attained wide national and international dimensions, when Mandela became a legend, hero and symbol of the liberation movement, the most open-minded representatives of South Africa, at the initiative of the then president, Frédéric de Klerk, found the only possible alternative. On February 11, 1990, after prolonged negotiations, the government decided the liberation from prison of Nelson Mandela and of his surviving associates. On May 2, 1990, President de Klerk made the historic decision to sit, together with his ministers, at the round table of the negotiations, facing Nelson Mandela and his partners. The central issue of the successful negotiations was the future of a new, democratic and non racial South Africa, under the high patronage of the African National Congress and of the majority of the black population. Thus, de Klerk transfered the chair of President to Nelson Mandela and, a little later, the position of a Vice President to Thabo Mbéki.

The first parliamentary elections in 1994, the following elections in 1999, as well as those held in 2004, gave two-third majority to the African National Congress (ANC), in coalition with the communists. Most of the black population ageed with the idea of Desmond Tutu, the Anglican pastor of South Africa, a Nobel Prize laureate, according to whom "there is no future without forgiveness" and with the idea of Nelson Mandela: "White people are our compatriots and I want them to be safe."

During the 15 years of implementation of the ANC's programme for the renewal of the country in the spirit of forgiveness and peaceful coexistence, for the rehabilitation and development of the economy, for the gradual downsising of inequalities between the black and white citizens, for the fulfillment of the agrarian reforms, South Africa entered new social ways.

In the domestic politics, Mandela and Mbéki got unexpected positive results. The gross domestic product per inhabitant increased from 2,800 dollars in 1990 to 9,736 dollars in 2007. The growth of the gross domestic product increased at a rate ranging between 3.2 - 4.2% per year. The inflation fell from 17.4% (in 1991) to 4.3% (in 2004). The budget deficit dropped from 5.1% (in 1994-1995) to 2.3% (in 2004-2005). South Africa has strengthened and expanded its economic power. It became the first world producer of gold, of metals within the group of platinum chromium, iron, of aluminium silicate, the world's second largest producer of vanadium, magnesium, the third largest global producer of African fruits, the world's fifth food producer.

South Africa has one of the most modern asphalt-coated roads, of which length is 59,753 km, it has over 25,000 km of railways, 142 airports with asphalt-coated runways and 6 ports.

Its industry is also rated as the most developed in Africa, capable of producing the widest range of industrial equipment, computers included.

However, the problem raised by the African National Congress (ABC) was how to achieve "some form of socialism" (Mandela), as long as 100% of the mining and banking institutions, and 80% of the lands were in the white bourgeoisie's possession? Studying the South African experience, I had the impression that its political leaders, who had got rid of dogmatism, wanted to bypass the strategic errors of the primitive socialism of Nkrumah, of Boumediene in Algeria, of Mugabe in Zimbabwe, who applied reforms in the agriculture by expelling the white owners of the lands, thus causing the food crisis.

They accepted their "positive discrimination" strategy in the industry, mines and banks. Banking and mining enterprises, under the pressure of their work ban, agreed to yield 26% of their capital by 2004, and 40% of the job-positions in favour of the black population till the end of 2009. The government promised the purchase in association and the distribution among the peasants of about 30% of the lands.[112]

It is expected that the owners of industrial enterprises agree with the gradual "Africanisation" of the private capital, but this is not the final point of the social progress.

When the accumulation of taxes, customs duties, other taxes and contributions is insufficient to meet the growing needs of the large social programmes, the society will have no outlet for further development than the repurchase of a portion of the private capital and the transition to the new higher stage of socialisation.

The progressive tansfer of the capital and of the companies management in the hands of the black people and the development of the "black capitalism" is also the potential path for the progressive socialisation of the private property, the long evolutionary path from capitalism to socialism. In the underdeveloped countries, capitalism, which has not exhausted its driving forces and still has progressive character, can be of more use to the people's interests than to the interests of capitalism development. What is wrong with building the socialism, without the violence of the primitive accumulation of capital, without public nationalisations, and on the expense of capitalism? The new pathways of the accumulation resources entirely open the novel prospects of social progress.

However, the path of socialism, as ascertained by the evolution of the social progress, is not only the way for the socialisation of private property. Mandela and Mbéki are the ones who have understood this long ago, since they stipulated these principles in the constitution: "Everyone has the right to life", "property rights", "the right to education", "the right to housing, and the right to health, nutrition, water, social security".

By following the solution of freedom and of equal right to life for all citizens, the African National Congress achieved, over 15 years, the free schooling of children, free lunches in primary schools, free medical insurance for children up to the age of 6 and for pregnant women, the electrification of the poor peripheral districts, the reducing of unemployment and other measures of social value. There's no doubt that not only roses bloom in South Africa. The heavy historical inheritance still marking 43 million black people, who live by the standards of the poorest countries in Africa, where the "assisted market" agrarian reform has not produced the expected results, where 35%, or 17 million people, are wandering idly in the streets, where the population is dissatisfied and hungry and are devoted to crime (in 2004, there were recorded about 20,000 murders, 30,000 attempted murders, 50,000 rapes and around 300,000 robberies)[113] – all these are very alarming signs, and they blame the too slow economic and social reforms.

It seems that President Mbeki, by applying the reform very slowly and, moreover, by making too many concessions to the white bourgeoisie, continued to anger not only the black population, but also the ruling party (ANC), inside. Recently, Mbeki lost the elections battle in the party congress. Jacob N'Zuma was appointed by democratic elections for the position of party chairman. He is more left oriented, and the black population await from him important changes not only at the top of the party, but also a possible victory in the presidential elections.

In South Africa's foreign policy, the South African President has assumed the historic responsibility for the "African revival", that is to reinstate the control of Africans on the internal social and economic structures, their role in economic development, in condemning the coups d'état, in defending human rights and fundamental freedoms, in developing economic cooperation and political relations with the countries in Southern Africa and with other countries in the world, based on the principles of egalitarian cooperation and mutual benefits.

In other words, in its foreign policy, as an extrapolation of the progressive domestic policy, South Africa places its bets on the card of supporting progressive ideas and the victory of the left-wing political parties, on the card of the evolution of social progress, of the evolution of socialism.

(i) Resuscitation of Rwanda, after the Genocide, on the Way to Independence and Social Progress

Rwanda, a small country of Eastern Africa, bordered along 650 km by the Great Lakes, an agrarian country, with 6.5 million inhabitants, a place of special sight-seeing beauty, almost unknown to the world until 1994, became famous after the genocide which caused the massacre of more than one million people of the Tutsi and Hutu ethnic groups, with some meddling of the French troops as well.

After the military victory (in July 1994) of the Rwandese Patriotic Front for national and social liberation from the French occupation, an anti-imperialistic, anti-colonial coalition government, headed by President Paul Kagame. In August and September 2003, the first presidential and parliamentary elections were organised according to the principle of multiple parties. The President, whose office time expires, and his Patriotic Front, won a brilliant victory, with 94.3% of the votes. The opposition parties could not win the trust of more than 1.5%, respectively 3.5% of the voters. The rate of participation hit a record figure: 80%.

The new government should have to find solutions for many vital issues of the population:

- Reintegration of more than two million refugees exiled since 1959 and management of over 100,000 detainees.
- Putting a plug on the great number of rebellion attempts among the ex-military and the Interahamwe militias.
- Providing elementary protection against the immune deficiency syndrome and malaria.
- Providing of drinking water supply.
- Fair distribution of farming produce and energy.
- Speeding-up the economic growth rate to 6-9% per year.
- Reinforcement of ethnic unity, of democracy, and development of culture and education for all children.

This progressive African programme, limited to its modest internal means, brought positive results. At present, after 13 years of reconstruction and national reconciliation, Rwanda is a country brought back to life, a stable country in point of economy and politics, a country that has left behind its colonial inheritance of ethnic discrimination, a country that has chosen a future for its children. The National Unity and Reconciliation Government succeeded in building up a feeling of national identity, a feeling of the birth of a new Rwandese nation. The decentralisation and the establishment of local councils, where the decisions on development are taken by the communities, expanded the participatory democracy.

The Rwandese economy recorded a yearly growth rate of the gross domestic product of 8%. The inflation fell to 3.2%, while the monetary depreciation amounted to 6.5%. The liberalisation of the currency exchange reinforced the banking system. The government programme "Vision 2020" aims at transforming the agrarian economy into a modern agrarian-industrial economy and the substantial increase of the living standard of the population.

(j) Zimbabwe at the Crossroads of Dogmatism, Democratic Socialism and Liberalism

Zimbabwe is the ex-colony in the south-western part of Africa, resulted from the disintegration in 1953-1954 of the federation formed by Rhodesia and Nyassaland, which gathered in one state alone, South Rhodesia, North Rhodesia and Nyassaland. The proclamation of the independence of these three national entities evolved gradually.

In 1964, the independence of South Rhodesia was proclaimed, under the new name of Zambia, followed then by the independence declaration of Nyassaland, which became the state of Malawi. In 1965, Ian Smith's government of white immigrants, which had appropriated with no right the fertile plains on top of the plateau, proclaimed single-sided the independence of South Rhodesia. Fifteen years later, after lengthy encounters between the National Liberation Movement and the Ian Smith's white coloniser, the British acknowledged finally, in 1980, the real independence of Rhodesia, under the new name of Zimbabwe. Robert Mugabe, the political leader of leftist Marxist incline, military and political leader of the liberation movement ZANU, became the president of the republic.

In his speech on the occasion of the proclamation of the independence in 1980, Mugabe promised five principles of his internal and external policies: national sovereignty and equality between nations, devotion to the achievement of a socialist, egalitarian and democratic society, the right to self-determination and independence for all peoples, no racial discrimination, positive neutrality and peaceful coexistence.[114]

Discontented by the distribution of power to the advantage of ZANU and by the direction taken by Zimbabwe to socialism, the nationalist movement ZAPU (National Patriotic Front) constituted the movement for national independence and declared a fratricide civil war that lasted for eight years (1980-1988). The war ended in favour of ZANU.

After the war had ended, the implementation of ZANU's new principles of social progress in the first decades of finding out the ways to freedom, democracy and socialism, gave positive results. The new State nationalised partially the capitals in industry, mining, banks, hotels and mass media. It implemented the extensive preparation programme of local cadres, built thousands of schools and clinics, rehabilitated thousands of destroyed roads, declared the mandatory and free primary teaching. All workers and clerks with a pay under 150 local dollars are granted free health insurance, etc.

Zimbabwe, which has earned a reputation as the granary of Southern Africa, has become an important cereal supplier for the PAM, the United Nations body dealing with the supply of food produce, and it seems to be the great hope for the rescue of the black population from perpetual misery and poverty.

In agriculture, the reforms bore, more or less, the sign of Marxist dogmatism and Talmudism. The organisation of the peasants in cooperatives, through repurchasing part of the land of the great landowners, caused an important exodus of the white population to Australia, New Zealand and South Africa, the fall of the agricultural production, which used to bring yearly roughly 1.5 billion dollars in foreign currency, that is about 75% of the budget income.

ZANU and Mugabe were faced with a hard to solve issue. How to get rid of racial discrimination and social inequality, on the way of seeking new solutions for the revolution in agriculture? "One man, one farm", this was the slogan of the ZANU liberation movement. Mugabe promised the distribution, along a three year time span, of lands expropriated from the whites, in favour of 162,000 peasant families. 19 years later, merely 72,000 families have turned into land owners.

At present, 4,200 white farmers still own 11 million hectares and are supplying 70% of the agricultural production, while millions of black people barely can survive on the infertile community lands. At mid-1998, Mugabe announced a new expropriation action, by the buy-back of 5 million hectares land and their distribution to 91,000 peasant families. Over two more years, the buy-back rate shrank to zero. The agricultural production began to decrease, the same as the budget resources ensured by exports, and the supply to the population, as well.

The involvement of Zimbabwe in the war in the Democratic Republic of Congo and the providing of military assistance (several thousand troops and the entire war equipment) for the benefit of Laurent Kabila, had the purpose of saving the regime from a new invasion from the North; Mugabe and Kabila considered this assistance as an expression of international solidarity. This war, which cost Zimbabwe 2.6 million dollars, deepened even more the economic, agricultural and social crisis.

The economic sanctions unjustly imposed by the USA and the European Union kindled the situation even more and contributed to the worsening of the crisis. The industrial and agricultural decrease, the inflation rise and with it its natural consequence – the dissatisfaction of the population.

Therefore, the resistance of the opposition multiplied, organised by the liberal nationalists, gathered round the Movement of Democratic Change and its leader, Morgan Tsvangirai.

The USA, England and other Western countries, which saw Zimbabwe as a country floating adrift, helped financially and morally the political opposition, in view of the organisation of street demonstrations and the dissolution of the Mugabe regime.

After difficult attempts of confrontation between the internal neo-colonial right-wing forces, with support from the outside, and the nationalist left-wing forces, Mugabe found himself at the crossroads of reminiscences of dogmatism, excessive authority of the democratic socialism and western liberalism.

In March 2008, under high social pressure, presidential and legislative elections were organised, in an atmosphere of often violent confrontation between the national leftist and the neo-colonial right-wing forces. In the second voting round, which was boycotted by the opposition, President Mugabe, whose office time had expired, confirmed his victory for one more mandate. In the legislative elections, ZANU – Mugabe's party – obtained 99 seats, the opposition party of MDC got 100 seats, and the opposition fractions – of which some had declared they were independent – other 10 seats. On the occasion of the swearing in before the President of the Republic, the members of the parliament elected the new speaker of the National Assembly, namely Lovemore Moyo, deputy of the MDC.

When I was ending the last proof reading of my manuscript, prior to depositing it with the publishing house, the battle had begun for the position of a Prime Minister and the forming of the government.

Robert Mugabe, President of the Republic, declared that, should the opposition be not willing to participate in the new government, he would form the government without the opposition. Most probably, the office of the Prime Minister will be caught by the opposition.

The people in Zimbabwe harbour the hope that good will vanquish ill, that their sacrifices along the 45 years of struggle will finally bear the long expected fruits.

(k) The Ivory Coast, at a Crossroad of Neocolonialism, National Independence and Socialism

Being a former French colony and a hunting zone for elephants, whose ivory tusks used to be exported, (hence the name of the country), the Ivory Coast spreads along an area of 332,500 km^2 in West Africa, in the Guinea Gulf, in the subequatorial area. From 3.5 million inhabitants in 1960, the Ivory Coast's population grew to 20 million, about 26% of which were coming from the neighbouring poor countries. Having a gross domestic product (GDP) per capita of 1000 dollars and an annual average growth rate of 8% during the years 1960 – 1980, it was rightly called “the African miracle”. The Ivory Coast became one of the most developed countries of Black Africa, the economic and financial coordinator and the driving motor of development of West Africa.

The industrial production of the light and food industries, which is in the hands of French monopolies, contributes by about 75% to the GDP, while another Lebanese part contributes by about 22%. The Ivory Coast became the first cocoa producer in the world, the third coffee producer and the first African producer of cotton, cashew nuts, sugar and palm oil.

Forty years of domination of a single party regime which sold at a low price its national assets to foreigners, especially to the French capital, a regime of general corruption and illicit enrichment of the new bureaucratic bourgeoisie, of political persecutions, restriction of freedom and early suppression of any opposition – typical for almost all the underdeveloped countries in the cause of neo-colonialism – brought about the quick development of capitalism and created the conditions for passing from the self-sufficient communitarian patriarchal economy to the market economy.

On a historic scale of axiology regarding the birth and development of capitalism and the new developing productive forces, we can surely say that it was a positive and remarkable process of social progress.

However, when analysing objectively the social evolution, we have to look at the second, hidden side of the "Ivory miracle". Along with the development of the corrupted capitalism, neo-colonialism brought about the opposite side of social progress: the unlimited exploitation of national wealth, the destruction of two-thirds of the forests, relative and absolute impoverishment of working masses, fast increase of unemployment and social injustice.

In their report of 1997, World Bank analysts showed misleading results. The percentage of the families living under the poverty limit rose from 11% in 1985 to 31.3% in 1993, amounting to 36. 8% in March until May 1995.[115] After 10 years of crisis, the poverty limit has reached most likely 55%. At the same time, 49% of school age children are not registered in the primary education system. Also, 49% of adults are illiterate. In addition, 62.1% of the population has no electricity. The great majority have no social protection. Only 7.6% of the poor population has access to drinking water. Life expectancy hardly reached the level of 54 years.[116] Child mortality, produced by the immune deficiency syndrome, tuberculosis and other diseases, breaks the African records.

The yearlong increase of the contradictions between wealth and social injustice, on the one hand and the poverty and dehumanisation on the other hand, smouldered for decades within the "Ivory Miracle", erupted to the surface of the society during the last two decades of the 20th century, like the lava of a volcano. The prerequisites for the great political and social changes on the way of decolonisation, democratisation, emancipation and poverty decrease, have become mature. At the same tine, the political opposition to the dictatorship of a single party and to the French dominance has also increased.

In 1982, the year when the long economic, financial and social crisis broke out, Laurent Gbagbo, history professor at the Abidjan University, political émigré in Paris, a charismatic and intelligent politician, assembled around him progressive persons, striving for changes. The Ivorian Popular Front (FPI), an illegal leftist party, of socialist orientation was organised. In April 1990, under the pressure of inner and external democratic forces, the FPI became legitimate. A little bit later, The Ivorian Party of Workers (PIT) was validated, being followed by the right wing political party resulted from the PDCI-RDA, The Republicans' Rally (RDR). Thus, democratisation, the multiparty system and national emancipation have become the new flag of social progress.

At the first democratic free elections of October 1995, the candidate of the Ivory Popular Front, Laurent Gbagbo, obtained the confidence of 18% of the electorate, while in the National Assembly, 15 deputy seats were won. At the next presidential and parliamentary elections of October 2000, after the first coup d'état, the candidate of the Popular Front won by 52% of votes. Thus, the popular Laurent Gbagbo became the first left wing socialist president of the Republic of Ivory Coast. At the parliamentary elections, FPI obtained 82 deputy places and in coalition with the Workers' Party and the independent, left oriented candidates, he obtained parliamentary majority.

FPI had an unexpected victory because, under the circumstances of a general economic degradation and brutal decrease of the living standard, he knew how to offer the electorate, disappointed by traditional politicians, a programme of re-establishing the social-economic and political system and of putting the national wealth to the service of the people.

After the electoral victory of the Ivory Popular Front, a new stage in the country's development had begun. The new left wing leading team gave priority to redoing all the social structures from their bases, to industrialising and electrifying the country, creating a real independence of the country and the state and popular sovereignty. Investment decentralisation was achieved by establishing 58 General Councils. Three hundred villages were electrified, the ransom of cocoa and coffee was liberalised and a part of the accumulation was handed over to the peasants' management system. On a social level, mandatory and free education was provided, the Universal Health Insurance Law (AMU) was voted and the salaries of the teachers and military staff were increased.

On the economic level of stimulating private investments, the National Investment Bank (BNI) was established to support the private sector. Other institutions like the Agricultural Bank, the National Fund for Solidarity (FNS) were set up for financing some micro-enterprises intended for the young unemployed, pupils dropped out from schools, etc. The Ivory Cost has started to pick the fruits of its left wing policy.

As seen from the very beginning, the new team has avoided the strategic mistakes made by the African pioneers of community socialism, of European social democracy and was relying on some experience of Arabic North-African socialism, they started to outline the possible ways of socialism.

Asked by a Senegalese journalist about the definition of socialism in his opinion, the president of the republic, Laurent Gbagbo, answered: "We do not have the monopoly over what is good in socialism or in many other currents of thought, but socialism means to do away with dogmatism."

"At present, in Africa, the first target of socialism is to attain democracy, a second one is to be able to provide bread to everyone, which would mean to find the ways of economic growth; a third target is to ensure education for everyone, because it is only by education that people will be less ignorant; a fourth target is health."[117]

President Gbagbo, a specialist in materialistic dialectics, also pointed out that the demands of socialism in Norway, for example, are totally different, depending on a country's level of development. However, as history teaches us, social progress has always faced the live resistance of the old surviving classes, everywhere in the world. It is easy to understand that the country's remaking from the basis and the national emancipation on the way to full independence, of social progress, were not convenient for the national bourgeoisie and so much the less for the extreme right bourgeoisie and the right neo-colonialist French forces from Elysée.

In September 2002, with the help of mercenaries recruited from abroad and of local rebels, supported, according to the republican press, by the right wing forces of President Jacques Chirac, a second coup d'état was organised in order to dismiss the government of national revival.

Although well prepared beforehand and financed from abroad, the coup d'état did not succeed because the army and the police officers, faithful to the republican left, rejected in a powerful way the attack, liquidating a part of the insurgents and pushing the others towards the North of the country. Thus, the country was divided into two parts: the northern part, unfertile and very poor, and the southern one, of the subequatorial area, very fertile, bearing rich national resources.

The numerous attempts of French neo-colonialism and its vassals around the right wing party to delay for five years the peaceful settlement of the conflict by the Linas Marcoussis Agreement failed. In addition, the first and second government of national unity failed too.[118]

The new strategy of the republican forces is to talk with the rebels, whose former leaders of FESCI (Student and School Federation of Ivory Coast), including their leader Guillaume Soro, the present Prime Minister, are of left wing orientation, and to establish a new government together with the rebels, in order to prepare the way to organising free, democratic, transparent elections, true bearers of great hopes. The elections will probably take place in June 2000.

Thus, the way to real independence was opened, so that the inhabitants of the Ivory Coast could exploit the country's riches for themselves. The great majority live with the hope that the elections will be won by the new, impartial African leader, the ideologist of national and social liberation, and by the leftist political forces and parties that defended with honour the national independence, peace, general development and prosperity of the country. These forces fight to transform the riches of the Ivory Coast into riches for all its citizens.

15. Australian Labour Socialism

When I finished editing this book and sent it to the publisher, the worldwide movement of socialism revival registered a new important victory. At the presidential and parliamentary elections of 2007, the most powerful opposition party (The Australian Labour Party – ALP) had a final victory, without any surprise. The victory was surely persuasive because ALP and its political leader, Kevin Rudd (50 years old), won the confidence of most voters, on a national scale and in the eight regional states as well.

For the first time in the history of young Australia, the victory was total. I have felt a moral duty to the Australian left wing and to my readers to reveal, multum in parvo, the historical roots of this great victory, as a new contribution to the social progress of our planet.

(a) History of the Labour Party

The history of the labour party is closely connected with the birth and development of the fifth continent of our planet. During the years 1605 – 1606, when the Dutch and Spanish sailors discovered that clouded continent, they had to fight with some hundreds of thousands Aborigines. During the years 1770 – 1868, the English colonists started to populate the fifth continent with free immigrants and English convicts to be the white slaves of the new settlers. The new capitalism, born in fire, blood and sweat, developed under conditions specific for the English colonisation.

Until the year 1830, the growing number of white slaves in concentration camps, called by J B Hrist "open penitentiaries", surpassed the number of free immigrants. Actually, these "open penitentiaries" were transformed into training schools for the groups of new workers who transmitted from one generation to another their ideas of liberation from alienation, as well as the humiliations and feelings of capital rejection.

After 120 years of transplanting the savage capitalism, of organising the young working class in trade unions and fighting to defend its daily interests, the "Australian Labour Party" was created. As a political advocate and moral guardian of the working class, the "Australian Labour Party" became soon one of the most powerful parties in Australia. In the year 1905, the Labour Party acknowledged the socialist character of its views and at the elections of 1910, winning the confidence of the Australians, the party formed the first labour government in the world, of leftist orientation. After the Paris Commune, this was the greatest event in the world, with historic and moral values which unfortunately did not find their right place in the history of the labour movement. The left wing culture of the working class was strongly built into the social and political structure of the workers, the trade unions and the Labour Party, that dominated the political scene of Australia in the 20th and in the early 21st century.

By its powerful leading positions, resulted from the electoral majority in the years 1905 – 1910, 1929 – 1933, 1941 – 1945, 1945 – 1949, 1972 – 1975, 1983 – 1996, the working class contributed to the achievement of the elementary social rights of the civil society in one of the most developed systems of social insurance and at one of the highest living standards in the world. For the first time in the world, Australia implemented the principle of alternating to power left wing with right wing political parties, alternation that became a universal principle and one of the most important driving forces of the development of our civilisation.

(b) Parliamentary and Associative Socialism

The Australian Labour Party took its name from its old metropolis, being of a more leftist orientation; it is different from the English Labour Party in some views, the latter featuring some deviations.

The analysts of Australian media consider the Labour Party as a social-democratic one which, according to its statute, is a socialist democratic party. The socialist character of the party and movement strengthened after the victory of the October Revolution. However, the Australian Labour Party never accepted the Soviet way of socialism (with a single exception in 1921, when the congress of the workers' trade union tried to nationalize the industry, distribution and exchanges). The Australian Communist Party, with only some hundreds followers and a minor influence on the workers' movement, often divided into two parties, removed itself gradually from the Moscow line. At the beginning, the Australian labour class and social–democratic movement were dominated by the ideas of parliamentary socialism. Historians point out the appearance of two tendencies of parliamentary socialism. The first tendency stresses the parliamentary action of the labour party, while the second one stresses the actions of a socialist character.

The socialist researchers Métin and Thompson performed a first analysis of the labour movement. "The image of Australia resulting from these researches, one being made by Métin in 1901 and the other by Thompson in 1919, is the image of a new and progressive society, a pioneer of the innovative social legislation, which provides the labour class movement with a large area of expression." (119). In his book, "How Labour Governs", V.G. Child criticised parliamentary socialism as being a nest of bureaucracy and corruption, launching the idea of corporative socialism which started to get roots in Australia. In Child's opinion, the goals of the labour class movement are: changing the social structure of the society, banning the exploitation of slave workers, by self-managing of workers by their party, and the peaceful creation of socialist Australia.

Child's fundamental idea, of peaceful, slow transition to the public sector of economy, on the way to gradual nationalisation and private property reimbursement, becomes so actual today that certain social-democratic leaders, bi-coloured Europeans and Australians, avoid this fundamental issue of social progress.

In the second rally, after the Second World War and after the big economic western boom, Gough Whitlam, president of the labour government in 1972-1975, attracted by the European wave of the socialist left wing, preferred the social intervention policy, while the presidents of the labour governments Bob Hawke and Paul Keating (1983-1996) moved rather towards the economic rationalism as an alternative of the "third way".

(c) The Great Success of Australian Political Alternation

The presence of powerful and omnipresent labour parties, with their success and failure, followed by the alternation of power of the left and right parties or, better said, the political and economic competition of those parties on the political stage, have become the motive power of social progress.

Although the class struggle, considered by Marxists as the fundamental motive power of social progress, has not disappeared yet from the social arena, it got the shape of political and economic competition on the way to the alternation to power of the left wing parties. This is the political expression of the evolutionistic form of the class struggle and competition between classes. We can surely say that Australia became a model of this competition.

With a population of 20 million inhabitants, Australia is at the same time a destination of immigration for 200 countries in the world. After the Second World War, it received over 6.5 million immigrants who blended in harmoniously with the old generations, into a new multicultural civilisation. The country of great democratic traditions is today among the most developed countries in the world. With a yearly average growth of the gross domestic product of 3 – 4%, Australia achieved in 2007 a gross domestic product per capita of 33,037 dollars and one of the highest living standards. According to the economic report of OCDE (Organisation for Economic Development and Cooperation), in the last 15 years, Australia's living standard surpassed the living standard of the most developed countries of the G 7 Group, excepting the USA.[120]

The inflation was stabilised to about 2.5% and the unemployment percentage to 5%. All the public debts were refunded. The taxes on goods and services (the equivalent of our value added tax, VAT) are the lowest in the world, amounting to only 10%.

By means of its own funds of investments, Australia is ranked as the fourth country in the world, with about 777 billion dollars obtained in 2006. It is the greatest worldwide exporter of coal, iron and wool, the second exporter of cotton and barley and the third exporter in the world of wheat.

The universal system of social security, particularly in point of the pension system (at a high level), is one of the most developed in the world.

Culture, sports and tourism also play an important part in Australia's policy of social progress. In other words, the special feature of Australian socialism consists in the coexistence of the private sector and the state intervention in distributing the national income as a social state policy. There is no doubt that the recent victory at the elections of 2007 of the Labour Party has given new hopes to the development and strengthening of the elements of Australian socialism.

(d) The electoral Programme of the Brilliant Victory of the Labour Party at the 2007 Elections

The electoral campaign of the Labour Party, under the leadership of Kevin Rudd, against the conservatory government of Prime Minister John Howard, was based on the party's political platform which is subjected to revision and updating every three years.

The platform provides the general political line of the future government and not the ways of its achievement. It is highlighted so that the "traditional values of labour should remain a constant value to be relied on by everybody". "Labour" will not allow the benefits of change to be concentrated in the hands of the privileged of collectivities or, at least, will not allow them to become available to the privileged of collectivities. The benefits should be distributed to all Australians and to the entire assembly of our regions". Further on, the platform stipulates the fact that "all the people are born equal in their right to dignity and respect and they will have to enjoy equal chances in fulfilling their potential."[121]

The platform pays special attention to the growing role of the state in the economic administration. "The government plays a crucial role, it ensures the equity in connection with: guaranteeing equal chances, banning unjustified discrimination and fulfillment of a more equitable distribution of wealth and income."

Often, in the course of the platform updating, the conservative fraction of the Labour Party, being more oriented towards the free market economy and understanding with the USA, enters into conflict with the left wing fraction that pays more attention to the state interventionism, being less enthusiastic about the entente with the USA.

During the electoral campaign of 2007, the two fractions made a compromise, which led to victory.

After the failure of the 1996 campaign, the Labour Party,

efficiently led by Kevin Rudd, performed the necessary changes to the electoral programme and oriented its electoral campaign more and more towards the actual claims of the civil society.

The implementation of the electoral programme will surely expand more and more the range of the social components of the Australian programme, contributing to the enrichment of the planetary treasure of experience and social progress on the way to socialism.

16. The 21st Century, the Century of Socialism in Most Countries of Our Planet

The civilisation of the human race has existed only in the organisation form as tribes, communities, peoples, nations, states, and as determined social-economic systems. It evolved according to the imminent laws of social progress, of passing from an inferior social-economic formation to another, superior one, more developed and more productive. The transition from an inferior social-economic to a superior formation was the result of the action of the general law of consonance of productive forces with the economic production relations, a law discovered by Marx and further adopted by all the socialist economic schools as a bearing for the social progress movement.

The productive forces of a social-economic formation (technique, technology, production organisation, labour productivity, etc.) have always been more mobile, in all systems. They develop and improve faster than the production relationships between people. The latter take the form of property, of economic phenomena, categories and processes in the areas of production, exchange and distribution. All the students of secondary economic schools know this historic hierarchy of organising our activity.

However, we have to draw our readers' attention to certain aspects of the social scale of progress that, under determined historic circumstances, can change the course of development.

If we compare the social progress of the inferior formation of social relations with the superior formation, as history generally goes on, the ranking system of the social-economic formations follows the mainstream of history's progress.

If we analyze each country or group of countries separately, we will see that there are exceptions, as in all processes of movement of matter and society. The USA did not pass through feudalism to reach capitalism. The African countries did not pass through feudalism to come later to liberalism and capitalism. The countries of former USSR and China did not pass through the school of developed capitalism to advance on the way to socialism. Some Latin-American countries did not know, in their evolution, about the stage of slavery, etc.

Such an order of transition, in which nations and peoples passed from a social formation to another, including also the possibility of jumping over an economic formation while passing from an inferior formation to a superior one, may lead to doubts in connection with the truth of the Marxist theory of all peoples and nations compulsorily passing through socialism. Could it be possible for some capitalist countries to by-pass socialism as a new social-economic order and to pass to another system that does not exist yet?

During a seminar of economic sciences held in Bucharest, already 30 years ago, a brilliant student called Popescu, asked me the same question. He wondered why, if it was possible for some countries and nations in the world to jump over a certain social-economic order, why would it not be possible just the same in the process of transition from socialism to capitalism. Instead of the transition from capitalism to socialism, what if we could imagine that some peoples pass from capitalism to another system that does not exist yet? The student Popescu had me embarrassed. I answered him briefly that the transition to a system, which does not exist yet, would mean the transition to the nothingness we do not know yet and that any logical and formal philosophy lacks a concrete basis and could lead us to prophecies.

However, the attempt to give an effective answer to that important theoretical question, the rational core of my student's questioning, haunted me years on end. The answer to that question raises an entirely new question. Could it be possible that socialism and its superior stage, called communism by Marx, which we shall call humanism, to be more consistent with the new changes, were the last social-economic formations or the terminal point of social progress? In other words, what will come after communism or humanism? A better social order, entirely unknown to us?

According to the present level of knowledge concerning the law of compliance of social production relations with the degree of development of productive forces, it seems that the result would be that socialism, as an inferior stage of communism, and communism in turn, as a superior stage of socialism, are purposefully organised systems in which the people master the laws of social progress and direct them to the intended results. According to the degree of impetus of productive forces, any socialist and communist society continuously improves its social production relations, adjusting them to the level of evolution of productive forces.

Thus, the permanent consonance of the ones to the others does not lead to a social revolution, to a new social order. However, if the society does not create the adequate immune mechanisms of defense against the deviation from the historic mainstream of compliance between production forces and relationships, then a social revolution might emerge. However, this is only an exception and not the general rule of social progress. Whereto would the possible exception advance in the following 200 – 300 years and more? Nobody can make such scientific predictions.

The extent of my research on social progress may be found in the following 50 – 100 years of latent revolution, of most peoples and nations' transition to socialism. Everything, which surpasses certain limits, can lead to Nostradams' predictions, which are by no means the object of my research. When I refer to the transition of "most peoples and nations of the world to socialism", I do not mean the transition to socialism of **each and every** people and nation in the world, I merely mean most of them. I take into consideration any possible unpredictable events that surpass my field of research.

As I observed many times, but under different angles, the way of transition to socialism of the majority of peoples and nations in the world is the way of a latent social revolution which gradually erodes and changes all the old social relationships and structures. Opposed to the violent socialist revolution, on the way of becoming extinct, yet not being extinct altogether, the latent revolution implies that certain important social issues should be solved, within the narrow limits of the old system, and that the power has to be conquered by general democratic and free elections, and that it has to be improved by the alternation of left wing and right wing parties. After the power is turned into the hands of the civil society, represented by left wing political parties and forces, the latent revolution goes further on its road of faster solving other great remaining issues on the way to the socialist revolution and the victory of socialism.

The latent, peaceful revolution has nothing in common with Trotki's theory of the permanent revolution. The latent revolution is not a permanent revolution but rather a cyclic revolution, evolving in waves, liberating more and more people of alienation, fetishism and the dominance of money over spirit, of the world's material domination.

The cyclic development of the revolution, as a result of the analysis of the history of all revolutions, suggests the idea according to which neither the linear, nor the perpetual development of the revolution can find their reason in the development of the contradictions of different pre-capitalist systems. The cyclic development of the revolution is rooted in the cyclic development of capitalism and neocolonialism. Whenever in a country or group of countries the fundamental contradictions of the system grow ripe, they will be followed by a period of social revolutions, which have been the driving force of history. We live and die with the legitimate belief and the biblical hope that, before the end of the 21st century, the social revolutions will pick the ripe fruits of social progress in most countries of our world, on the way to democratic, liberal and humanitarian socialism.

References

1. Robert Hue. Communisme, un nouveau projet. Stock Paris, 1999, p. 89, 90.
2. Henri Weber, De quoi débattent les socialistes?, Le Monde, Paris, 18 Novembre 2005, p. 22.
3. Blaz Boskovic, Osnove polit-ekonomskog sistema humanog drustva, SD Publik, Belgrade, 2004, p. 117.

4. Vanessa Sojilkovic, www.tolosart, org/nessakovic.
5. Le livre noir du communisme, Robert Laffont, Paris, 1997, pp. 561, 573, 574, 584.
6. Lech Walesa, Un chemin d'espoir, Fayard, Paris, 1987, pp. 326, 327.
7. The 2000 Elections, Le Monde, March 2000.
8. Jacques Allaman, Vladimir Poutine et le poutinisme, Editeur L'Harmattan, Paris, 2004, pp. 5, 6.
9. Eugeni Primakov, Au coeur du pouvoir. Ed. des Syrtes, Paris, 2002, p. 20.
10. Roj Medvedev, Poutine, Povratak Russije, Novosti, Belgrade, 2007, p. 196.
11. Hélène Novaille, Vladimir Poutine: Une certaine idée de la Russie, www.leosthene.com, art. 225.
12. Jean-Marie Chauvier, Le Monde diplomatique, February 2007, p. 196.
13. Gennady Zyuganov quoted by Roj Medvedev, p. 238.
14. Georges Sokoloff, Métamorphose de la Russie, 1994-2000, Fayard, Paris, pp. 595, 596.
15. http://fr.wikipedia.org/wiki/Vladimir Poutine.
16. V.Z.Balikoev, Obschaya ekonomicheskaya teoriya. Lada, Moscow, 2000, p. 654.
17. Youri Roubinski, Les éclats de l'Empire ou la Communauté des Etats indépendants, IFRI, Paris, 2001, p. 11.
18. Jean Christophe Romer, Géopolitique de la Russie, Economica, Paris, 1999, p. 55.
19. Claire Mouradian, La CEI: un nouvel acteur sur la scène internationale, La Documentation Française, Série Russie n° 124, p. 4.
20. Gennady Zyuganov, La Russie après l'an 2000, p. 234.
21. Jacques Allaman, ditto, p. 4.
22. L´Ukraine, nouvel acteur du jeu international, sous la direction de Anne de Tigney, Bruylant, Bruxelles, LGDJ Paris, 2000, p. 24.
23. Http:// wikipedia.org, Biélorussie, Kazakhstan, Ouzbékistan www.Moldavia.
24. Marcin Frybes, Une nouvelle Europe Centrale, La Découverte, Paris. 1998, pp. 123, 125.

25. Ivan Krastev, Que cache la vague populiste? Le Monde, June 23, 2006.
26. François Julien, Revue le Monde, 2005, n° 94.
27. Yu Guangyuan. La modernisation socialiste de la Chine. Foreign Language Editions, Beijing 1983, pp. 6-7.
28. Joseph Stiglitz, La grande désillusion, Fayard. Paris, 2002, pag. 298.
29. China, 2000, Foreign Language Editions, Beijing, pp. 104, 105.
30. Deng Xiaoping, Les questions fondamentales d'aujourd'hui. Beijing, Foreign Language Editions 1987, p. 111.
31. The 17th National Congress of the Communist Party of China, Foreign Language Editions, Beijing, 2007, pp. 2, 9, 10, 13..
32. Le défi chinois, Le Monde, June 15, 2005.
33. Gennady Zyuganov, ditto, p. 176.
34. Jiang Zemin, quoted by Alain Peyrefitte, La Chine s'est éveillée, Paris, 1977, p. 611.
35. Alain Peyrefitte, ditto, pag. 611.
36. Mohandas Gandhi, Tous les hommes sont frères, Gallimard, Paris, 1990, p. 151.
37. Bipan Chandra, Mridula Mukherjee, Aditya Mukherjee, India After Independence 1947-2000, Penguin Books, New Delhi, 2002, pp. 173, 177.
38. Rajiv Gandhi, Le Monde, May 1, 1985, Nov. 1, 1986.
39. *Ibid.*
40. India Development Raport 2004, Indira Gandhi Institute of Development Research, New Delhi, 2004, pp. 36, 125.
41. Christophe Feuché, Stéphane Dovert & Benoît de Tréglodé, Contemporary Vietnam (Viet-Nam contemporain), IRASEC / Les Indes Savantes, Paris, 2004, p. 239.
42. Christophe Feuché, Stéphane Dovert et Benoît de Tréglodé, ditto., p. 232.
43. Philippe Papin, Viet-Nam. Parcours d'une nation, Belin, Paris, 2003, pp. 202, 173.
44. Christophe Feuché, ditto, pp. 24, 245.
45. www.Nepalliberation.com/bridge/sylvian.
46. www.Nepal/secours.bi/nepalhistoirib.
47. Http://fr.wikipedia.org/wiki/Parti du peuple Pakistan.

48. Http://fr.wikipedia/wiki/Pakistan.
49. http://preseci.com.
50. www.France24.com opposition-malaisie-avance Gouvernement-leg.
51. Le Monde, October 18, 2002.
52. Pierre Mauroy, Voyage au cœur de l'Internationale Socialiste, Paris, 1998, p.18.
53. Marc Lazăr, La gauche en Europe depuis 1945, PUF, Paris, 1999, pp. 20, 21.
54. Pierre Rosanvallon, Entretien. Le Monde, 22 noiembrie 2005.
55. Robert Hue, ditto, p. 19.
56. Olivier Besancenot. La révolution, Flammarion, Paris, 2005, p. 9.
57. Manifeste pour une Europe sociale, Desclée de Brouwer, Paris 2004, p. 7.
58. Laurent Fabius. Libération, April 5, 2005.
59. Patrice Cohen Seat, Communisme: l'avenir d'une espérance, Calmann-Lévy, Paris, 2007, p. 55.
60. Rolf Nordling, Suède socialiste et libre entreprise, Fayard-Mame, Paris, 1970. pp. 18, 19, 154.
61. Diana L. Raby, Democracy and Revolution, Latin America and Socialism, Pluto Press, London, 2006.
62. Histoire générale du socialisme, Vol. 4, Presses Universitaires de France, Paris, 1978, p. 223.
63. Fidel Castro, Le Monde, 18 august 1995.
64. Hugo Chavez, Interview, Jeune Afrique, l'Intelligent, November 14-20, 2000, p. 58.
65. Jean Jacques Jouvin, Problèmes d'Amérique Latine, Paris, 2006, N° 4006-4007, p. 14.
66. Libération, Paris, September 10, 2003, p. 3, 4.
67. Marta Lagos, quoted by Christian Lionet, Les Chiliens aux urnes pour enterrer les années noires, Libération, Paris, December 11 & 12. 1993, p. 16.
68. Le Monde, 17. 01. 2006.
69. Hugo Chavez, ditto, p. 59.
70. Vanessa Stojilkovic, ditto, p. 3.
71. Hugo Chavez, op.cit, p. 59.

72. www.Bresil.ci/br l.
73. Christian Dutilleux, Express, Paris, March 21, 2003..
74. www.bresil.ci/bra pauvreté. httl.
75. Lucrecia Escudero-Chauvel & Diana Quattrocchi, Http/hns-info.
76. www.Calpa-Paris.org/article, php article 246.
77. Jorge Marrirodriga, El Pais, Madrid, reproduced in Courrier International, December 7, 2005, p. 43.
78. Lucretia Escudero Chauval °i Diana Quattoci, ditto
79. Quote from Jean Claude Boucher, after the assassination of nine leaders of the leftist movement. Le Monde, January 29, 1989.
80. www.diplomate.gouv.fr, Bolivia, May 9, 2006.
81. Ignacio Romanet, www.Monde diplomatique, Fr. 2003,10472.
82. Ramon Pajuelo Teves, Pérou: Crise politique permanente et nouvelles protestations sociales. http:/risal.colectifs.net/1381.
83. Le Monde, August 7, 2002.
84. Ivan Cepeda et Claudia Giron Ortiz. Comment des milliers des militants ont été liquidés en Colombie. www.Monde-diplomatique.fr, 12196.
85. www.fitk.glaval.CA/axl/nicaragua.
86. http:/fr.wikipedia.org/wiki Nicaragua.
87. Jack Eduard Alvis, Politique générale, Sena, Haitians.www.org.
88. Erasmo Saenz Carrete. Et si Mexique virait a gauche. Monde diplomatique, June 2006, p. 2.
89. Erasmo Saenz Carrete, ditto, p. 3.
90. http:/fr.wikepedia,org./wiki/Mexique.
91. Ignacio Ramonet. Le Mexique fracturé; www.Le.Monde diplomatique.fr.2006/08.
92. Zyad Liman, Obama, une révolution américaine. Afrique magazine. March 2008.
93. Barack Obama. Les mémoires. Quoted by the daily L'inter, Abidjan, 20.03.2008.
94. David Gakunzi, Ad'Obe Obe. Rencontres avec Julius Nyerere, Descartes et Cie, Paris, 1955. p. 53.
95. Histoire générale du socialisme, Presses Universitaires de France, vol 4, Paris, 1978, PUF. p. 342.

96. Julius Nyerere; What Now? Development - Dialogue 1973 Nr.1-2, p. 59.
97. David Gakunzi, Ad'Obe Obe, ditto, pp. 61, 62.
98. Carlos Belli Bello, Interview, Notre Voie, Abidjan, February 23, 2006.
99. Embassy of France in South Africa, Economic Mission 19/12/07.
100. Angola Press Agency, Luanda, 9.02.2007.
101. www.Skolinternational.Com, Angola.
102. Philippe Meymarie. Le Monde Diplomatique, 24 noiembrie 2001.
103. Suzie Boulanger and Patrick Martineau, Congo, www.alternative.ca/art. 2 459.
104. Pascal Airault, Une économie à genoux, Jeune Afrique, June 18-24, 2006, p. 66.
105. Julius Nyerere, Socialisme, démocratie et l'unité Africaine, La declaration d'Arusha, Présence Africaine, Paris, pp. 82, 83.
106. www.tfg.ulavalca.
107. Daniel Jouanneau. Le Mozambique, Karthala, Paris, 1995, pp. 103-107.
108. Daniel Jouanneau, ditto, p. 115.
109. www.infoexport/le services des délégués commerciaux du Canada..
110. Alfred Bosch, Nelson Mandela, le dernier Titan, L'Harmattan, Paris, 1996, p. 49, 55.
111. Fatima Meer, Plus haut que l'espoir. Présence Africaine, Paris, p. 27.
112. The South Africain Story, chapter 2, www.info.
113. www.fr wikipedia.org. Afrique du Sud.
114. Hassu Patel, Travaux et documents, Paris, May 2, 1987, pp. 11, 12.
115. World Bank Report n° 15 640, June 14, 1997.
116. Gouverner autrement la Côte d'Ivoire, L'Harmattan, Paris, 2000, pp. 102, 103.
117. Laurent Gbagbo, Notre Voie, Abidjan, March 4-5, 2006.
118. Laurent Gbagbo, Speech at the promotion of his son's work: "La Côte d'Ivoire, un air de changement", L'Inter, April 2008.
119. Robert Aldrich, Le mouvement social, L'Atelier, N° 167, p. 150.
120. Australia in Brief, Australian Department of Foreign Affairs and Trade, Sydney, 2007, p. 69.
121. http://en.wikipedia.org./wiki/Australian Labour Par.

3

New Elements of the Theory and Practice of Society Development

1. Informational and Biotechnological Revolution and Social Progress

(a) The New Age of Technical-Scientific and Technological Discoveries

The Second World War was not yet over, when the explosion of the first atomic bombs dropped on Hiroshima announced the discovery of the atom fission and fusion and their recombining in the most terrible destructive power of our civilisation. The discovery of the atomic power and the inter-continental rockets makes the entire world frightened by the prospect of a new nuclear catastrophe and becomes, on the other hand, the guardian of eternal peace – opening new prospects to the great energy revolution of the 21st century, designed to serve the future of our planet.

Sixteen years later, after the explosion of the first atomic bomb, Yuri Gagarin flew into space, thus announcing to the world the new revolution of space travel. In the 1960s, colour television came on the market, as well as the great revolution in visual communication and information. The 1970s were the years of the discovery of computers, which replace partly the human mind. In the 1980s, mobile telephones conquered our planet and turned it into some kind of a planetary village.

In the second third of the 20th century, the automation of the production process was completed in the developed industrial countries. Robot implementation gradually replaced the mechanised work in production processes. Along with the appearance and spreading of robots, the social progress went through a new age, the age of change in the technological production systems.

The bio-technological revolution replaces oil and lubricants with new bio-fuels, replaces the chemical components of plastics with bio-components and achieves a wide application in the pollution control industry, in the electronic and pharmaceutical industries. A new era, beyond oil and without oil, began to level the way for new energy sources. The bio-technological revolution will shatter and largely alter the structure of the old, classical technologies.

In the building industry, which is the oldest in the world, the classic technology of reinforced concrete and burnt bricks is replaced to an ever larger extent by steel structures, polystyrene, laminated plasterboards, aluminium joinery and outer finishes in opaque glass.

In transports, the jet planes, the high speed trains, and the computerised automobiles shorten the distances between villages, towns, cities and countries, and speed up the exchange of goods and of knowledge. The most recent American discovery is the supersonic plane, with a speed of 11,000 km/hour, far superior to the speed of sound. The research scientists announce the mass production of private helicopters, Shaikar electric cars with a speed of 550 km/hour.

All these technical and scientific discoveries of our age, as well as many others of the kind, which the human imagination could not have dreamt of 100 years ago, were born during a record time span of only 70 years.

(b) Deficiencies of the Informational and Bio-Technological Revolutions

The technical and bio-technical revolution is still in its very beginning stage. Just as, according to Rostov's sayings, for the first industrial revolution there were needed 30-40 years until its extended implementation, for the new industrial revolution, too, there will be needed at least 70-80 years for its large-scale implementation, which will probably extend beyond the 21st century.

What we can certainly state, is the undisputable fact that the informational and bio-technological revolution will last much longer that the first industrial revolution, for the simple reason that the first one did not encounter the opposition of the leading classes and structures, since it created innumerable jobs, while the second one is disposing of manpower, consequently generating unemployment in ever larger proportion.

For the leading classes, the unemployment turns not only into the threatening sword menacing their existence, but also the main handicap for the extended practical implementation of the new industrial revolution.

However, the leading classes can not put a stop to the course of history. In the files of the scientific research institutions lie hidden fantastic projects of the newest scientific and technical discoveries, the implementation of which in the real production, exchange and social distribution will undoubtedly change the production techniques and technology and, consequently, will alter even the technological production system, all social, state, political and ethic inter-human relations.

In other words, we are facing a historical transition process of the world nations and countries to a new social order, resulting from the ruins of the totalitarian socialism, of the decaying, metastasised imperialism and of the failing neo-colonialism.

It is difficult, almost impossible, to foresee every new technical and technological effect all over the world, up to the end of the 21st century. As per the estimations of sociologists and futurologists, no matter what scientific, actually possible prognosis, could extend, over a 30 years interval. The 50-year forecasts imply 30% risks and, for intervals exceeding 50 years, the risk factor rises to 50% and even more.

However, in this survey I undertake to make social forecasts that do not resemble the future imagined by Jules Verne, on the contrary, they foresee something totally possible, approaching reality, something that will change the vital core of evolution, something born from the imagination, soul, heart and life of the common people, who dream of the world of more wealth, more freedom, more justice and more humanity.

I would like to show to my readers my thoughts, analyses, researches in the late 20th and the early 21st centuries with regard to the social-economic evolution of the developed West, of the medium-developed East and the under-developed South, under the shadows of a new technical and technological revolution.

What are the consequences of this new revolution for the development of the economic, state and social structures, for the development of the social inter-human relations, for the moulding of new morals and new dimensions of the living standard and the quality of life of the people on our planet?

What are the consequences of this revolution for the ideological and theoretical foundations of the social movements, of the changes in the ways, forms and methods of the progress of the new society?

(c) Changes in the Technological Production Systems

We may make the ad-hoc statement of a historical truth. Just as the first industrial revolution of the 18th and 19th centuries erased the feudal relations and left its print on the capitalist relations in the social structure, just the same, based on the same logical thread of thought and on the same development laws of the society, the new revolution will erase the capitalist relations and leave its mark on the socialist relations in the social structures. This is the beginning and the end, the one and everything of the revolution and the evolution of our civilisation. Any other praise of the perennial capitalism, of the new economy, of the popular capitalism and of the third way, is nothing more than an attempt to lull the people in, with their ideological drugs.

One of the best known sociologists in the world, the American Peter Drucker, wrote in his book "Beyond Capitalism": "In the span of 50 years, a new society will appear before our eyes. The world that will come forth from the present remodelling of values, beliefs, social and economic structures, political ideas and regimes, briefly, from the remodelling of our concept on the world, will not at all resemble to what we could imagine today."[1]

If we clear Drucker's analyses of his ideological dislike for socialism and his partiality for "post-capitalism" which, in his opinion, is neither the "anti-capitalist" society, nor the "non-capitalist" one, then we may say that more of his analyses and summaries on the results of the new industrial revolution are not empty words.

Yes, the world will change fundamentally in the coming 50-100 years, but not in the direction of Drucker's "post-capitalism", since capitalism can not be followed again by capitalism, but rather by a new, completely novel social structure, whose ideas and movements have designed the way of mankind, from Rousseau to Saint-Simon, Owen, Marx, Engels, Proudhon, Lenin, Trotsky, Mao Zedong, Deng Xiaoping, Jaurès, Mitterand, Putin, Lula da Silva, Laurent Gbagbo, and other socialist thinkers more. Certainly, this will be socialism.

Therefore, capitalism, as a social-economic system, will not last forever. It has a beginning, a middle and an end, as all other previous social systems. At present, the vital question is not to know whether capitalism will have an end, but rather to know when this end will be, how it will come and in what historical period it will happen.

The most pessimistic analyst of our future, the American Robert Heilbroner, wrote in his book "Vision on the Future": "Capitalism will not last forever. Its inner dynamics are too powerful to let us imagine the capitalist system navigating the waters of the future, like a gigantic submersible ship. Change is the very essence of capitalism – technological, social and political change and economic change – which hits the eye in the historical observation of no matter which capitalist nation."[2]

To the question about getting to know the changes which we might expect in a nearer or farther future, Robert Heilbroner answers relatively reserved and pessimistic: "Is it possible to imagine already, reasonably, an obviously superior system to our system? Certainly not in the time span we have called tomorrow", that is "the next century or the next two centuries of turmoil".[3]

But, what social-economic system could replace the capitalist system? To this vital ideological question Robert

Heilbroner has no answer at all. Robert Heilbroner is not a sociologist of international importance and, hence, can not offer answer of global importance.

2. State, Revolution and Democracy

(a) New approach to the Theory of State, Revolution and Democracy

In this chapter we approach under multiple theoretical risks, one of the crucial issues of the contemporary theory and praxis of the international workers, socialist and communist movement. We are speaking about the matter of the state, revolution and democracy, an issue debated at the middle of the 19th and the beginning of the 20th centuries between the front of the working class, the social-democratic and the socialist movement, on the one hand, and the communist front on the other hand. The first one, gathered around the 2nd International, and the second one around the 3rd International. But, as the popular saying goes: "Who's afraid of the wolf should not go to the woods".

It is a common knowledge that Marx and Engels expressed in the most concise way and defended to the extreme the concept of the objective necessity of the violent revolution, of the "destruction" and the "demolition" of the old bourgeois state machinery and its replacement by "organising the workers class, as a dominant class", that is by the state of the "dictatorship of the proletariat".

After 70 years of evolution of the working class and of internal battles between Marxism and opportunism in the matter of the state, the revolution and the democracy, Lenin sustained vehemently, in his book "The State and the Revolution (1917)", the principles of the founders of scientific socialism.

Then, their concepts had an objective historical sound. The ruthless criticism of the theory of the ideological leaders of those times, of a part of the working class with regard to the role of the bourgeois state in reconciling the class interests, with regard to the peaceful turning of capitalism into socialism by means of the universal voting right, supported by Bernstein, Kautsky, Scheidemann and other supporters of social-reformism, and conquering the power by violent revolution, all which at that moment was the justified historical way to social progress.

The basic issue of each revolution is the matter of power. Which is the class, which are the classes, which are stepping down from power? Which is or which are the ones climbing into the power position? This question is vital for any revolution, which means that the revolution destroys the old social-economic systems and gradually sets up new ones, throughout a very long transition period. This quality jump, from one state to another, in the then historical circumstances, could have been achieved only through violent revolution. Consequently, Marx was then duly right when he wrote that violence gives birth to new society, which the old society is carrying in her womb.

But in the Marxist perspective, the violent revolution was not the exclusive feature of social progress. Marx has never been exclusive, even less a metaphysician of the existing state. Marx was a great master and founder of materialist dialectic, which always observes the phenomena and processes of social progress in their continuous movement and change. Marx did not close the potential ways of the peaceful revolution. Where there are conditions for the taking over of power by free and democratic elections, there is no room for violence and armed revolution.

"For instance, in England – wrote Marx – the road leading to political power is open for the working class. Where the political trouble could achieve it promptly and securedly, an armed rebellion would have failed."[4]

At the time, speaking and writing about the power take-over by elections, when the western world, as a whole, except Great Britain, was falling under the yoke of totalitarian tyrannies, when only Liebknecht and Bebel in Germany were the first popular deputies in the world, was quite abnormal and opportunistic and was lacking any real foundation.

Only in the eve and in the wake of the Second World War, could the ways of democratisation, the road of the peaceful revolution, be opened as a result of the pressure of the working class and democratic movements and of the bourgeois political compromises.

b. Peaceful Social Revolution

The age of armed revolutions is slowly receding back into history. Given a certain development stand of the production forces as well as the culture and the collective social conscience and the democracy under the new historical circumstances, revolutions embrace the features of peaceful revolution.

The power take-over, by the socialist and social-democratic parties, by the popular workers', communist parties and their green allies, is possible then by peaceful ways. The bullets and machine-gun fire are replaced by the voters' lists. In the new historical circumstances, free elections are the highest form of the conflict of classes. They are the expressions of the latent peaceful revolution. By secret vote, the citizens choose freely their representatives, by presidential, parliamentary and local elections, thus establishing the power of the civil society by peaceful means.

After the Second World War, elections play a new historical role in the progress of society, as a result of the informational and bio-technological revolution, of the intensifying of the contradictions of capitalism, of the strengthening of the social conscience of the working class and as a result of the efficient struggle of the left-wing parties for the expansion of liberal democracy. A new trend appears in the evolution of political domination of the bourgeoisie in power.

The incapacity of the leading classes to settle the capital issues of society, as well as unemployment, pushing aside are ever greater poverty of part of the population, the incapacity of the state to provide each citizen with his own dwelling, to provide the youth with decent education and schooling, all that pushed the citizens more and more to the left. The absolute and irrevocable domination of the bourgeoisie in power sinks back into history.

The class of the owners must give in and accept compromises, must share the power with the representatives of the left-wing parties, or must pass the power to the left-wing parties for a time span of 5 or 10 years, following free and democratic elections. So, the flag of bourgeois democratisation changes hands, being taken over by the people's majority.

As a result of such mutations, radical shifts occur in the relationship between the violent and the peaceful revolutions. Some extreme left leaders accept the democratic sentence of the elections, but there is one thing they never accept, namely that the freely expressed will of the people should not be achieved entirely because the leading classes prevent it by means of force.[5]

But time is over changing. From now on, the dominant historical circumstances of the past are already part of the history. They do not dictate any longer the rules of the revolution. The violent revolution becomes only an exceptional event, while the peaceful revolution becomes the general rule of the advancement of social progress.

Now-a-days, in most of the countries, the bourgeoisie must accept the popular sentence of the success of the socialist, the social-democratic, the working class and other left-wing parties. This is the reflection of the major popular will to change society by appropriate progressive reforms, by the latent peaceful social revolution and by gradual evolution of the social progress.

After carefully reading the text, the readers, specialised in social and political sciences, will notice that the terminology of the latent social revolution differs, to some extent, from that of the socialist revolution, both in its content and directions.

The latent social revolution is not a violent one. Neither is it a permanent revolution according to Trotsky or Lenin, taken for a certain country, nor is it the social-democratic evolution of reformism. It is the latent, peaceful, social and simultaneous revolution of socialism revival and globalisation, the basis and integral part of the socialist revolution.

It is latent because at a certain level of capitalist development, it erodes the material substance of the private monopolist property or as Schumpeter points out, it devitalizes the property of joint stock companies. It is a social revolution because it tries to solve, within the narrow limits of liberalism, certain important social problems. Its actions can be slowed down or stepped up according to the capacity of the left wing political parties to pick and put together the fruit of this revolution.

(c) Demolishing or Democratising and Adjusting the Old State Apparatus

The alternation between the dominance of the left and right wings until the final victory and consolidation of the left wing is a new phenomenon; we can even say it is a new law of the social revolution. This law of alternation is the fruit of new political and social changes, an expression of the bourgeoisie's withdrawal from the attack of the leftist electorate against the existing order.

Therefore, the theses issued by the founders of scientific socialism referring to violent revolution and dictatorship of the proletariat as well as those concerning the abolition of the old state apparatus and its replacement by a wholly new one, is now a history.

In "The State and the Revolution", Lenin exposed his views, on the one hand, on the issue of the removal of the old state apparatus by abolishing the parliamentary system and the three powers of the state: legislative, executive and judicial, and on the other hand, on the removal of bureaucracy and clerk system by gradually replacing and rotating all the society members and also by abolishing the historical form of social division of labour in direct production labour and labour at state leadership level.

As history has proved it, those views are not only the Russian expression of that time concerning the relations between state, revolution and democracy, but they also show how bureaucracy and totalitarianism came into being and were developed.

The peaceful revolution does not need the demolition and abolition of the bourgeois state but its democratisation and gradual adjustment according to the needs and demands of social progress and also the demolition and abolition of old administration methods. The state apparatus of developed states that has been improved and specialised for hundreds of years, has its own contradictions and faults that hinder social progress. Therefore, the social reforms, the adjustment of the old state apparatus to new necessities, the demolition and abolition of the old administration methods are important demands of the social-democratic, socialist and communist movement.

The accommodation of the old state apparatus to the new requirements of social progress will have to go through a continuous struggle of the leftist forces, parties and movements, without any deviation, for the expansion of the bourgeois democracy not only in the developed countries but also in the underdeveloped ones.

Liberty and democracy, which have always been the symbols of the bourgeois revolution, will become grave diggers for the old system, and symbols of the social revolutions, just as the 20th century free market has denied itself asserting the expansion of the social production in the 21st century.

Although two views on the development of democracy appeared later on, namely: those defended by the communist parties and those of the social-democratic and socialist parties, history gave its verdict, as Pierre Mauroy points out:

"The contradictions we are talking about have become more and more artificial. An alleged democracy by holding free and pluralist elections has spread. During the latest decades, democracy has spread over many continents, so that new stakes appeared."[6]

Liberal and humanitarian socialism will be attained only by democratising the society and the state, by gradual economic, state and political reforms.

Democratisation, as a basis of social progress, demands updating and adjusting the constitutional systems to the new necessities of the civil society, the real separation of the executive, legislative and judicial powers, total democratisation of parliamentary systems and development of participatory democracy, regional decentralisation and socio-economic self-management.

The liberation of the seventh power from the monopoly of financial oligarchies, the right to work guaranteed by constitution, the democratisation of the by-laws of anonymous companies, social insurance system take-over by insurants and many other elements of social progress are parts of the democratisation process.

(d) Participatory Democracy, the New Future

The fundamental issue of the society democratisation

process is to involve more the society in state decisions, promoting participatory democracy. Participatory democracy is a type of democracy in which the most important decisions of social progress are not taken from the top of the political pyramid of different classes but from the bottom, from the depth of the civil society from the resources of social progress. The expansion of participatory democracy has been included in the programs of some socialist, social-democratic and communist parties and in other leftist parties as well but some forms and ways of its implementation are still being researched in order to find viable solutions.

In 2007, the French socialist party introduced in its electoral programmes the requirement of putting in place a participatory democracy: "Introducing participatory democracy to all public communities (juries, citizens, participating budgets, etc.). The citizens that collected one million signatures will be entitled to examine a text of law."[7]

Ségolène Royal, a failed candidate in the 2007 elections, published in 1996 in her book, "The truth of a woman", in which she wrote that "today our country is a society of citizens who wish to be listened to and be involved in thinking and in decision making but tomorrow it will be much more".[8]

In her electoral campaign, Ségolène Royal explained to the French people, the meaning, the advantages and the future of participatory democracy, as a genuine social revolution.

History left only a few patterns of participatory democracy. Such patterns of participatory democracy can be found in the Iroquois, a tribal people living in the primitive commune, in the forums of ancient Carthage and in the Athenian republics. They can also be found in the meetings of the Paris Commune, of the members of political parties for working out electoral programs and in modern contemporary bourgeois democracy, where very few referendums in connection with some strategic decision-making processes of leading parties were organised.

The former Yugoslav system of social self-management had experimented for a long period of time a symbiosis of parliamentary democracy and participatory democracy. Before voting the most important laws in Parliament, deputies had to consult with their electorate, to obtain their adhesion or disapproval and to vote in favour of or against the projects of some laws. This means that when taking their decisions, the deputies are not subjected to their political top the decisions of which may be right or wrong. They are rather subjected to their electors and any state apparatus is subjected to the people's control. The people's control in the decision-making process is the very expression of genuine popular democracy.

It is not impossible for the creative collective genius of people to find the best ways of implementing the actual participatory democracy until the end of the 21st century. Participatory democracy is the future of our civilisation.

In addition to the long process of society's evolution, the development of democracy, the revolutions and evolutions are integral parts of society's movement. Relying on what we have learned from the past, we should be aware that democratisation and evolution would become the main weapons to social progress.

Mastering the tools and levers of democracy, of latent revolution, of evolution, of private property and its socialisation, of competition, production of goods as well as the development of social non-commercial production, the exchange and distribution are as important as the state power take-over. The peaceful latent revolution without gradual reforms is voided of its revolutionary content.

Only when we understand the essence of the contradictory unity between revolution and evolution replacing the spontaneous development by the conscious and organised action of left wing political parties and of millions of followers, only then will we be able to say that the victory is on the part of civil society and of the people.

3. Reformism, Reforms and Revolutionary Evolution

(a) Reforms Epidemic

The changes attracted by the new industrial revolution in the dynamics of the economic, structural, state and political developments, are not at all indifferent to the forms and methods of their performance. Those forms and methods are searched by politicians both in the left wing and in the right one, according to the interests of the classes they are representing.

Both in the right and in the left wing, the politicians are looking for instruments adequate for social reforms. The word reform that is being repeated millions of times in programs, articles, essays, conferences and talks of the left and right politicians, has become the new flag of the political and ideological struggle for the dominance and orientation of the social conscience of society's majority.

Hence derives the necessity to actually put the reforms into practice, namely: administrative and judicial reforms, reforms referring to the security of the citizens, to financial structures, education, social security, etc. In one word, all fields of the economic and social activity are in need of reforms. The reform epidemic has caught almost all the countries of our planet.

The inability of the dominant classes to solve the numerous contradictions of the social progress is subjected to the pressure of the civil society that is looking for adequate changes. The popular pressure forces them to rehabilitate the cracks of the system by blunted social reforms. In fact, such reforms represent the will of the bourgeois classes and of one of their satellites derived from the old social democracy, to keep the existing state by reformism. They do not express any advance of the social progress.

The contemporary leftist movement is not against the reform of the existing social system, but rather against reformism, collateral reforms, and against those reforms that do not change the essence of the existing state.

Unfortunately, certain social-democratic, social and labour parties have not completely abolished reformism. In France, Italy, Germany, and in other countries, the rising political currents had a more leftist orientation. The objective effervescence towards the left of the peoples of those countries resulted in a positive process of revitalising the left wing in Europe; moreover, not only in Europe, but also in Latin America, South-Eastern Asia and in Africa, too.

(b) The Reforms and the Revolutionary Evolution

The change of the relation of forces between classes, at both national and global level, to the benefit of the progressive movements of the national and social liberation, opens up new historical prospects for more vital and more revolutionary reforms, favourable to social progress. Such reforms enlisted into the programmes of the socialist, labour, social-democratic and communist parties, are an integral part of the social revolution, of evolution, of gradual quantitative changes on the way to social progress.

The resistance of the left extremist parties and organisations to the gradual quantitative and qualitative changes as an integral part of the evolution of the society is as harmful as the blunt reforms and the collateral ones of the rich classes. Marxism was never against evolution. Marx had underlined many times that evolution is a part of the revolution often calling it "revolutionary evolution". The forgotten thesis of "revolutionary evolution that had been understood by Jean Jaurès as a moment of history, can contribute to clarify the attitudes of the leftist parties as against the binomial revolution-evolution.

"Today, as half a century ago, said Jaurès, you have to beware of revolutionary phrases and to profoundly understand the laws of the revolutionary evolution in modern times. Thus, I have always guided myself by what Marx had called "revolutionary evolution".

In my opinion, it consists in introducing into today's society certain forms of ownership that invalidate and surpass it, forecasting and preparing the new society and through their organic forces they lead to the breakdown of the old world. In my opinion, reforms should not be only sweeteners – but also preparatory means. This is the method of socialist achievement."[9]

By writing these lines about the new dimensions of the revolution, I don't mean to deny the revolution in its essence. The only thing I do is to revive Marx' concept on the "revolutionary evolution", supported by Jaurès, deemed to be one of the efficient methods of the social revolution.

Before and after power taking over, the left wing parties fight ever stronger, reuniting their forces to carry out more radical social reforms by expanding the new social relations. These are the alpha and omega of the contemporary strategy of the progressive social movements.

(c) The Main Directions of the Revolutionary Reforms

It is important for the readers belonging to the pluralist left wing and their professional leaders to better understand what types of reforms are available and which reforms are we favouring, and to avoid any possible doubts, even if well intentioned and sincere, concerning our objective synthesis over the real movement, we'll try to outline a few of the main elements of the reforms that lead to revitalising the dimensions of the society's development on its way to "the revolutionary evolution".

The main direction of these changes consists in the total democratisation of the existing civil society or, as Jack Lang puts it in his book, the implementation of a new political regime by changing the constitutional framework of the society.[10]

The constitutions of the capitalist countries that reflect the evolution of the bourgeois democracy represent the fundamental law of defending the judicial system of the bourgeoisie's private ownership, expressing its implacable right to "usufructus" and "abusus". They are the expression of the evolution of the bourgeois revolution. They contain more or less reminiscences of the limited democracy, more exactly of cosmetic dictatorship.

The liberal constitutions do not guarantee the elementary principles of Montesquieu, of complete separation of powers. They limit the parliamentary initiative, the control of the society over the activities of the executive power. They no longer guarantee the primordial rights of man, of the citizen in a modern society, the right to work. Neither do they guarantee the protection of the citizen against violence, banditry and terrorism. They no longer forbid arms wearing. They do not guarantee the defence of the society against the traffic of drugs, alcohol and cigarette addiction. They do not guarantee the contribution of the church and the state to the ideological, theological and ethical formation of the new coming generations.

4. The Intellectuals, the New Class of Social Progress of the Developed Countries, the New Strategy of Alliances

(a) The Working Class – historic mission fulfilled

For 250 years, the civilisation of our planet was built at the expense of industrial workers. The industrial revolution of the 18th century involved ever more workers in the production of goods due to its extensive development. If, at the end of the 18th century, the percentage of the industrial workers in the developed industrial countries amounted to only 7-10%, as against the active population, until the beginning of the information and bio-technological revolution of the 1960, this share reached the upper limit of 40 - 50%. The percentage of the industrial workers is one of the most important parameters describing a country's level of modern development.

The starting point of the classical economic theories of Quesney, Smith, Ricardo, Marx, of the neoclassical theories of Mill, Jevons, Walras, and of the theory of Pareto, was based on analyses of phenomena, categories, economic processes and social relations between labour and capital. In the development of the proletariat and the industrial workers, Marx saw the main social revolutionary force for establishing a new social order. Therefore, Marx considered the working class as the "grave-digger of capitalism".

In the contemporary period, the working class of the developed countries fulfilled its historic mission to a great extent. By intransigent fighting, the working class succeeded to obtain the five days working week, to legalize the minimal guaranteed wages, tuition-free education, to increase the salary according to inflation, etc.

Our civilisation has been created by means of handiwork, by labour, by the sweat of the working class. The working class, organised in trade unions and political parties made its first Great October Revolution in Russia and then in the countries of the former Russian Empire.

During the years 1941-1950, the working class has contributed to a great extent to the popular revolution in

China, Vietnam, North Korea, Cuba, the former Yugoslavia and Albania. It has started to build the basis of the first socialist country in the world.

The working class made the great social revolution in China where it built the solid basis of Chinese socialism and also in lots of Asian countries. It has also contributed to the liberation of many underdeveloped countries like Cuba, Brazil, Venezuela, Algeria, Tunisia, Libya, Angola, Zimbabwe, The Democratic Republic of Congo and other neo-colonial countries.

(b) Changes of the Class Structure. The Intellectuals, the New Leading Class of Social Progress

After the Second World War, the class structure has gradually changed. In the developed industrial countries, the process of absolute and relative growth of the population has been closed, attaining its maximum limits of 65–75% of the population. This is a great anonymous army to the benefit of social progress in the history of our civilisation.

The growth of the active population was not synonymous to the growth of the proletariat and the development of the working class, according to the way traced by Marx. Totally opposed to Marx' forecasts, who stipulated the quantitative growth of the working class and its main core – the industrial workers (perfectly justified during an entire historic period), under the actual historic circumstances, the growth of the active population does no longer lead to general expansion of the proletariat. At present, the growth of the active population takes an opposite course. It is the course of gradual disappearance of the industrial workers as a revolutionary core of the working class and of their turning into intellectuals, as an intermediate layer between the working class and the bourgeoisie, into a new leading class of social progress.

The intellectual class, resulting from the working class and from its own roots, gradually assumes two roles in the development of the society. On the one hand, it keeps its historic role of a driving force of the information and bio-technological revolution and, on the other hand, it assumes the role of transmitting the mission of the working class to conclude the social revolution on our planet.

According to Jeremy Rifkin, an American sociologist and economist in the 1950's, the American industry employed 33% of the total active population. In the 1960's it employed 30%, while in the 1980's this percentage fell to less than 17%.[11]

This objective historic process is not only the result of the most developed countries in the western world. According to a research made by A. Madison, cited by Roland Garnier, during 117 years (1870 -1987), the percentage of workers and clerks in the primary sector, in 16 industrialised countries fell from 48.8% in 1870, to 24.7% in 1950 to eventually reach a limit of 6% of the active population in 1987.[12]

From that date on, until the end of our century, may be even earlier, the main core of the working class, formed by industrial workers, will fall in the developed countries to 5%, while the industrial workers will no longer have the role of the most revolutionary class on the political scene. The only workers that will remain will be those specialised in the maintenance of machines and installations, in the maintenance of areas of transportation and in those operations that cannot be replaced by automated, robotised and computerised production lines.

Just as the first industrial revolution eliminated by massive introduction of machines in agriculture, most of the peasants as a class, cutting them down to only 2.5%– 5% of the active population, the new informational and bio-technological revolution will reduce the number of workers occupied in industrial production to 5% of the active population, according to the same economic logic. On the contrary, the number of workers employed in services, commerce, public food industry, tourism, education, management, area maintenance, etc. will largely increase.

The metamorphosis of the working class and the decrease of the number of industrial workers in the developed countries represent a long historic process that will probably last until the end of the 21st century and in some countries until the first half of the 22nd century.

Where will the removed workers go? A part of them will naturally withdraw by retiring. A second part of them will be employed in services. A third part will complete the labour reserve army up to the optimum limit. The fourth part will be retrained, improving their knowledge and changing their professional standard.

The new phenomena of metamorphosis have undergone several intellectual negativist interpretations, far from the real development of the society. They consider that "the machines are the new proletariat", that "this is the death of all workers", "the end of the socialist illusions", and "the end of human labour", etc.

All those well-intentioned or biased interpretations contain a grain of truth, according to the ideology of the person who does the interpretation, before the grain germinates, grows and fructifies.

In interpreting the new phenomena, one must always start from the extrapolation of the rational essence of truth. The machines are not the new proletariat, neither in the etymologic nor in the material sense. The materialistic interpretation considers that the machines are dead objects put in motion only when they are animated by human labour. Either directly activated by human labour like in the age of Arkwright and Foulton, or indirectly by Bill Gates' computers, machines will be machines. The difference between the two ages consists in the fact that in the first age, the proletariat operated directly the machines while in the second age, the intellectuals create computer programs that will be put in motion by machines.

Thus, human labour does not disappear, rather the form of labour by which "the machines are put in motion". The workers do not disappear, it is only the direction in which human labour evolves – namely in the direction of labour consumed by the intellectual class. The labour movement does not vanish, it is being engulfed within the great movements of the civil society.

Marxism will not be extinguished, only some of its outdated theories. Socialism will not be extinguished, only its outdated forms of manifestation.

The historic tendency of transforming the class structure in the developed countries does not end along with the birth, development and the entire assertion of the new intellectual class.

(c) The New Role of the Workers in the Tertiary Area, the New Strategy of Alliances

The evolution of the class structure is not only partial but also global. It includes all the fields of social reproduction of the primary, secondary and tertiary areas. It includes the industry, agriculture and the services of social reproduction. The services comprise managing, health, banking and financial services, trading, food, handicrafts, tourism and others.

The services of the tertiary area do not produce material goods or commodities. They serve in a useful way the production of material goods and the development of the primary and secondary areas. The activity of the hard working agents of services is not assessed as productive work but as useful work for the two areas of social reproduction.

In the age of the birth and development of the early capitalism, in the 18-th and 19-th centuries, the percentage of unproductive but useful labour of the services sector represented 5%-10% of the total social labour. That is why the political economy of Petit, Smith, Ricardo and Marx did not include the social services in the area of reproduction as an important factor of social progress.

Nevertheless, material reproduction was not stagnant. The development of the production forces and social progress furthered by the first and then by the second and now even by the third industrial revolution, comprised ever more all the employees of the tertiary area in the field of expanded reproduction. In 2004, the percentage of the active labour force in the tertiary area attained 50% - 60% in the Western developed countries.

Of course, the metamorphosis of the primary and tertiary sector is a long historic process that totally changes Marx's old concepts about the alliance of the working class with the peasantry as a sine qua non condition of the successful social revolution.

The left-wing progressive forces of the developed countries are facing a new historic alternative, a new strategy of alliances of the class of intellectuals undergoing development together with the everlasting influential metamorphosed working class. In the underdeveloped countries, these forces are facing the alternative of achieving a consistent alliance of the developing working class with the masses of peasants and the new developing intellectuals.

There is no doubt that the achievement of the new strategy of alliances in the process of social progress is the fundamental condition of the planetary revival and globalisation of socialism.

(d) The Class Struggle and the Cooperation between Classes

The gradual metamorphosis of the working class on the scene of history and the genesis of a new class of intellectuals was an opportunity for some analysts of new social changes to renew the old theories referring to the disappearance of the class struggle and the appearance of a new age of peace and cooperation between classes.

Some social development analysts are launching a new theory referring to remuneration, social relations, and the disappearance of the bourgeoisie. They are shifting the class struggle to the field of the mass of employees (workers and clerks).

As Guillaume Duval put it, "Today, because of the quasi-disappearance of the non-employees (the bourgeoisie and the KGV petite-bourgeoisie), the contradictions among the mass of employees are the main divisions structuring the social dynamics." And furthermore: "Today, the greatest part of the conflicts of interests that structure the social and economic life, the class struggle, "as it used to be called a long time ago" has been shifted to the mass of employees."[13]

Firstly, the gradual disappearance of the most revolutionary layers of the working class does not mean that the working folk have totally disappeared or in the second place, that the bourgeoisie disappeared from the historic scene. In the third place, this disappearance does not mean that the interests of the new class, the intellectuals, who take over the flag of the revolutionary struggle, are in contradiction with the interests of the big bourgeoisie.

Now we can say without the risk of being wrong, that all the intellectuals use their entire creative power for the sake of the technical and technological revolution, of social progress.

We can say that almost half and probably even more of the intellectuals in the developed countries are not passive observers of the political progress but active and creative protagonists of the social progress.

Therefore, the theories referring to the disappearance of the class struggle among the working class, the intellectuals and the bourgeoisie are pointless.

In his article, "The class struggle is not dead", published in "Le Monde", François Galichet wrote that it doesn't matter if the class struggle disappeared, but to know the significance of the class struggle concept in the context of the globalised economy, taking into account the way in which capitalism is being structured today."[14]

As long as the social division will be present in distinct classes, separated by different interests, the class struggle will still exist. In the societies based on private property, the class struggle has an antagonistic character. In those societies based on community property, the class struggle will have a non-antagonistic character, as long as different classes will be present. The class struggle will disappear only after the disappearance of the classes and the homogenisation of the interests of the entire society. We are still very far from the disappearance of the classes and the class struggle.

Thus, in the very theory and practice of the class struggle, modern society faces important changes both in form and in content.

The gradual reforms of the economic and social system are the expression of the political compromise between the big bourgeoisie and the civil society. They are also the expression of the class struggle.

In addition, street strikes and manifestations, indignation meetings as well as several public protests are the expression of class struggle.

The election campaigns taking place every five years represent the highest expression of the class struggle between the left and the right forces for power taking over. Political meetings and round table conferences are also the expression of the class struggle.

Another form of class struggle is represented by social, political and cultural debates, shown on TV, between the left and right-wing forces, as well as the journalist interpretations of social, political, economic and cultural problems. The western industry of public opinion formation is also the expression of class struggle. Essayists or writers, when publishing their works, have to be concerned with the problems facing our society. They will have to decide on whose side they will be– the left or the right wing. Neutrality in this great planetary confrontation between progress and retrograde forces has made a big step backwards.

One of the greatest changes in the relations between classes, between the leftist and right-wing forces, refers not only to the form and content of the class struggle, but also to the change of the relations between the class struggle and the cooperation between classes.

Marxism of the 18th and 19th centuries never accepted, because of objective reasons of that period, the possibility to cooperate with the bourgeoisie due to the place of the leading class. Any attempt of ideological or political cooperation with the leading classes was qualified as opportunism and a big treason of the working movement.

Nevertheless, time is changing and, along with it, the political strategy of the revolutionary classes. Although the rich class increased in financial power, it diminished in quantity by a few percents of the population of the developed countries after capital centralisation. In point of politics, it ceased to have the exclusive monopoly of power.

Its economic programmes are in a deadlock. Its social programmes do not correspond to the interests of an important mass of the population. Just because of the failure of its economic and social policy, the civil society demands reforms that are more radical. In this case, the bourgeoisie has to compromise and carry on dialogues. To put it differently, it is forced to make a step backwards.

The economic and political compromises between the right and left forces become a more frequent phenomenon in the daily life of social progress. In the countries where there is a balance between the right and left forces, a new governing form is emerging by the cooperation between the right wing president and the parliamentary leftist majority appointing its government and vice versa.

If the political compromises of the left parties, forces and movements with the leading class are done for the sake of social progress, then they have a positive character.

As an expression of the cooperation between classes, reciprocal compromises can be also seen in numerous economic solutions, in setting up foundations and in increasing charitable actions.

Bill Gates, the inventor of the computer, the wealthiest man in the world, with a fortune of 70 billion dollars, set up the "Bill and Melinda Gates" foundation, the budget of which amounts to 30 billion dollars, for the purpose of helping the poor and sick children.

Warren Buffett, the second wealthiest man in the world (44 billion dollars), declared on the 25th of June 2006, that he will donate 85% of his fortune to five humanitarian foundations. The Mexican Carlos Slim, the third wealthiest man in the world (30 billion dollars), dedicated himself to the leftist movements in Latin America. As an admirer of the Brazilian president Lula, on the 2nd of July 2006, he sustained Lopez Obrador, the candidate of the leftist party of the democratic revolution, in his electoral campaign. The thousands of foundations financed by the big bourgeoisie for charitable purposes are no longer instruments intended to cover the big bourgeoisie's exploitation character but, on the contrary, an instrument with tendencies of compromise between labour and capital.

Just because of the political and economic compromises and of the cooperation with a part of the bourgeoisie, the political leaders of the social-democratic parties, socialist parties and other moderate leftist parties, not considering the left extreme, are replacing more often the phrase "class struggle" by the term of "social dialogue". If a change seems to be needed to mirror the changing of the ratio of forces between classes, then they are legitimately right.

We cannot agree to reciprocal compromises, on the way to social progress, keeping the old terminology of violent revolution and class struggle. The peaceful revolution, the class struggle and the cooperation between classes correspond to the contemporary evolution of social dynamics. It is not important if a cat is black or white, it is important that it should catch mice, as Deng Xiaoping used to say.

5. The Church, the Sate and the Left-Wing Political Parties

(a) The Church, the First Cradle of Civilisation and Culture

When I tried to find a right title to the 5th subchapter, I was aware that I was approaching one of the most complex problems – that of revising the role of the church and theology in .society. When I say "revision", I don't mean the eternal dialogue between science and theology, between Marx' and Feuerbach's materialism and Hegel's idealism, or the issue of knowing if the world evolves by the laws of theology or materialistic philosophy.

The answer to this question is not only a matter of scientific knowledge but also of social practising, of most people's belief in the theological formation of human conscience.

Today, 70% of Europe's inhabitants, about 76% of the two Americas' population and of Australia and, most probably, the same percentage of Asia and Africa, believe in the theological interpretation and in the theological profile of the people of our planet.

In this world of clamant social iniquities, of big losses and disappointments, which are even bigger when welfare is sought in the terrestrial kingdom, people need divine protection for their biological and spiritual needs and spiritual redemption.

In the entire history of our civilisation, the church, theology, Christianity, Islam, Buddhism, Hinduism and the entire scaffolding of their structures have spread confession and love, hope in a better tomorrow of our life. The church, theology and their humanitarian civilising actions were the first carriers of our culture and education, founders of schools, universities, libraries, carriers of our spiritual lives.

The ecclesiastical organisations were the forerunners of the formation of the social regional, state and political structures. Thus, during the Middle Ages, after the fall of the Roman Empire, in Europe and much earlier in Asia, appeared the tendency of subordinating the feeble early social structures under the fosterage of the church, a tendency that was later on transformed into absolutism. Through its inner synergic nature, absolutism turned over the centuries into despotism and the Inquisition.

The Inquisition – the darkest period of our history – although it destroyed the elite of the progressive creative intelligence, it still could not stop the course of history.

(b) The Secularisation and its Limits

The development of production forces, strengthening the structures and statehood, as well as the genuine intellectual and social revolution during the 16th and 17th centuries, culminating in Europe with the French Revolution of 1789, required a new Magna Charta against the absolutism of the church, its separation from the state and the liberation of the society's creative forces to the benefit of social, technical and economic progress.

The separation of the state from the church and self-financing and privatising its activities opened new areas for the development of technique and technology, for revitalising the industrial revolution for the revival and prosperity of sciences, education and culture.

In a certain stage of social development, the positive context of secularity, that had dominated the movements of the society for more than 130 years, turned to the opposite, actually hindering social progress. Ever since the 20th century, a religious crisis has begun to develop which, as Karl Jaspers put it, plays an important role in the spiritual crisis of human conscience.

By having excluded catechism and theological ethics from school, without replacing it by ethics, sociology and civil philosophy, which could have influenced the formation of the new generations in a positive way, the young people have to orient themselves towards the technical and technocratic education which will change them into obedient robots of the big economic profit making machinery.

In fact, the education of the young people is no longer done only by family and school, being left to the influence of the street, the TV and the cosmopolitan and thriller movies, leading to the vulgarisation of the extremist American culture present in all its aspects of banditry, criminality and individualism.

New extensive areas have been opened to create the effect of massive and collective exaltation by the consumption of drugs, sexual debauchery, homosexuality, violence and minor delinquencies in the schools and districts of the outskirts, of banditry and moral decadence.

Abandoned in the street, with no ideals, no juvenile pride, no jobs, faithless and hopeless, a part of the young people find refuge in communities characterised by attitudes of negativism and social debauchery.

The moral and general cultural decadence of the western society is a warning for the left-wing political leaders of the necessity to revise the relations between the church, the state and the left wing political parties. It is only the church and faith in God by its sound theological, philosophical and sociological education and by cooperation with the state and the leftist political parties that can save the society from moral collapse.

The profound debates in the French political, religious, cultural and journalistic circles over the matter of the Islamic veil worn in schools, debates that took place during the years 1996-2003 and were published in the press under the title "Should the law of separation between the church and the state be revised?", with the subtitle "France is no longer secular", are a proof that times are changing. Along with these changes, the claims of the civil society for "modernising the secularity" are gradually replaced by the cooperation and the complicity between the church and the state and the left-wing political parties.

(c) Revision of Secularity. The complicity between the Church, the State and Progressive Parties

In his book "The Church and the State in France", Dominique le Tourneau writes:

"The mutations undergone by the French society in the early 3rd millennium, in relation with the unification and edification of the European area, will really lead to the necessity of revising the type of state separated from the church, as it exists now in a French style. More than half of the paragraphs of the laws dating from 1905, which control the principle of secularisation, have become void."[15]

In fact, this regime of separation between the church and the state is far from being final, as it would seem in the verbal war between the supporters and opponents of secularisation.

The French state already takes 12% from the tax budget, while Germany uses about 10% in order to finance the catholic church, mainly for the conservation of churches as historical monuments.

Poland, Austria, Hungary, Spain, Italy and a series of other European countries are lighting the spark of the surviving secularisation that had been simmering. In Venezuela, Peru, Guatemala, Brazil, Algeria, Libya, the Ivory Coast, the cooperation of the state, the church and the left-wing parties is an integral part of the daily policy of these countries.

By introducing theology and theological ethics in schools, financing the clerical teaching staff, representing the church in the parliament and the local organs of power, bringing back to life charitable organisations, such as, restaurants for the marginalised members of society, old age homes, nurseries for children, humanitarian associations and many other actions would bring about the reorientation of the new generation towards the revival of the great ethical values of our old civilisation.

The cooperation of the clergy with the left-wing political parties and with all those who in their memory still keep feelings of social justice is neither in contradiction to the objectives of the church, nor to the majority of the civil society.

The declaration of the French episcopate in October 1972, after two years of talks between 40 Bishops and the representatives of the labour movement, legitimize a historic truth: Christianity recognizes for its followers the freedom to public opinion, the existence of the class struggle and the agreement of the church with democratic socialism.

The decadence of the developed Western world and the stagnation of most underdeveloped southern countries, as well as the incapacity of the old outdated social systems to settle numerous contradictions, made it possible to spread more quickly the new liberation ideas of the pluralist left-wingers. They acted like a general accelerator in the transformation of the social conscience and in reuniting the great majority of believers around the idea of social and spiritual liberation.

The new social movements in the history of the left-wing thinking have sobered up a part of the clergy to come closer to socialism. Among the Christian clergy–Catholic, Protestant and Slavic, often appear new revolutionary ideas, which blame the economic domination of the big capital and support the cause of the weak in order to meet their social demands.

The ecumenical council of Christians in Uppsala, held in 1968, expressed the solidarity of the Christians with the peoples and classes fighting for their liberation. New movements appeared, like: "The social doctrine of the church", "Social Catholicism", "Looking for new active participation of factory workers", "Increasing the participation of the public power in a more righteous redistribution", "Socialisation of certain means of production", etc.[16]

Pope John Paul II was the closest to the leftist conception over the relationship of labour and capital, in which the capital has to serve the labour and not vice versa. In his Encyclical, the Pope states openly and directly:

"The means of production could not be owned against labour, neither can they be owned just for the sake of possession, because the only legitimate title of their private or public ownership should serve labour alone."

The years 1970s – 1980s have been obviously marked by a new historic period of closeness between the left-wing ideas and movements and the humanitarian and theological aspirations of Christianity.

George Hourdin pointed out : "The idea of a change in the society is obviously necessary, as it has an effect on both partners involved. The meeting of the Christians and socialists has effects not only on the future of socialism, but also on the future of the church".[17]

All the left-wing parties and movements should eventually accept the ideas according to which worldwide socialism is rooted not only in the doctrine of utopian and scientific socialism but also in the primordial sources of Christianity, Islamism and Buddhism. The left-wing parties and movements should reject secularism and the outdated view of the separation between the state and church.

Now, more than ever, only the alliance of the three great social forces, the church, the state, and the political parties of the pluralist left can become a gigantic force of civilisation to save our civilisation from decay and collapse, in order to lead our planet to a new world of solidarity.

6. Ideological Revolution and Social Consciousness

The new industrial, informational and biotechnological revolution is about to change not only the economic, sociological and political dimension of the social development but also outdated ideologies, revolutionising the way of thinking and the very concept of social progress.

The radical change of the theory of scientific socialism constitutes an objective phenomenon of social progress. My goal is not to discover here and now the elements of the changes necessary for the socialist ideology (this being the goal of the global character of my judgment). The purpose of my research is to prove the objective necessity of revolutionising the ideology and theory of scientific socialism and to contribute to find new ways to form the awareness of the fighters and defenders of socialism; at the same time, I want to point out certain gaps between the ideology and formation of the social consciousness.

The Western society spends hundreds of billions of dollars, yens and Euros to orient the social consciousness of citizens to a thought-out direction.

The United States consumes annually for public opinion formation almost as much as it invests in the industry of modern weapons for the so-called self-defense. The other developed countries are not far from the United States. The oversized army of public opinion formers cost as much as the military army.

An entire industry of public opinion formers has emerged. Under the circumstances of the alternation between the left and right wing political parties, the battle for the public opinion formation takes place on one of the most important shooting ranges, between the advanced forces and the backward ones of contemporary society.

The powerful financial oligarchy owns the most important newspapers, the TV, most of the publishing houses, audio-video companies, most of the education and schooling of the young people and probably a part of that clergy that serves the omnipotent capital more than the heavenly divinity.

The Western public opinion formation industry can transform the greatest lies into changed reality.

At the time when The United States were preparing the Iraq war, they were spending billions of dollars to prove the American citizens that the war was justified, being intended to destroy the Iraqi nuclear weapons and to save the humanity from a possible nuclear adventure.

The war started. Saddam Hussein's army was destroyed but the nuclear weapon installations could not be found because no nuclear arming had ever been tried in Iraq. This was the greatest cheat of the new history of our civilisation making the majority of Americans believe in the necessity of an American invasion at the cost of tens of thousands of lives of both parts of the barricade. In fact, the American military machinery serving the financial oligarchy, intended to lay hands on one of the biggest petroleum deposits as the American petroleum resources will be exhausted in 7 or 15 years.

In today's world of the dominance of the financial oligarchy of the big western powers, there is no justice whatsoever. The world is being fed more with lies than with the truth.

However, what is the truth? The philosophy and anatomy of the truth teach us that social sciences contain three kinds of truth. What is true for the exploiting classes is not for the exploited ones. What is true for the exploited classes is not for the exploiting ones. However, does objective truth really exist or as people usually say, is it "the real truth"?

Historic materialism discovers the existence of the objective historic truth. After cleaning a phenomenon from its outer layer of classes and penetrating into its substance, the objective historic truth will be unveiled. This is the truth. It does not have a political class character similar to the truth of mathematics, physics, chemistry or astronomy.

It is in the name of the truth, especially in the name of the historic truth, and of the real truth, that the political movements of the socialist, communist, social-democratic left wing and other progressive parties should find the means and ways of creating a powerful industry of public opinion information and formation. But how and by what means will they do it, as long as the financial possibilities of the left wing parties and movements are not enough to counteract the powerful industries of public opinion formation of the big patronage.

In Brazil, the Universal Church of the Kingdom of God owns a complex of private companies, including its own television company and tens of newspapers and magazines sponsored by the donations of its followers. If the catholic church and the other churches can claim from their followers the tithing, i.e. 10% of their net income, why shouldn't the community of left wing parties followers ask for a voluntary contribution of, say, 2% of their income? In this case, the solidarity fund in France, for example, could count on an annual aid of some billions of Euros for the creation and development of its own industry of social consciousness formation.

If the left wing oriented French people wish real changes in social relations and the protection of their interests – this being valid for all the other countries – then, mere street protests and strikes are not enough. Neither is it enough to vote every five years for the support of electoral programs. The left-wing-oriented people should provide the material circumstances for the creation and reinforcement of the public opinion formation industry that could be capable of opposing in both quality and quantity the powerful media of right wing political parties.

In that case, the spontaneous formation of the left wing electorate's public opinion would turn into an organised strategy of the great ideological offensive.

Although social consciousness does not define the social relations but rather the social relations define the formation and development of the social consciousness, the latter becomes an enormous force of speeding up social progress from the very moment it imposes itself on the masses.

7. For the Durable Unity of the Left Wing Parties and Movements. The New Left International Movement

(a) Positive Effects of Totalitarian Ideology Collapse

In the 2nd chapter, I have tried to show my readers the new turning taken by the pluralist left movement on our planet on the way to the revival of democratic socialism that occurred during the last two decades. Today, over two-thirds of the inhabitants of our planet have chosen the way of their own existence, the way of our future, of the future of our children and grand children.

This is not only the objective immediate result of the social progress of our civilisation, but also, the result of subjective factors, brought about by increasing the social consciousness, of organising the advanced left wing forces and of their capability to overcome somehow the split that had dominated the socialist, communist and labour movement for more than 140 years.

The dissolution of the 3rd Socialist International was followed by that of Kominform (Information Bureau of communist and labour parties) dominated by Stalinism. The dissolution of the Soviet totalitarian socialism and Stalinism and the collapse of the ideology of the past had a decisive role in the expansion of the ideological, political and strategic unity of the left wing movements and parties, in opening up new ways of social progress.

The tendency of ideological closeness among the social-democratic, socialist, communist and labour parties spreading on a worldwide scale as well as increasing the unity of the main goals of movements had a great contribution to the planetary revival of socialism.

(b) Proliferation of Left Wing Parties and Movements

What is the relationship between scientific socialism and

the proliferation of the left wing political parties and movements? Obviously, pluralism of the left wing parties and political movements is an objective process based on the diverse nature of the society and political movements. It is the reflection of social progress. The unique party of the left wing political movements goes back to history. However, at a certain level of pluralism, the proliferation of the multiparty system can become a brake to social progress when important strategic decisions of history are taken and there is no unity of action in these movements.

The most recent failure of the French left wing in the presidential and parliamentary elections as well as the failure of the Portuguese and Italian parties proves my theses. The French left wing was divided into six parties at the first round of elections of May 2002, namely: the Socialist Party, the Communist Party, the Labour Struggle, the Revolutionary Communist League, the Green Party and the fraction of the Socialist Party of Chevénement. During presidential elections, the right wing candidate Jacques Chirac, hardly surpassed the 22% limit in the first round. His potential competitor, the candidate of the Socialist Party, Lionel Jospin, obtained only 17% of the suffrages because of the negative effects of the Chevénement fraction, which took 6% of his votes. Thus he lost the battle for the 2nd round which he would have won with the support of the other left wing parties and movements.

The unexpected rise of Le Pen, of far right orientation, who won a part of the poorest electorate of the socialist party is the result of the surviving "reformist complex" and of "social liberalism" of the French socialist party that could not solve the vital fundamental issues of the civil society.

Analysing the objective causes of the electoral catastrophe, a group of 11 well-known French leaders – deputies of the people, members of the Socialist Party, published in the newspaper "Le Monde" a survey about the reasons of the defeat. They say that those reasons should be found in "the split of pluralist left wing, the campaign's lack of dynamism, the political deadlock in the first round of presidential elections. All these are interrelated with deep-rooted causes like: the persuasive silence referring to fundamental issues facing our citizens, a project which had little to say to the popular layers, especially the employees, the disability to trace the force lines of a great project for our country."[18]

The split of the French left wing and the lack of accuracy in applying a clear and coherent program appeared again two years after the elections at the referendum on the Constitution of the European Union, either for a Constitution of liberal Europe or for a Constitution of social Europe. The left wing on the top of the socialist party pushed the electors to vote against liberal Europe while the centre-left wing pushed them to vote for liberal Europe. The other French left parties also voted against the constitution of liberal Europe.

This time, however, the right wing of the socialist party, together with the right of Jacques Chirac, lost the battle. 53% of the votes were against liberal Europe and for social Europe. In Holland, the failure of the right was even bigger. There is no doubt that if the other European countries had consulted the civil society by a referendum and not by parliamentary ways, the battle for social Europe would have been won. This new phenomenon of the political movement in Europe proves the increase of people's unity in choosing ways to social progress. This unity shows the divided left parties the only possible way to social progress.

Maybe the Brazilian experience of Lula da Silva, president of the labour party in Brazil and president of the Republic, in organising the unity of all left parties and movements together with the theological movement of the "Ray of God" church, could help the French left wing and the other European left wings in finding the best ways of unity in diversity, of social progress.

(c) Left Wing Parties and Movements of all Countries, Unite!

The time has come to replace the Marxist quotation "Proletarians of all countries, unite!" expressed in the Manifesto of the Communist Party, by a new formula of the left wing parties: ***"Left Wing Parties and Movements of all Countries, Unite!***

The labour, intellectual and peasant movements formed their unity in the struggle for national and social liberation. However, in some countries, the leaders of political parties that do not agree, keep a distance. Is it because the invisible hands of the right wing apply the slogan "split and divide" or because some left leaders are incapable of leading such a big movement? It is certainly difficult to give an affirmative answer. Still, how long will internal division dominate the left wing parties and movements? To this question, there is only one answer. It is time for important strategic actions of all left parties and movements to achieve the social revolution.

The general tendency of uniting the left parties brings about, in an objective way, a very new approach of their union, relying on new ideologies and strategies, in a consultative International of the left parties and movements.

After the dissolution of the 3rd Communist International and of Kominform agency of the communist and labour parties, the 4th Socialist International which regrouped 120 parties, played an important part in mobilising the social-democratic, socialist parties and movements and other parties and left wing movements, in the experience exchange according to the guidelines of these parties and movements to the required direction.

The 4th International could have become the symbol of the international union of all parties and movements, which still isn't as such. It is hard to understand that other communist, labour, Trotzkian, left wing green parties and others should remain at the edge of the international union.

Without analysing the sectarianism of those parties and movements, the left wing parties and movements should follow the new logic of internationalism, which is the logic of the union of all left parties and movements. The recent formation of a unique worldwide trade union of labourers shows the new way to the unity of the left wing movements.

Considering the process of globalisation of the financial oligarchy and the union of the bourgeois parties, the left wing parties and movements should be the perfect, new and indubitable union of social dynamics.

The development of the international progressive movement in the era of worldwide revival and globalisation of socialism put onto the agenda two working assumptions of the international union. Either to recompose the Socialist International into a new International of all left wing parties and movements or to dissolve the Socialist International and to form a unique (single) consultative International of left wing parties and movements.

The question is: what way will the international union of left wing parties and movements take? History will give its verdict in the nearest future.

Waiting for the verdict of history, we disagree with the idea of forming two Internationals, which had cost us many victims, misunderstandings and defeats.

Left Wing Parties and Movements of all Countries, Unite!

References

1. Peter Drucker, Au-delà du capitalisme, Dunod, Paris, 1994, p. 35.
2. Robert Heilbroner, Visions du futur, Economica, Paris, pp. 96, 113.
3. Robert Heilbroner, ditto, pp. 113, 114.
4. Karl Marx, interview in a New York World daily, quoted by Jacques Attali: "Marx, l'esprit du monde", ditto, p. 205
5. Olivier Besancenot. La révolution, Flammarion, Paris, 2003, p.105.
6. Pierre Mauroy, ditto, pp.18, 19.
7. Libération, Paris, February 27, 2007.
8. Ségolène Royal, quoted by Laurent Pfastatt in his work, Décripté de A-Z City/Document Paris, 2006, p. 62
9. Jean Jaures, Etudes Sociales, Ressources, Paris, 1979, p. XIX.
10. Jack Lang. Un nouveau régime politique pour la France, Odile Jacob, Paris, 2004, p. 230.
11. Jeremy Rifkin, La fin du travail, La Découverte, Paris, 1996, p. 27.
12. Roland Garnier, Croissance et Cycles, Ellipses, Paris, 1995, p. 72.

13. Guillaume Duval, Le libéralisme n'a pas d'avenir, La Découverte, Paris 2003, pp. 138, 140.
14. François Galichet, La lutte des classes n'est pas morte, Le Monde, January 30, 2009.
15. Dominique le Tourneau, L'Église et l'État en France, PUF, Paris, 2000, p. 120.
16. Quoted from Robert Chapuis, Les Chrétiens et le socialisme, Calmann-Lévy, Paris, 1976, p. 18.
17. Georges Hourdin, Catholiques et Socialistes, Grasset at Fasquelle, Paris, 1973, p. 230.
18. Le Monde, October 18, 2002, Jean Marc Ayrault, Bertrand Delanoe, Eric Besson, Jean Glavany, Elisabeth Guigou, Bruno Le Roux, Martine Lignières-Cassou, François Rebsamen, Daniel Vaillant.

4

Progressive Socialisation of Private Property and Redistribution of National Income

1. The Socialisation of Private Property in the Theory and Practice of Social Progress

(a) Against the Social Progress Defeatism

By the presentation on the social progress path that I have made so far, I have tried to demonstrate the evolution of the socialism as an idea turned into a scientific theory and as a social-political movement in favour of changing the existing condition. Have I managed to make understandable for my readers the objective historical processes of birth and metamorphosis of the great social movement to socialism, its contradictions, strengths and weaknesses? Only readers themselves will judge upon. In my exploits, I have tried to release the phenomena of our progressive movement from the adjacent and nonessential elements of our consciousness. Thus, I have shown the readers the essential trends of the social progress in a crystalline, pure and simplified form.

My following reviews get us closer to the main goal of all the left-wing movements on our planet, namely to the birth and development of new social-economic relations, released from exploitation and alienation, from selfishness and envy, relations which all left-wing people, notwithstanding the differences between them, call the new mode of production, namely the socialist mode of production.

From the very beginning, I feel the moral need to get the readers' and left-wing militants' attention on the imminence of the struggle against the defeatism of some leaders who undermine their own initial socialist identity. The left-wing progressive movements reject defeatism of certain political leaders who continue to deem themselves socialists, but think that the socialist mode of production is by far outdated.[1]

It is true that the totalitarian socialism in the former Soviet states has failed precisely for it has deviated from the line of the democratic, liberal and humanitarian socialism, but it is equally true that the peoples in that area and in the Eastern Europe countries, who lived deep disappointment during the twelve years of transition to capitalism, have opted for the revival of the democratic, liberal and humanitarian socialism. Learning from an outdated historical era, the peoples in a number of countries in Eastern Europe impart more and more confidence to the socialist, social democratic and communist parties. In most Western European countries, the socialist and social democratic parties are in power. The large China has taken over the flag of the world movement of national and social liberation.

The social democratic and communist parties in India are the driving force of the revival. Latin America burns in the fires of national and social revolutions, from Venezuela, Brazil, Chile, Bolivia, Argentine down to Uruguay etc.

After the success of the revolutions in Algeria, Tunisia, Libya, Angola and Zaire, and in anticipation of the revolution in the Ivory Coast, Africa raises the flag of the struggle for national independence, for democracy and socialism.

The great international movement for socialism revival marks the trends of social progress, leading to the establishment of a new mode of production.

Some leaders of the Socialist Party have expressed doubts over the possibility of establishing socialism in France. They rejected the great message of François Mitterrand, who had said that "socialism is possible in France, despite the claims of those who think that capitalism is always able to overcome its contradictions and crises ...; consequently, socialism is possible in France, and the ways and means to achieve it will necessarily be different from those in other countries."[2]

(b) Five Levers to Socialize the Private Property

The mode of socialist production, exchange and distribution is based on the gradual socialisation of the main means of production, on the transformation of the private property into social property through structural reforms.

The objective need of socialisation, of the transformation of private property into public property is not only the basis of the Marxist theory, but it also finds its place even in the theological interpretation by the clergy.

According to Pope John XXIII : "The socialisation is one of the characteristics of our age. It is the progressive multiplication of the relations in the community life: it involves different forms of life and associated activities, as well as institutions of law."[3]

The socialisation of the private ownership of the major means of production currently covers five basic forms:

The first form: the gradual socialisation through the State participation in the capital of the large public companies.

The second form: a broader participation of the workers, clerks and middle-class in the capital of the public companies.

The third form: the increasing of the pension funds participation by the capitalisation of their contribution into public companies.

The fourth form: the continuing growth of the State role in the redistribution of the national income in favour of the civil society and the limitation of the power of the upper middle-class by means of the economic mechanisms of society control.

The fifth form: the development of the associative, social and joint economy structures.

A detailed review of channels for the metamorphosis of the private property into social property, a process most probably lasting until the end of the 21st century, would help to clarify various concrete aspects of the social progress.

2. The Social Shareholding and the Nationalisation of the Private Property

(a) From the Private Shareholding to the Public Shareholding

The historical development of the capitalist private property, through the channels of concentration and centralisation of the production and of the capital, lured the young capitalism into the nets of setting up public companies, as a means of concentration and centralisation of the capital, of increasing the scale of production and the profits.

The growth of the public companies marked the transformation of the property owned by private individuals into capitalist associative and collective property.

During that era, the discovery of a new kind of property organisation, as public companies, as the dominant element of ownership, was a major economic breakthrough, which we may compare with Newton's theory of gravity.

Walter Lippmann wrote in his book "The Free City": "The modern capitalism could not develop if the joint-stock company had not existed."[4].

Walter Lippmann is entirely right. The joint-stock companies, which took the form of trusts and cartels during the period of capitalism, and of holding companies and multinational corporations now-a-days, have become the dominant forms of ownership, the leading economic force that shakes the entire economy and society in the Western developed countries and even in the subordinated countries of the South.

According to UNCTAD, there currently exist in the world 63,000 multinational companies that control 800,000 branches all over our planet, of which 500 giants such as General Electric, General Motors, Ford, IBM (USA), Daimler Chrysler (Germany), Royal Dutch / Shell (The Netherlands and England), BP (England), Toyota (Japan), Total Fina Elf (France), Nestlé (Switzerland), etc.[5]

Large and medium public companies mainly act according to the principle: "one voice, one share". By means of a low number of shares they are holding, which often falls below

15%, they control the entire activity of the company. Basing their policy on the principles of the minor shareholders' domination over the majority, in this way they mobilise the capital shares held by tens of millions of small shareholders of the civil society.

The concentration, the invisible centralisation of the capital and the competition among the large companies, which require huge financial resources to renew the technology, in correlation with the decreasing trend in the rate of profits, impose the financial oligarchy to mobilize not only the petty bourgeoisie's financial means, but also the savings of the civil society.

The genesis, the existence, the development and the flourishing of all these multinational companies and of thousands of other national companies have been possible, thanks to the mobilisation of the capital through stock exchange sales, of which value often aims for 10 US dollars or Euros. General Motors have mobilised the capital of several million of shareholders to build their empire, which exploits about 165,000 employees worldwide.

In France, England, The Netherlands, Italy and other countries, the large national and multinational companies have made fortunes and imposed their domination based on the same principles of mobilising the savings of the small shareholders.

In France, immediately after the Second World War, the annual savings of the families exceeded by far the annual gross savings of the private companies. Between the years 1959-1973, they amounted to 42% of the annual global economy, while the savings of the private companies reached 25.7% only.[6] In almost all Western developed countries, the mass of the annual savings of the civil society highly exceeds that of the capital held by the important major shareholders.

(b) The citizens, Potential Owners of the Capital Stock

This new phenomenon in the evolution of the national wealth in favour of the civil society is still one of the important clues of the major changes in the relationship between labour and the capital, in favour of the labour.

Most members of the civil society have invested a part of

their modest savings in the purchase of shares issued by the companies which they used to work for or by others.

Therefore, after the Second World War, during the Thirty Glorious years, the ideological sponsors of the West updated the theory of the popular capitalism, which essentially consists in attracting a larger part of the civil society on the way of the financial ownership. In 1983, in the U.S.A, 76 million workers and clerks were holding 19% of the total shares. In France, according to a survey conducted in 2001 in the top forty public companies, the number of the worker- and clerk-shareholders reached 1.6 million. During the same year, their cumulative investments amounted to 520 billion Euros, namely 10% of the total capital of the private companies.

According to the newspaper Le Monde, in the largest forty French joint-stock companies, 25-80% of the workers and clerks were shareholders in the companies where they were working; Total Fina Elf – 77%, Air France – 72%, PNB-Paribas – 80%, France Télécom – 76%, Orange – 64%, Renault – 80%, Alcatel – 51%, Crédit Lyonnais – 73%, Aventis – 58%, Pechiney – 43%, Lafarge – 45%, Suez – 34%, Saint Gobain – 25%, Bouygues – 25%, etc.[7]

The sale of a portion of the capital stock of the largest public company, EDF-GDF (electricity and gas), during July-November 2005, was an unprecedented success. Five million French people, most of them civilian shareholders, bought the State's shares.[8]

Their financial participation in the capital stock is much smaller than their will, desire and consciousness to influence, in a certain manner, as shareholders of their companies, the company's decisions that would affect their interests. Their participation ranges between 2.5% – 10%, in some cases amounting to 20%, which is, economically, perfectly justified in the present moment, when the net nominal wages and the relatively high prices of the apartments, rental, transport and cultural services do not leave enough room for more savings and investments in public companies.

In these most recent years, due to the slowing growth of the economic field and of the revenues of the civil society, there has been noticed the decline in the savings of the small shareholders.

In the United States, at the end of the 1990s wretched years, the people's savings rate dropped to 4.6% of available resources in 1995, to 3.6% in 1997, to 2.3% in 2000, to reach 1.2% in 2004.[9] Similar such trends are recorded, in different proportions, in other developed countries in Europe.

The phenomenon of temporary loss of the civil society's savings was favourable at a time for some Western analysts of the economic development, who expressed their pessimism about the future of the workers and clerks ownership. Without citing them – for, in general, this is not my method of ideological dialogue – they say that the civil shareholding is a stupid idea, which has no future, that it is a matter of luxury intended to the best paid employees etc. Consequently, their thinking is like this: the militancy of the left-wing parties and of their leaders, who see the shareholding development as a way to socialize the capital and to protect the interests of the working classes, has no future.

(c) The Citizens, the Actual Potential Major Owners of the Joint-Stock Companies

The proponents of the thesis which does not support the citizens' shareholding judge the evolution according to Feuerbach's metaphysics and not to the legitimate dialectics of the historical materialism. It is true that, towards the end of the 20th century, the percentage of civil society's savings became relatively low, as a result of the stagnation and decline of the population's purchasing power. But it is equally true that, in the evolution of Western society over the next 50 years – even if the economic growth rate will be at the level of the rate calculated by Joseph Schumpeter, a 2% rate, which has been taken as a general rule for the Western development – we can expect, excluding a catastrophe, the GDP per capita and, respectively, the personal income of the civil society to double, and, during the next one hundred years, to grow about four times.

Let's have a brief look at History! In France, the GDP calculated on the basis of the prices during the year 1980 increased 3.58 times in 40 years, between 1949 and 1989.[10] In the U.S.A., according to Schumpeter's calculations, the total available production increased 2.7 times in 50 years, between 1928 and 1978. Notwithstanding the postwar years of exceptional growth, if we reduce the calculations to the traditional increase rate of 2%, the gross domestic product per inhabitant will grow at least 2 times in 50 years. By extrapolating the traditional rate for the next 50 years, we expect to double the GDP, in the pessimistic variant, and to triple it, in the optimistic version. If the price conditions and the demographic pressures do not change, in France, the current gross domestic product per inhabitant will probably rise, according to the first variant, from 28,000 Euros in 2000 to about 56,000 Euros in 2050.

It is quite understandable that the evolution of the gross domestic product growth will be proportionately reflected in employees' salaries. If in 2000, the average salary in France was about 1,500 Euros and a family income - for, most often, both spouses are working – amounted to about 3,000 Euros, it will rise, in the pessimistic version, to 6,000 Euros per month for the next 50 years, namely to 72,000 per year. If a four-member family's expenses for food, housing, transport and cultural needs increase in absolute terms, then, in the future, they will reduce relatively. In this case, we may predict, with more or less risk, a noticeable increase in the volume of savings.

Therefore, any version we may apply for the future salary growth, we can hope for the civil society's savings increase up to at least 25-30% of their personal income. In 1975, in the U.S.A., and in 1969, in France, this percentage reached the level of 13%. And no one in their right mind could deny the savings growth over the next 50 years, not to mention the next 100 years! At that time, the will and desire of the civil society – which are already obviously noticeable morally and mentally – of investing a minimum share of their savings in the purchase of shares issued by the companies which they are working for, will become one of the major propelling forces for the socialisation of the private property and for the social progress. This will become to be in ways that Marx had not guessed, and could not have imagined. The employees will then enjoy two kinds of personal income, one from their own salary and the other one from the dividends resulted from their capacity as shareholders.

"Certainly, Marx did not imagine - Philippe Manière wrote : The capitalist system, which he absolutely detested, would become one day the driving belt of his social project! The victory of the market economy, which has practically buried the state-related utopias, truly opens the way for a genuinely new collective ideal, which rightfully claims, similarly to Marxism, for the subordination of the economic power to higher purposes. Dispersed in many hands - our hands - but featuring unlimited virtual strength, the power of the capital is currently a fearsome weapon against power abuses and against assaults on the values we love. From now on, the employers have found their masters: all of us."[11]

(d) The Public Companies, Transmission Belts Toward Socialism

Considering the evolution of the current Western developed society, the surveys prepared by Philippe Manière are not prophetic, they are rather deeply scientific.

The increased participation of the civil society in the joint-stock capital gradually changes the character of the private property, reduces the amount of private capital and relatively and absolutely increases the registered capital and, in correlation with it, all the other rights and powers of use, usufruct and abuse. It gradually changes the relationships between labour and the capital, and mitigates their mutual antagonism and eventually leads to the homogenisation of the society and to the disappearance of the classes and of the class differences in a distant historical perspective.

Joseph Schumpeter predicted the fate of the stock companies long before Philippe Manière, namely 50 years earlier, and – it is true - with less precision, for it could not be otherwise ... "The modern joint-stock company, although an offspring of the capitalist evolution, transforms the bourgeoisie's mentality toward the socialism, it gradually narrows the area where the capitalist initiatives may be exercised – moreover, it will end up by destroying the very roots of this regime." .. "The capitalist evolution shapes the phenomena and souls on account of the socialism."[12]

Thus, the joint-stock companies, which were the mainstay of the development and strengthening of the private property, the essential ring of the capitalist chain development, convert to their opposite. Gradually, they become what Philippe Manière called the "driving belts" of the socialism, or, as Joseph Schumpeter wrote, "the evaporator of the material substance of the property". To be clear, the public companies become the main form of socialisation for the private property and of its transformation into social property.

"As Peter Drucker had predicted - Philippe Manière wrote – the shareholding capitalism is the only one that actually can put into practice the collective ownership over the means of production. However, it is also the sole to give the workers the word and the power, even off the economic sphere: from now on, the employers will live under the constant pressure of their shareholders, who, directly and indirectly, are their employees, too. So, the market is the one achieving the promise of the proletarian dictatorship, which, in the eyes of a democrat, is admissible in respect of the market role."[13]

At the dawn of the 21st century civilisation, completely new horizons are opening toward the socialisation of the private property and toward the expanding of the new integration social relations, as well as toward the abolition of the exploitation of man by man, toward the elimination of any market mystification of the human species. But let's not forget History!

In the most decisive moments, the question persists: "Who will win over whom?" The fetishistic power of money, of the capital and of the training techniques of the consciousness of a nation and of their underground networks of information may release from exclusion, as in 1929 - 1933 in Europe, their extreme right-wing parties. Then, the transfer of the dictatorship of the economy finance capital to the politics of the peoples and nations may lead to the degeneration of the revolution into a counter-revolution.

But we live with the great hope that the peoples, trained by the history of the fascist counter-revolution, will develop in due time the social immunity, for this is able to provide the unbeatable ways of the social progress.

3. The Retired Persons as Major Investors in Joint-Stock Companies

(a) The Role of the Pension Funds in the Socialisation of the Stock Capital

The increasing participation of the workers and clerks in the capital of the public companies is the potential virtual force of the socialisation of private property. The payments made by the employees to pension funds in the Anglo-Saxon areas, USA, England, Netherlands, Denmark, Switzerland and Ireland – as in other countries they are still in their setting-up phase – signal the trend of the major domination by the pensioners' capital in the public companies of these countries, its actual potential in accelerating the process of socialisation of the private property.

In the USA, according to Olivier Pastré and Michel Vigier, the assets of the retirees' private companies were worth 30,000 billion in 2002, namely two and a half times more than the financial public companies capitalisation with the stock-exchanges, or two and a half times more than the GDP of the USA in 2004.[14]

According to experts, in England, the ethical investments – as so often called – amounted in London, in 2000, to just over 100 billion US Dollars, in the Netherlands to over 160 billion Dollars etc.

These are huge private companies that collect the employees' payments to the pension funds and invest them as their own capital in joint-stock companies. From several dozen companies thirty years ago, they have multiplied like mushrooms after rain. Hundreds of new public companies, under the common names of pension insurance funds, have begun to shake the economy of the developed capitalist countries.

In the USA, the largest pension fund is Fidelity, in Boston, which is worth around 900 billion Dollars, three times more than the national budget of France.

Further on, there are the Capital Group in Los Angeles, worth about 500 billion Dollars, Calpers, with 180 billion Dollars, Scudler in New York, which has a capital of 130 billion Dollars. In England, the pension funds in Edinburgh are worth 370 billion Dollars, etc.[15]

A few decades ago, the human mind could not imagine, and much less would have designed the fantastic dimensions of the retirement insurance funds. Undoubtedly, they are fabulous financial resources of the working class and of the retired persons, invested in the public companies of retirement funds and, therefore, they express, de facto, but not legally, the socialisation of the private property and its gradual transition to the collective property.

Commenting on the role of the pension funds in the property socialisation, Peter Drucker wrote:

"If we defined socialism as "the employees' ownership of the means of production"–and this is also the orthodox definition and the sole rigorous definition–, the USA are the first true socialist country."[16]

Drucker was right when he discovered the possible trends of the retirement funds evolution. I would only add an essential correction. Through the pension funds, the USA, is potentially the first country that can transform the capitalist private ownership over the shares into socialist collective ownership.

However, between the potential possibilities and the actual reality, there is always the great gap between the oligarchic employers, who are opposing the democratisation of the management of the pension funds and joint-stock companies, and the will of civil society, which wants to control the mentioned funds.

How are the contradictions between the interests of some and others acting practically? The answer to this question reveals the very substance of the extraordinary invention of the retirement insurance funds.

Climbing down from the masked and fuzzy face of the pension funds to the clear and naked essence of the American mechanism of capitalisation of the retirees' contributions, we may find out two sides of the same coin: a positive one, which objectively leads to the socialisation of private property, and a second, negative one, that removes the pensioners and their representatives from the participation in the general meetings and the boards of directors of the joint-stock companies, for they are the effective owners of their funds.

In other words, the workers, the clerks and the pensioners are, de facto, the main co-owners of the public companies and, in legal terms, they are just the source for the collection of the monthly dues into the pay desks of the joint-stock companies that manage the pension funds as if their own property. Their only legal right is to collect, after they retire, a part of the annuity as a pension.

Each future retiree pays the private pension funds a monthly amount, comprised in the range of 3-7% of their wages. When they reach retirement, the workers and clerks who invested in pension funds receive a certain annuity as a pension. However, they are not the nominal owners of their savings invested in joint-stock companies. When a pensioner dies, their savings, invested in joint-stock companies, do not return to their successors, but rather to the mentioned companies. In this manner, to the extent of the dues collection, the pension capital doubled after the one generation was replaced by another one, entering the retirement insurance funds and not those of the civil society. In substance, the companies managing pension funds do acquire the capital intended to the pension rights, use it and reinvest it in joint-stock companies as if their own capital and as to their own choice. Prospective investor-pensioners are volunteer donors of money, they are an inexhaustible source of capital accumulation for the public companies and they are the beneficiaries of only a portion of their work product.

(b) The way of Pension Funds Capitalisation in the Latin-Germanic Area

In France and in the other countries of the Latin-Germanic area, the establishment of the pension insurance funds, based on the principle of the dues capitalisation, is still in the stage of gestation.

In the countries of the Latin-Germanic area, the workers and taxpayers pay, until their retirement, the pension funds from where, every month, after the age of 65, pensions are extracted for payment to the retired people. In principle, the extension of the life expectancy to 77, and, over the next 20-50 years, to the age of 80, will increase the army of retirees and will create major disruptions in the normal operating mechanism of the retirement insurance. Therefore, the transition to the Anglo-Saxon mechanism becomes an objective necessity of the action of the natural demographic laws of the society progress.

Although France has not capitalisation for the retirement insurance funds yet, Guillaume Duval writes, "this is no hindrance for it being in the first row of this movement, especially through the FEFSI (the European Federation of Funds Managers), the first European country to manage collective retirement insurance funds, with 889 billion Euros under way of settlement, as compared to the 370 in Great Britain."[17]

4. Privatisation, the Partial Socialisation of the Capital of Large Businesses and Redistribution of National Income

(a) Privatisation Contrary to the Interests of the Civil Society

As we have found out by reading the previous chapters, the ways of the social property emergence and development, as the economic basis for the socialism of the 21st century, are quite different from those of the 19th and the 20th centuries. The nationalisation of the main means of production, as the only way to socialise the property, as well as the collectivisation of the agriculture, are now a matter of history, with all of the past obsolete inventory.

Thus, when we talk about the partial socialisation, we do not deny the nationalisation totally. We stress upon the need for nationalisation only in economic sectors that can serve the longest and the best the interests of the civil society. Therefore, the occurrence and development of the public sector of the economic and social activity in all social-economic systems are and remain the first and main division of labour in the public and private sectors.

At the end of the Second World War, under the influence of the catastrophic consequences of the global economic crisis of 1929 - 1933 and of the damages caused by the war in Europe and also of the inability of the private sector to revive the economic growth, in the developed countries a wave of the left-wing parties grew ever stronger in favour of the partial nationalisation of some social-economic objectives, as a possible effective lever of the State for a new and accelerated economic development of Europe.

Thus, in France, they nationalised some of the energy, transport, telecommunications and banks. In England, the Workers Party nationalised the mining industry, part of the energy and transport. In Germany, the state controlled the entire cash flow, nationalising the Zentrale Deutsche Bank. In the 1970s and 1980s, the "state" companies in the public sector owned about 25-35% of the total economic activity of Western Europe.

Indeed, we may say today, taking a step back into history, that the public sector, the state economic sector and the increase of the state role in the redistribution of the national wealth in favour of the socialisation of labour and not to the benefit of the capital are the elements which, in the 1960s-1980s, were the strong vectors of Europe's economic boom.

If we consider the development of the state sector from the point of the theoretical analyses of the partial nationalisation processes, we will be inclined to believe that just the public sector development and the socialisation of the national income redistribution in favour of the civil society were the foundation of the genesis of the economic basis of socialism.

The American financial tycoons and other representatives of the capitalism globalisation understood this much earlier than some Marxists, social democrats etc., when they developed, through the International Monetary Fund and the World Bank, the total privatisation strategy, which has acquired worldwide dimensions.

In fact, the main purpose of the privatisation was not to make the enterprises profitable, but to destroy the potential roots of socialism, not only in the developed Western countries, but also in the medium developed countries in the East (after the collapse of socialism) and in the underdeveloped countries in the South.

Unfortunately, many socialist and social democratic parties in Europe have been fooled by the privatisation. After the first wave of privatisation, the state public sector of the economy has declined from 25%-35% to 5%-20%.

Alain Griotteray divided the European Union countries into three groups, according to the size – now-a-days diminished – of the public sector.[18]

- France and Italy, Portugal and Greece, 18%-24%
- Germany, Spain, Ireland, Denmark, Belgium and The Netherlands, 9%-12%
- Great Britain and Luxemburg, 4%-8%

The privatisation has had, on the one hand, negative effects by the actual economic slowdown and, on the other hand, by the depletion of the state treasuries, largely needed to cover social needs. The privatisation directly limited and affected the interests of the civil society.

(b) The Objective Need for Socialisation

The re-nationalisation of the privatised companies and the partial socialisation, up to the optimal limit, of the state participation in the capital stock of the enterprises are not a subjective nostalgia of the extreme left-wing and, much less, a utopian requirement of the civil society. It has its roots in the contemporary needs of the society, in view of ending the perpetual budget deficits, which have already reached fabulous amounts of about 5% – 8% of the GDP, in order to cover the increasing financial needs of the society for the development of infrastructures, of education, science, culture, of social security.

At this stage of the right- and left-wing forces ratio, the optimal limit of the state participation in the capital of the large enterprises may be limited, in the future, by the major capital of the shareholder who owns the main package of shares. If a main shareholder is holding, let's say, 32% of the shares, the state could redeem part of shares held by the other shareholders, in a proportion of, let's say, 25%. It will be a compromise that does not affect the vital interests of the main shareholder, but ensures the vital interests of the population and the additional revenues of the state in order to meet the ever increasing social needs.

However, the wheel of history does not stop turning here. In our scientific projections, we have no moral right to stop at the way third or half. In the not too distant history of the social progress perspective, perhaps within 35 and even 50 years and more, the left-wing civil society may raise the matter of the State major participation in the registered capital of the large companies.

Indeed, the major participation of the State in the registered capital will change from bottom to top the role of the large companies in the development of the economy and of the society. It is the very matter of the essence of the public companies bases. In this manner, the decisions monopoly passes into the hands of the State, of the society.

Under such circumstances, we may ensure and guarantee the participation of the trade unions and of the associate producers in the boards of administration of the enterprises. Consequently, in this way, the major participation of the state and of the civil society in the registered capital of the large companies becomes the new decisive and irrevocable vector of the transition from capitalism to socialism.

(c) The Socialisation of the National Wealth Redistribution

By analysing the process of the spontaneous redistribution of the national wealth and the metamorphosis of the general law of the capitalist accumulation, we enter a new area of redistribution of the national wealth (GDP), or of secondary distribution, which goes more and more in favour of labour, and less and less in favour of the capital.

The national wealth is redistributed as the state budget, by the force of the state law and of its specialised structures. So that, it was and still is a matter of the state superstructure and of these parties and political classes that hold the power. It always plays a certain role in the development of the economic basis of these classes, or of other classes holding the power.

The redistribution of the national wealth acts as the mandatory collection to the central state budget and to the regional budgets of the companies' taxes on profit, of the taxes on real estates, of the import-export customs duties, of the VAT and of the companies' contributions to the social insurance and of the taxes on the employees' salaries, as well as of the various municipal fees.

Unlike the primary distribution, the redistribution of the national wealth is a conscious, organised action of these classes and social segments holding the power. Therefore, it may have two tendencies. The right-wing parties, when holding the power, try to exercise the redistribution in their classes, and the left-wing ones, when holding the power, in the interest of the classes they represent - as much as possible.

During the period of alternation in power between the left- and right-wing parties, the left-wing parties, when holding the power, exercise the redistribution much more in the interest of the civil society. A new phenomenon of the social progress can be noted, the general trend of socialising the redistribution of the national wealth.

The general trend of socialising is not my scientific discovery. Since the 1980s of the 20th century, the professional analysts of the economic boom of the developed West realised the new phenomenon of the socialisation of the national income redistribution. In his book, "The economic history of the 20th century", Jean-Charles Asselin analyzes the increasing share of the public expenditures in the distribution of gross domestic product (GDP) in the most developed Western countries. The author presents data according to which the state's share within the distribution increased in the OECD countries from 32.3% of the GDP in 1968-1973, to 43.8%, in 1990. France, which, during the same period, increased the state participation in the distribution to 50%, is approaching the top of the redistribution line. Japan, by its 32.3% of the GDP, shows the lowest level of state participation in the redistribution.[19]

It is obvious that the way of rescue consists in opening the taps for new sources of collecting a portion of the profits of the private public companies into the State's treasuries, in order to balance the inflows and outflows of money and to meet the constantly growing social needs of the society. These are the alpha and omega of social progress.

(d) The New Role of the State in the Economic Development of the Society

The relentless growth of the productive forces of the developed capitalist countries, the evolution and modernisation of their economic basis have had positive effects on the social changes of the social superstructure and, first of all, on the state's economic role in the development of the society. The state, as the most conservative and more stable part of the social superstructure, is living its positive metamorphosis, despite the opposition shown by the wealthier classes.

From its role as a creator of the legal, economic and super-structure conditions needed to perpetuate the existing system, and from the role of defender of the class interests, the State becomes one of the most active vectors, the instrument of the social progress of the alienated, marginalised and exploited classes.

The metamorphosis of the economic role of the State in the development of the society meets some tough resistance from the wealthier classes belonging to the financial plutocracy, who see the state as the main danger of limitation and restriction of their economic and political domination. Therefore, the political, ideological and praxeologic attacks, against the state property, so that it should be privatised, and against the economic expansion of the State's role, sustained under the logo "the less State, the more efficiency", are actually directed against the economic interests of the civil society.

Today, even the veterans, most convinced of the unlimited role of the market in the societies of the developed West, begin to see the limits of the market. Considering this, Joseph E. Stiglitz wrote: "Simultaneously with the globalisation, the problems I have just mentioned, the fair role of the state, the market boundaries, the way the economy shapes the behaviour of individuals and the society, are discussed all over the world ... the globalisation affects the type of society that is currently setting up on the planet ... Is there a different perspective, based on global social justice and on the balance between the state and the market? We have to fight for this very perspective!"[20]

The political dialogue between the left- and the right-wing parties and their theoretical interpretations on the theme of the economic role of the state lose their meaning, for the practice has already passed a verdict. Today, the state's economic role in the society development grows more and more in all countries. This role gains an ever more positive character. In the hands of the progressive classes of the society, the state becomes the most powerful tool for the big changes on the way of the revival of socialism.

The general decadence of the developed capitalism and the transition to socialism update an old ideological problem, in a unique manner. "What is the destiny of the state's economic role during the transition from capitalism to socialism? Have Marx's concepts about the "disappearance of the state" and the state replacement by the associations of producers, which Lenin took over later and developed in his famous work "The State and the Revolution", and which Kardelj, the ex-Yugoslavian, adapted to the specific conditions of the Yugoslavian self-managing socialism, adequate historical resonances over the birth and development of the Western socialism? Answering this key-question opens a new site for the theoretical scientific research.

Checking in practice the reflections I did on the dangerous and thorny way of the research has convinced me, more and more, of the fact that the disappearance of the state and of its economic functions refer to a distant future. The laws of the genesis, development and disappearance of a social-economic phenomenon prove that, in principle, the disappearance of a phenomenon or of a category, as the final stage of a process, cannot interfere in the starting phase, but only in the final phase. The state will be replaced by associations of producers. It is a long-lasting objective historical process and toward this horizon the generations of our planet's nations are advancing slowly, but surely. Time is not so much important as is the objective process of social progress.

5. The Associative, Social and Joint Economy

(a) The Associative Joint Economy – an Integral Part of the Socialisation

The first associations of non-union and non-political nature appeared in Europe in the late 19th century, at the end of the first industrial revolution, as an attempt of the civil society to diversify its instruments of solidarity in the defense against the attacks by the bourgeoisie against its vital interests. Therefore, particularly after the French Revolution, there have come forward and have more and more multiplied the associations, the clubs of artists, of writers, of public employees, of students, of health professionals, the cooperative associations of farmers etc., which expressed their solidarity in defending their particular interests. They exceeded often the limits of the social and economic solidarity and vexed the political and economic interests of the ruling classes.

In 1810, in order to limit the new associative movement and bring it under his control, Napoleon introduced in the new criminal law the obligation of legally certifying all the associations and clubs with more than 20 members, provided they should comply with the restrictive clauses stipulated in the new criminal laws. The restrictions imposed by Napoleon to the expanding of the associative movements remained in force for over 90 years.

Thus, Napoleon's criminal law has created a vacuum in the structures of the social organisations of the French resistance, as well as some structural differences as compared to the Anglo-Saxon area, where the associative movement reached larger sizes.

Only the transition from the free competition capitalism to imperialism, as well as the transformation of the workers, unionist and socialist movement into a new political force for progress, through the democratisation of the social relations, freed France from the Code of Napoleon, opening new spaces for the development of the associative movement of solidarity.

Between the two world wars, the associative movement in Europe diminished more or less, almost disappearing in the areas of fascist Europe. Only with the defeat of the fascism and the victory of democracy, after the economic boom of the 1960s and 1970s, the movement of the European associative movement reached exponential proportions.

In France, in 1990-1992, according to a survey of CREDOC *[the Research Center for the Study and Survey of Life*

Conditions], every citizen was a member of one or more associations. More specifically, 45.6% of the active population aged over 18, or a number of 20 million people out of about 30 million employees, were associated in one or more organisations. The associative movement – according to the same investigation – numbers about 2 million employees and has an annual budget of around 50 billion Euros.

The scopes of the solidarity association organisations cover the largest area of social interests and, consequently, the types of associations are widely different from each other. They include sports, cultural, educational, charitable activities, student and youth, family, consumers, environmental activities, women's rights to equal work and equal wages, agricultural cooperative and commercial organisations, and many others.

In the field of the primary agricultural and handicraft production, of the transport and trade, their protagonists are united in cooperatives, which they consider an effective means of maintaining their independence from the large companies. The cooperative movement has won, almost all over Europe, sizes large enough.

In the agriculture area, there actively operate 3,700 cooperatives, which achieve an annual turnover of 66 billion Euros. Nine of ten French farmers are organised into cooperatives. The primary production is organised as family farms and the marketing is the competence of the cooperative organisations. The production cooperatives (19,000 members) are not too entrenched, for the large agricultural farms, which require considerable investments, are not part of the French farmers' tradition.

One hundred thousand artisans are members of handicraft cooperatives. Seventy thousand citizens are members of cooperative apartment owners, 60,000 citizens are members of HLM (moderate rental housing) cooperatives, 1,500,000 citizens are members of consumer cooperatives, 13.1 million citizens are members of credit cooperatives etc.[20]

(b) Principles and Scopes of the Joint Economy Organisations

The principles of the joint social economy organisations, as seen from Thierry Jeantet's point of view, are the following:

- "Free adhesion of the individuals
- Democratic management (one person, one voice)
- Non-individual accumulation of profits (fair distribution of the surplus)
- Establishment of a collective patrimony (absence of capital for associations and also for mutual organisations, non-shareable reserves for cooperatives)
- Solidarity
- Usefulness and quality of services and products (accessibility of prices, respect for the persons' health, for the environment ...)
- Autonomy from the State".[21]

The extraordinary pressure of the associations and cooperatives may be interpreted by the rising of the social consciousness of the civil society for the need to reinforce the defense against the assaults of the dominant classes.

The association scopes have not only a social-defensive, cultural, moral and educational character, but also, most often, an economic character, a character of association in production, distribution, transports and recreation.

As Jean-Louis Laval wrote, the main objective of the symbiosis of the social, cultural and moral values of the associations with the economic incentives is the "re-composition of the economic and social relations .... that passes through the strengthening of the activities which are developing under the effect of a 'drive for reciprocity', thanks to a cross between the human resources (employees and volunteers) and financial resources (subsidies, fees, donations, revenues from sales of services)".[22]

The development of the associative and social solidarity is a new phenomenon of the social progress in the socialisation of the private property off the property and not inside companies. In fact, this is the process of protecting the small and medium private properties and of placing them in the field of the social movement. This new phenomenon of the pressure increasing in geometric progression by the social solidarity associations, springing from the new industrial and informatics revolution on the background of the negative effects of the market economy, exceeds the social dimensions and penetrates deeper into the economic sphere.

In the social-economic, educational, cultural, social and productive sphere of the social activity, the associative enterprises occupy quite a place. They are one of the major vectors of the mutual stimulation and of the social solidarity emulation, for strengthening the social cohesion of the marginalised classes and segments of the society.

Therefore, they must find their rightful place in the social progress. They must take a firm stand in the social-cultural and social-political pyramid of the social movements. They raise the legitimate question of knowing their own position in the social progress of the future.

The primordial issue of the distant prospects of the development of the social solidarity and cultural movement over the next 50 years is not just a matter of forecasting, but also a matter of choice for the left-wing parties with regard to their strategy on the social solidarity economy. Is the social solidarity economy an integral part of the birth and development of the new social-economic production way, or is it just an alternative economy that serves to protect certain everyday interests of the society?

The answer to this question is logical and historical. If today, at the beginning of the 21st century, the solidarity movements are the most effective instruments for the protection against the attacks of the large capital against their interests, tomorrow they will objectively turn into social-political movements, and the day after into new social-economic relationships, as part of the new mode of production.

References

1. Lioı əl Jospin, Cent ans de parti socialiste français, Le Monde, April 23, 2005.
2. François Mitterrand, Oeuvres complètes. Rencontre, Paris, 1994, p. 73.
3. Qouted from Robert Chapuis, Les chrétiens et le socialisme, Calmann-Lévy, Paris, p. 108.
4. Quoted from Raymond Barre. Économie politique, P U F, 1955, p. 412.

5. Jean Ziegler, Les nouveaux maîtres du monde, Fayard, Paris, 2002, p. 108.
6. Thomas Piketty, L'économie des inégalités, La Découverte, Paris, 1997, p. 153.
7. Le Monde, Paris, October 4, 2002.
8. Le Monde, Paris, November 19, 2005.
9. Courrier International, December 2004, p. 31.
10. Roland Garnier, Croissance et Cycles, Ellipses, Paris, 1995, p. 54.
11. Philippe Manière, Marx à la corbeille, Stock, Paris, 1999, p. 11.
12. Joseph Schumpeter, Capitalisme, Socialisme et Démocratie, Payot, Paris, 1990, pp. 218, 304.
13. Philippe Manière, ditto, p. 258.
14. Olivier Pastré, Michel Vigier, Le capitalisme déboussolé, La Découverte, Paris, 2003, p. 134.
15. Philippe Manière, ditto, p. 74.
16. Peter Drucker, The Unseen Revolution: How Pension Fund Socalism Came to America, Harper & Row, 1976, p. 78.
17. Guillaume Duval, Le libéralisme n'a pas d´avenir. La Découverte, Paris, 2003, p. 12.
18. Allain Griotteray, Mieux privatiser, La Découverte. Paris, 1999, p. 198.
19. Jean-Charles Asselain, Histoire économique du XXème siècle, Presses de Sciences Po & Dalloz, Paris, p. 410.
20. Joseph Stiglitz, Quand le capitalisme perd la tête. Fayard, Paris, 2003, pp. 376, 383.
21. Thierry Jeantet, L'économie sociale face au XXIème siècle, La Documentation Française, Paris, 2001, p. 54.
22. Thierry Jeantet, ditto, Introduction générale, p. 3.

[illegible] 1998.

5. Jean Ziegler, [illegible], Paris, 2002, p. 108.

6. [illegible] La Découverte, Paris, [illegible], p. 118.

7. Le Monde, Paris, [illegible].

8. Le Monde, Paris, November [illegible].

9. Courrier International, December [illegible].

10. [illegible] Paris, 1998, [illegible].

11. [illegible] 1998, p. 24.

12. Joseph [illegible] Paris, [illegible], pp. 213-[illegible].

13. [illegible], op. cit., p. 238.

14. [illegible] La mondialisation [illegible].

15. [illegible] op. cit., p. [illegible].

16. Peter Drucker, The [illegible] Revolution [illegible].

17. [illegible], Paris, [illegible].

18. [illegible], Paris, [illegible].

20. [illegible].

21. [illegible].

22. [illegible], Paris, [illegible].

23. [illegible].

5

The Global Reorganisation of Inter-State Relationships and their New Collaboration and Cooperation Relations

1. Global Development of Socialism and International and Social Integration

(a) Global Revival of Socialism, a Foundation for Socialist Globalisation

As demonstrated by our previous analyses, the global revival of socialism is not a figment of my imagination. The analysis, presented in this book, depicts real processes, emerged out of the ever-growing internal and external contradictions of the developed West, of the moderately-developed East and of the under-developed South.

What I have been trying to seize from the contemporary reality of the processes going on in the global society is the substance, the very essence of our civilisation's actual movements. I have been trying to depict these movements in their purest forms, when get to be intelligible and tangible for all people concerned about their own future, namely about the common fate of mankind.

The revival of socialism brings the re-establishment of all the virtues of the socialist theories: social movement and determined social relationship, which open up new approaching towards solving the many handicaps that had to be faced during the implementation of socialist ideas. The revival of socialism doesn't imply only making available the existing virtues, but also (or even more so) discovering new values and dimensions of socialism, emerging from the implementation of all the processes which accompany social progress.

The resuscitation of socialism becomes a globalised phenomenon. It arises from an objective need, from actions, from the general laws of social progress; it emerges from the latent social revolution, called upon to replace the old social relationships with new ones. The revival of socialism can have, though, a violent nature in circumstances lacking enough freedom and democracy, in societies where the ruling classes oppress the will of the people. Each old democracy gives birth to a new one, just as all ancient violence brings forth new violence.

The revival of socialism advances gradually, in waves, with each wave engulfing another group of countries. This revival expresses different types of content, different shapes and different ways to attain the goals. At the same time, these waves are a synthesis of the main objectives' unity. Finally, the revival of socialism provides all the objective conditions of socialism globalisation.

Without a worldwide revival of socialism, the globalisation of socialism is out of the question. In other words, the socialism's worldwide revival is the foundation of its globalisation.

Our readers will probably ask (justifiably so) what is the fundamental difference between planetary revival and the globalisation of socialism.

The first difference is that this revival is the product of the lengthy process of the socialism's birth, development and maturity, with each country's specific features, with all the specific establishments generated by the different traditional, cultural and economic circumstances of the human existence. Once socialism covers a larger group of countries, it assumes a worldwide trait, namely that of the globalisation of socialism.

(b) Fundamental Differences Between the Two Types of Globalisation

The globalisation of socialism is an expression of the fundamental principles governing social relations within a group of countries, extending outwards, in the global scene of relations between peoples, nations and countries.

We cannot search for the origins and the social-economic signification of the socialism's "globalisation" in contemporary economic and politic literature, and even less so in the well-established dictionaries and encyclopedias. This new historical process is only at its debut and, as such, is rarely and vaguely represented in the circuit followed by novel social science ideas.

That is precisely why, in my attempts to define the main features of socialism's globalisation, I need to use deductive mechanisms and extract the new concept out of that of the globalisation of capitalism, which already is amply and thoroughly interpreted.

At first, the globalisation of capitalism took the form of the social and economic re-integration of the developed western countries, of the reciprocal merge of capitals, and it has dragged less-developed countries on the imperialist and neo-colonist path.

After the Second World War and after the former colonial powers, such as Britain, Japan, France, Belgium, Spain and Portugal, have grown weaker, and as the United States had quickly become a bigger economic and military power, globalisation became the new expression of the American desire to dominate the world. Under the pretense of economic relief, "structural reforms" and a so-called reduction of poverty and economic gaps, the American financial oligarchy, together with the other oligarchies in the western developed countries, controlling the World Bank, The International Monetary Fund and the other major financial institutions, have contributed considerably to the increase of economic gaps, world hunger, thirst and poverty.

"Globalisation or "mondialisation" – said Jean Ziegler – is, thus, far from adequate for a truly generalised economic development. On the contrary, it only leads to localised development, limited to three major business centers, where the large companies are localised: banks, insurance companies, marketing and communication services, financial markets... Globalisation also draws some sort of skeletal network across the globe, connecting a few large areas which are concentrating, among others, welfare – the areas where one can witness, now, the "advancement of the desert"... the reality of the globalised world consists of a network of welfare and richness islets, floating in an ocean of agonising peoples."[1]

Globalisation has had disastrous consequences upon the development of under-developed countries. Instead of reducing poverty it has rather slowed down industrialisation, agricultural modernisation, and social emancipation.

The globalisation of socialism emerges by means of the implacable action of economic laws, processes and principles inherent to social progress and, as such, it has a whole set of new effects in economic relations among the countries. Globalisation is an expression of the aspiration of our planet's civil society towards definitive emancipation from exploitation, social injustice and poverty.

The globalisation of socialism is also an expression of the diminution and annulment of economic differences between developed and underdeveloped countries; we can speak, in this case, of an institutionalisation of equal cooperation and collaboration between countries, of the establishment of a strong foundation for real, generalised support for the developing countries. The globalisation of socialism also aspires towards reducing and eradicating the arms race and all other non-productive expenses, towards integrating peoples, nations and states in a common labour and capital market, in a scientific and cultural community, towards the establishing of permanent peace and the ever increasing wellbeing of all the people on our planet.

(c) Principles of the Joint Economic Cooperation

The very opposite of the capitalist globalisation process, in which domination and subordination relations are exacerbated, in which exploitation, disintegration and unfair cooperation, as well as social discrimination, injustice and poverty are taken to unimaginable levels, the globalisation of socialism involves in theory, entirely new concepts of international cooperation, not depending on the condition of mutual help.

At the end of the Second World War, in the Bandung Conference (held between April 18th-24th, 1955, at the initiative of Nehru, Chu En Lay, Tito and Sukarno), 29 underdeveloped countries of the third world have set up the new major principles of cooperation between third world countries, including equality of rights, cooperation and reciprocal support, respect for national autonomy and disinterested, multi-lateral cooperation between peoples and states.

Unfortunately, with a few exceptions, the principles established during the Bandung Conference have never been implemented. The great imperialist powers have shattered the unity of underdeveloped countries, buying corrupt regimes and integrating them in the net of financial dependence of the IMF, World Bank and other multi-national financial structures.

The few exceptions I have mentioned are related to the People's Republic of China, which has applied and continues applying the principles outlined during the Bandung Conference, in its relations with some African and Asian states, providing low-interest or non-interest loans, for building railways, bridges, and factories, cultural and administrative centers.

The Chinese are currently involved in almost all African tenders related to the development of ample infrastructural and industrial projects. They are rapidly winning most of the tenders, by providing prices up to two or three times smaller than the Western offers.

Most sea ports, dams, barrages and railways are taken over by the Chinese.

During President Hu Jintao's recent visit in Mozambique, the People's Republic of China has provided a long-term loan for the development of Africa. The 15 billion dollars, plus an additional 10 billion dollars loaned to the People's Republic of the Congo, will be used for infrastructure refurbishment and for starting mineral ore exploitation. Until the year 2020, China will become the largest investor in Africa and Africa's largest commercial partner. China will outrun by far (at least three or four times over) the cumulated investments of Western countries.

Bi-lateral commerce between China and Africa has already surpassed 10 billion dollars in 2000, 100 billion dollars in 2010, and will probably amount to more than 500 billion dollars by 2020, as per expert prognoses.

At the very beginning of the 21st century, with the electoral victory of the leftist forces in numerous Latin American countries (namely Venezuela, Brazil, Bolivia, Argentina, Chile, Peru, and Uruguay), new elements of international solidarity have surfaced between the South-American countries. In April 2006, Cuba, Venezuela and Bolivia have signed, in Havana, the "Treaty for Peoples' Commerce" (T.P.C.) which has more than strictly commercial dimensions. The new commercial treaty, open to all countries, is considered, according to the Bolivian Minster of Foreign Affairs, a "space of integration" for the Latin American countries, as the opposite of the American integration (ALCA).

At the beginning of 2006, following the nationalisation of gas deposits in Bolivia, another summit between Bolivia, Brazil, Argentina and Venezuela was held in Puerto Iguaz, culminating with the signing of a treaty for preferential supply of Bolivian gas to these countries. A new giant project was envisioned, for the establishment of a gas pipe along South America, as a symbol of the new anti-imperialist collaboration and cooperation.

According to Brazilian president Lula da Silva, "Brazil is not looking for hegemony, nor is Argentina or Bolivia. We are building a continental alliance and this is how we are going to face the world by the time of the next meeting, in Vienna, on May 12th."[2]

Hugo Chavez is fighting for establishing the Latin-American television – Telsur, independent of the American CNN, for establishing a Latin-American oil block, for the establishment of a fund for the diminution of poverty, as well as for a Latin-American bank for development.

On December 8th, 2004, the "Cuzco Declaration", signed by twelve Latin-American countries, has signaled the beginning of establishing new ways of cooperation and collaboration, of a new Latin-American solidarity.

The recent South-South international conference held on the Ivory Coast is another confirmation of the birth of a new cooperation system and mechanism.

The USA, France, Portugal, Belgium, as former neo-colonialist countries, preoccupied by the burden of their own financial troubles, have lost the battle in Latin America and in

Africa. China, India, Russia, Brazil are the new masters of the world, working towards the beginning of the new world.

Of course, as the revival of socialism is spreading all over the world, the new forms of international cooperation and collaboration will become the major factors in the globalisation of the forces animating social progress.

2. Reducing the North-South Gaps and the Gradual Eradication of Poverty

(a) The Increasing Gaps between Developed and Underdeveloped Countries

The narrowing of economic gaps and the trend of economic equalisation between various countries in the West and in the South are not just an economic race of David against Goliath. It is not only a matter of international, worldwide ethics and equality. It is a matter, rather, of an objective economic law for the development of our civilisation. Unequal and inconsistent development of capitalist countries, active in an era of colonial conquests and imperialism, is being gradually replaced by the law of balancing out the level of development among countries in the West and in the South.

An ever larger number of under-developed countries, such as the People's Republic of China, India, Russia, South Korea, Saudi Arabia, Venezuela, Brazil, Mexico, Argentina, Chile, South Africa and other more, are now joining the family of medium-developed countries. In these countries, a material basis is being established for reducing the differences in economic development, for cutting-down the poverty and for increasing the peoples' standard of living.

Reducing the gaps between developed and under-developed third world countries is a stated objective of programmes set up by the United Nations, the IMF, the World Bank and its branch, the Society for International Financing. It is also an aim of the European Union and of tens and hundreds of international forums and conferences, dedicated to the development of the third world. This is fully justified, as the international organisations and forums, which are supposed to represent the interests of all of the planet's countries, peoples and social classes, adapt their programmes to the possibilities and objective requirements of developments, based on the interests of the world's financial oligarchies.

The history of these economic and political programmes unveils, however, another perspective, seldom taken into account. It is important to know what development programmes are adopted, but is even more important to know how they are actually put in place. Unfortunately – which isn't at all encouraging – we must witness the fact that, with very few exceptions, no major strategic project or programme for the emancipation and elevation of the third world countries has been finalised by the United Nation, World Bank or IMF.

The results of post-war development unveil the defeatist idea known, today, not only to political and state leaders of developed and under-developed countries and of the seventh power, but also to the majority of the citizens of these two entities, namely the fact that the differences between developed and under-developed countries and, as a consequence, the rift between them, are becoming ever larger.

I have no intention to burden the memory of my readers with an abundance of statistical data. My purpose here is to present, based on primary comparative information, the extent of the drama leading us to a possible catastrophe and, based on already existing tendencies, to make an attempt at drawing up ways and directions for the decreasing of these differences in the following decades.

The increasing rift between development and economic stagnation or regress is the visible manifestation of the 21st century's main contradiction, namely the contradiction between metropolis and semi-colonies, between the capitalist, developed countries and the under-developed countries, which have only recently left behind the traditional exchange system and entered the actually free market economy. The conflict between the old and the new systems, as an outer manifestation of the main contradiction, is the vital animating force of our civilisation and the source of third-level and second-level contradictions, as well as of other contradictions in the social development.

(b) Ways to Decrease the Economic Gap

The under-developed countries can become free of neo-colonialism, poverty, misery, if they rely on their internal forces, before asking for external loans. Using internal forces is not the same thing as economic autarchy, nor does it mean refusing any help from abroad.

After all, all the loans from the World Bank, the IMF, the FED (European Development Fund), as well as the bi-lateral loans contracted so far were no gifts, nor an expression of the Western charitable and altruist attitude. They were the expression of the inability of corrupt leaders of the wealthy classes in under-developed countries to mobilize internal means and forces to act towards an independent development. Debts of hundreds of billions of dollars, with huge interest rates, to be paid by under-developed countries two or three times over, are the fruit of the third world peoples' labour, sweat and privations. The loans are poisoned gifts. They have to be returned two or three times over. As such, they are the embodiment of their own work. Why wouldn't the third world peoples take the opposite, far less expensive way, and develop according to their own internal resources, based on the labour of their own people, and only afterwards start looking for more convenient loans, negotiating from independent and equal positions?

Is such a way a utopia, or is it the hope for their future development? In my opinion, it's far from being a utopia or a widely broadcast maneuver of the leftist revolutionary forces. The peoples of Venezuela, Brazil, Angola, Algeria, Tunis, Libya, The People's Republic of Congo and others, have chosen to tread this road. It is the same path followed by the great China, by Vietnam, Cuba, North Korea. The peoples of the former Soviet states, of Poland, Hungary, the former Czechoslovakia, as well as those of Romania and Bulgaria (former socialist countries), have gone through this stage. In these countries, socialism hasn't collapsed because of independent development and lack of foreign loans. Socialism has fallen precisely because of the opening of all the frontiers for the penetration of foreign debts and the restoration of liberalism.

Considering these new circumstances in the relations between developed and under-developed countries, the World Bank, the International Monetary Fund, the European

Development Fund and other funds providers will have to adapt their crediting financial strategies, without imposing preliminary subordination conditions. From world guardians of neocolonialism, they will simply have to convert, some day, to money sellers, as every other bank in this world. The financial institutions in Bretton Wood will have a vital interest of selling their money, just as peasants are interested in selling their tomatoes in the market. There will be a time when the world's bankers will roam one developing country after another, so as to make available their services.

As for the present, already the foundation of our future, the under-developed countries are furiously trying to have their debts annulled, as in some countries debts account for 30% to even 50% of overall exports. The degree of annual increase of the debts, which is a ratio between the total amount reimbursed and the sum of all exports, was, in 2004, of 32.3% in Kazakhstan, 36.9% in Argentina, 38% in Uruguay, 38.6% in Iraq, 40.4% in Turkey, 40.9% in Zimbabwe, 48% in Brazil and 49.6% in Lebanon.[3] Hence, this is the main handicap in the development of these countries. Getting rid of this handicap is not only a matter of charity, of erasing a debt, but one relating to the enhancing of actions in these countries, aimed at drastically reducing and annulling debt, as a recognition of their lawful right to the restoration of the riches exported to the developed countries over the dozens of generations of colonial and neo-colonial domination.

(c) Controlling the Demographics Associated with Economic Growth

One of the most important factors of reducing the gap between under-developed and developed countries is controlling the demographics, the birth rate increase, and squeezing it in the pre-set frame of dispatching the economic growth.

Between the increase of birth rate and the increase of material and intellectual wealth we find the same cause and effect connection as in the case of increasing national wealth or stimulating the expansion of hardship, hunger and poverty. The higher the birth rate, the higher material poverty becomes, and vice versa. This major scientific discovery has been presented to the international public by Thomas Robert

Malthus, in his paper "An Essay on the Principle of Population", published in London in 1798. The paper has long lost its effect in highly and moderately-developed countries. However, the strong reminiscence of Malthusian effects is still looming around like a haunting menace of our planet, over most of the under-developed countries.

How could the potential effects of Malthusianism be confirmed in most of the under-developed countries? The demographic and economic logic inherent to the relationship between cause and effect is fairly simple. The economic growth rate has its limits, placed somewhere between 2 and 8% and, in rare cases, up to 10%. The growth rate of the population, expressed not as a percentage, but rather as the number of children per couple, ranges somewhere from 1 to 15 children. The physiological demographic interval of population growth is far wider than that of increase in social production. In most of the African and Arab countries, the tradition is to have 8-10 children, but cases of couples with 15-20 children are not a rarity. In these countries, the wealth of a family is not measured in terms of material wealth, but in the richness of human fecundity.

In the developed western countries, annual rate ranges is traditionally – after the post-war boom – in the 1-3% span; in most of the under-developed countries, between 2-5%, and in some other countries in the 10-12% span. If the annual population growth rate is larger than the economic growth rate, the increase of the gap between developed and under-developed countries is an objective economic and demographic truth. If the annual population growth rate matches the economic growth, the gap between developed and under-developed countries is stagnating. Only if the annual population growth rate is far smaller than the economic growth rate can we expect a rapid narrowing of the gap between developed and under-developed countries.

(d) Delivery from Financial Tyranny of the Bretton Wood Institutions

Overcoming the high debt is only one, albeit major, link in the process of liberation. A second link, even more important, in the chain of liberating actions from dependence and subordination, is to become free of the administrative and financial dictatorship of the Bretton Wood institutions. They impose, on third world countries, the trap of privatisation of all public businesses and banks, established by these countries over decades of significant sacrifices, so as to strengthen national independence. After all, behind a mask of incapacity to properly run the businesses, we can find extensive privatisation, depriving third world governments and peoples of a vital tool in their struggle for national independence and social progress.

This explains the third world peoples' aspiration towards restitution, by means of redeeming, of an important part of the national privatised patrimony or towards partial nationalisation of privatised businesses. This is a righteous aspiration of peoples in third world countries towards establishing their own state-owned, jointly owned and private businesses, so as to provide their own capital accumulation.

Sustaining the development of national and private businesses and, firstly, of SMEs and micro-businesses, with all kinds of state incentives, is the best option for getting rid of under-development. This explains the endeavour, under such circumstances, of those nations, to attain real national independence, to establish equal collaboration and cooperation relations with the business circles and the developed states.

Under-developed states are not denying the need for economic cooperation with the developed states but, as recently stated by Laurent Gbagbo, president of the Republic of the Ivory Coast, it is a cooperation based on equality and mutual respect. These countries would be content if the 0.7% they are supplied out of the Gross Domestic Product of the developed countries, based on an agreement for supporting the development of under-developed countries, would be raised to the value of 1.5%, which in fact is far less than the overall military expenditure of the developed countries.

According to the "Le Courier International" magazine, the Gross Domestic Product of the 26 highly and medium-developed countries in the world amounted, in 2004, to 34.6 thousand of billions of dollars. Excluding China, Russia, Poland, Romania and other medium-developed countries, the global annual support for under-developed countries would be (calculated based on a 0.7% share of the Gross Domestic Product) of around 217 billion dollars, provided the developed countries abide by the agreement. If we include medium-developed countries in the economic circuit and if we apply a 1.5 percentage, based on the current levels of the Gross Domestic Products, the annual loans for developing countries would amount to 500 billion dollars and, in 30 years, to somewhere around 1000 billion dollars. If anybody thinks these figures are not real, they would be wrong. Investments would account for only 1.5% of the Gross Domestic Product of developed and medium developed countries in 2004, covering only a small portion of the third world countries' needs. But it would be, however, an entirely different image of the relationship between the North and the South, an entirely different image of the new economic development possibilities.

The western financial circles already understand that, in the following 15-20 years, their economy will get stuck in its own dirt, unless they start focusing on investments in the third world. This is precisely why – not due to charitable impulses – the western countries have initiated new economic cooperation programmes, dubbed NEPAD, a new, more subtle system of capital exports. As for the under-developed countries, they should consider more seriously revising the old codes of foreign investments, and establish, following China's example, industrial areas exempt from profit taxes, patent taxes and value added taxes.

Consequently, foreign support, as a secondary development source, and thorough mobilisation of internal wealth, as a primary source of development, would attain completely new dimensions. They could speed up economic and social development and could gradually reduce economic gaps between developed and under-developed countries, between the rich and the poor. That is why intensive education, industrialisation, electrification, agricultural modernisation and enhancement, with a high annual growth rate, between 6% and 12%, are the sine qua non prerequisits of social progress. This is the main link of social development, a means to abolish eternal poverty.

Some day, in the not very far future, political leaders, businessmen and bankers in the developed countries in the

West will understand that preparing a new strategy of cooperation with third world countries, accounting for over 4.5 billion people, which are expected to raise to billion people in 30 years' time, is the only way to open a new market for ever flowing capital, technology and consumer goods exports.

In fact, that is the only way for their own salvation, because, with no expanding market to sell its products, the West will suffocate in the ever narrower spaces of its own creation. This moment is not so far from now, as the moment of the great social transformations is also growing nearer.

I am no Nostradamus, nor any prophet reading the future in the stars. My readings are in the past, in the seeds which clearly show the prospects of our future.

3. The New Order of Super-Powers, the End of American Domination

(a) The United States of America, the New Masters of the World, or the New Cancer-Ridden Empire?

In 2002, Jean Ziegler, special rapporteur for the United Nations for the peoples' right to nourishment and, simultaneously, author of several works about the third world, published in Paris, an extensive and extremely well-documented book under the title: "The New Masters of the World". I have read it almost in one breath, looking for new elements of change in the relationship between capitalism and socialism, inside and outside of capitalism. Following the fall of the Berlin Wall, the thawing and the dissolution of the Soviet Union and the overall bankruptcy of the totalitarian system in the USSR and Eastern European countries, the economic and military power balance has drastically leaned in favour of the USA and other Western countries.

Since then, 18 years of American financial oligarchic offensive have gone by, so as to enhance the influence, the expansion and the domination of the USA and its allies in the United Nations, within the World Bank and its branches, within the IMF, the International Trade Organisation, NATO and other political, military and economic structures.

This situation presented Jean Ziegler with the opportunity to write his book and to paint, with an abundance of information, the ascension of these new masters of the world and of the new empire's alarming methods to enforce its domination.

After all, even now, the Americans do not have the monopoly on atomic and inter-continental weaponry. Russian atomic weaponry and rockets have maintained their potential power, even after the fall of dictatorships. Chinese atomic weaponry and rockets are not surpassed by the American and Russian ones. The European Union also has a powerful strike force, with missiles and atomic weapons. As for India, its super-sophisticated weaponry has become a guardian of peace, against blackmail exerted by the United States of America. In other words, in 2008, after the financial bankruptcy and the deep economic crisis, to speak of an American domination of the world, is an aberration without any support whatsoever.

So that, when we speak and write of a change in the balance of power and in the American domination, we needn't look only at the change in the balance of power between the most developed countries. We must also take into account new vectors in left- and right-wing political relationships.

Moreover, we must also take into account the decline and fall of neo-colonialism in most of the Latin American countries and in almost half of the African countries. We mustn't also forget about the nearing end of American, French and Belgian domination over under-developed countries. We mustn't omit the increasing solidarity between China, India, Russia and the recently freed countries in Latin America, Africa and Oceania. We must take into account, in this case and in general, the increase in the solidarity of national and social freedom movements of peoples all over the planet.

The brief period of imbalance in military, economical and political relationships, favouring the United States of America, right after the collapse of the Soviet Union and of the Warsaw Pact, is slowly compensated by the course of history. This means that we should not, when tracing a strategy of potential super-powers, now entering the scene of history, over-estimate the decaying American empire – just as we should not under-estimate it.

In estimating the actual power balance between the great

powers and the potential forces of the emerging countries, we must keep full objectivity. We must respect the new power balances, in constant motion and tuning in the international arena. We must, therefore, take into account the rapid growth of the economic potential of the four largest states in the world, namely China, India, Russia and Brazil, which account for nearly half of the globe's population.

(b) China, India, Russia and Brazil: the Great Powers of Social Progress

In 2007, China's Gross Domestic Product amounted at roughly 3,280 billion dollars. With an average growth rate around 8%, its GDP may double over the next ten years. In 2017, it may reach 6,560 billion dollars, in 2027 13,120 billion dollars, and in 2037 – and probably much sooner – it might reach 26,240 billion dollars and, therefore, leave far behind the current American level of 12,280 billion dollars, and reach and surpass its future level. In 2047, China's Gross Domestic Product might reach the cumulated GDP of the United States and the European Union.

My previsions are on par with those of Lee Kuan Yew, the parent of the Singapore dragon, according to whom China's Gross Domestic Product will reach, in 2050, the level of USA and EU's GDP, provided a peaceful evolution of national and international relations will follow.

In recent years, India has reached, based on total national independence and on industrialisation, an average yearly GDP growth of 6%-7%.

In 2007, India's Gross Domestic Product amounted to 1,171 billion dollars. It could double every 12 years, should it keep the same growth rate. In 2020, it can reach 2,240 billion dollars, in 2031 it might reach 4,480 billion dollars, in 2043 – 8,980 billion dollars, and may also getting close to USA's current level.

Aware of China and India's rivalry and of losing the world super-power monopoly, the C.I.A., following a proposal of the top leadership of American administration, delegated the National Intelligence Council, comprising well-recognised diplomats and intelligence officers, with drawing up a comparative study on economic relations between the world powers at the end of 2020. This geo-strategic survey has been prepared by a few thousand experts, who have submitted, in 2005, the results of their research.

Under the supervision of historian Alexandre Adler, the French have published the full report, in a book entitled "The C.I.A. Report: How Will the World Be in 2020?".

The general conclusion of American futurologists is that the power balance between the USA and the other developing countries will be, in 2020, nothing like what was in 2005. The 21st century will be, probably, perceived as the time when Asia, lead by China and India, will enter its own century, just as the hundred years before have been generally dubbed by commentators as the "American century". In these two great nations, China and India, the combination between a sustained economic growth, expanding military capability and numerous population will become the foundation of a high-rate growth, both economically- and politically-wise.[4]

American analysts avoid the subject of Russia's economic recovery (under the leadership of Vladimir Putin), which, emerging from the chaos it inherited and from its decrease in productivity, currently reaches high levels of economic growth, around 6%-7%, becoming one of the world's leading producers of steel, iron, oil and gas. With a GDP nearly equaling that of India, by 2020 Russia might become the fourth world power, should it maintain the same rate of economic growth.

With 220 billion people and a surface almost matching that of Europe, Brazil – the eighth world power – could become, in twenty years' time, the world's fifth economic power.

The patching up of the broken ship which was the Soviet Union and the restoration of the economic union of former USSR countries lifts out of the ashes an entirely new and modern power of the international triangle comprising China, India and Russia. There is no doubt, in a not so distant economic perspective this triangle will shake the world and will enforce a new world order of free collaboration and cooperation, based on mutual interest.

My projections of the future development of our planet are not a utopian vision of a dreamer fantasising about desirable programmes for our civilisation, but instead are the actual process already visibly budding and growing in the ample breeding nursery of our future.

A huge project has been carried on in November 2005, involving the consulting of representatives of half the civilisations on our planet, joined by representatives of China, Russia, Pakistan, Iran, Mongolia, Kazakhstan, Kyrgyzstan, Uzbekistan, Tajikistan, and other countries in the Regional Euro-Asian cooperation organisation, established in Shanghai a few years back. This organisation is becoming a new world union of Euro-Asian states and nations, becoming an anti-NATO alliance.

The recent military maneuvers carried on by China and Russia, as well as the transmission of nuclear military technique to India, and the military and technical cooperation of the three new emerging powers, clearly show the new geo-strategic policy of the great Euro-Asian super-powers. Is the new military alliance going to be established? That does not depend as much on the three peaceful, non-aggressive Euro-Asian super powers, joined by other Asian forces.

With the global rebirth of socialism, the China-India-Russia triumvirate, joined by Brazil, Venezuela, Iran and a lot of other freed countries, will thusly establish the World Union of free and independent countries, liberating the world of local armies and wars, of militarism and poverty.

The world will probably not develop precisely according to this scenario, and the deviation from this scheme will only confirm the diversity of ways in which society progresses, the great river of planetary rebirth which is eventually joined by all its effluents

4. The Metamorphosis of the United Nations and Their New Role in the International Cooperation

(a) The United Nations, USA's and the Great Western Powers' Instrument of Domination

With the defeat, in 1945, of the military-fascist forces of the Rome-Berlin-Tokyo axis and the establishment of a new world order which makes practically impossible the revival of vengeful policies – since Germany, Japan and Italy are currently under the control of international peace-keeping forces – a new international organisation was established, namely that of the United Nations. On June 26th 1945, the United Nations Chart has been unanimously adopted during the San Francisco Conference; its main objective was safekeeping international peace and security, organising efficient collaboration and cooperation between peoples and nations.

The highest body within the United Nations is the General Assembly which, at the time of the organisation's establishment, only comprised 51 states. At this time, 60 years after its establishment, the organisation includes 180 members, nearly every country on our planet.

The increase of the number of states adhering to the United Nations is an effect of the great changes which took part all over the world, evoking the fall of the former colonial system and the birth of new independent states in the under-developed countries, of which many have become prey to neocolonialism.

Although the member states of the United Nations have grown to 180, its original functional structure has remained nearly unchanged, over the course of 60 years. The Security Council, having 5 permanent members (the USA, China, Russia, Britain and France) and 15 non-permanent members, is the United Nations' executive arm and has, at its disposal, around 60,000 Blue Helmets for the enforcement of peace all over the world.

Sixty years have passed since the United Nations' Organisation has been established. Until now, the world constellation of states has gone through radical changes, including changes in the power balance between the developed and under-developed countries.

There is no doubt of the United Nations' at least partial contribution to peacekeeping and international cooperation. The organisation's role in providing humanitarian relief to starving third world populations cannot be contested. However, according to the writings of Jean-François Revel, "they have completely failed in their main task – that of having peace, human rights and democracy prevail."[5]

Unfortunately, we are left to assess a reality: The United Nations maintain the power balance on the international scene, protecting and developing the interests of the United States of

America and those of other Western super powers.

They still reflect the former power balances, which have taken shape after the Second World War and have been modified to suit the interests of the American financial oligarchy. The United Nations have not been able to prevent the American aggression in North Korea, nor the French war in Algeria, nor the French, at first, then American war in Vietnam, nor the invasion of Iraq by the United States, nor the tens of local wars in Latin America and Africa. The actions of the United Nations are not adequate to the ample changes which have taken place in a continuously emancipating and developing world.

The General Assembly of the United Nation currently has 180 members, of which approximately two-thirds are comprised of developing countries. They continue living in the shadow of the great powers. The great powers have shattered the union of the third world countries, rallied around the organisation of un-aligned countries, established by Nehru, Nasser, Sukarno and Tito in the 50's. Although the old colonial system has become extinct since the 60's, the former great colonial – and, now, neocolonial – powers have re-split the world in neocolonialist spheres of interest. The world wars carried for a new splitting of the world have now been replaced with local wars, with coups d'état and with the financing of arming one rival faction or another in the third world countries.

In fact, the General Assembly of the United Nations Organisation continues acting based on the principle of anonymous societies, in which shareholders with the largest participation determine the fate of our planet, according to the right to veto exercised by the great powers.

The ways of solving our planet's most significant problems, such as nuclear disarming, reduction of the greenhouse effect, reducing and eradicating unemployment, ending world hunger and reducing poverty, canceling most of the debts held by under-developed countries, putting an end to local wars, defending democracy, enforcing all the human rights and many other pressing matters, continue to lack both support and good will from the great powers.

(b) The Need to Review the United Nations' Charter

The United Nations' Charter, established by the General Assembly 60 years ago, has in the meantime become unfit in so many respects. It reflects the former power balances between the great powers, dominated by the USA, France and Great Britain which, using their financial authority and lobbying, have enforced their will upon the peoples of the world.

"A reviewing of the Charter – wrote Pierre-Edouard Deldique – would also allow for the inclusion of a new word: democracy."

"That in the first years of the third millennium, the United Nations' Charter, the articles of constitution of the world peace-keeping organisation, do not reference even once democracy, is at the very least astonishing."[6]

The very delicate question of knowing whether the UN should be dissolved, the author of the very well-documented book pleads for global reform and, mostly, for reforming the Security Council.

Although the Second World War has ended 60 years ago, and the number of members has grown from 51 to 180, the structure of the Security Council has remained unchanged, with its five permanent members, which hold an inviolable right to veto any decision, blocking every single positive initiative. There is no chance to ever reach – be it today, tomorrow or in 200 years – a 100% consensus in all the problems our civilisation is facing. The dictatorship of the most powerful is established precisely where the right to veto is applied, the unique principle of decision.

The right to veto is, in fact, the right to dictate, and has only existed in totalitarian regimes. Changing the power balance in the international scene, in the near future, gives us the conviction that the right to veto will need to be replaced someday, by the democratic principle of a two-thirds majority. This requires, and leaves no other option than, objectively extending the number of permanent members in the Security Council.

A radical reform of the Security Council remains, however, a faithful prayer.

(c) The UN's Real Role in Economic Cooperation and in Peace Keeping

A radical reform of the UN takes into account its new role in the collaboration and economic cooperation between the world's peoples and nations. Economic help for under-developed countries, by means of the existing UN structures, is only limited to the role of a fireman extinguishing the cries of the starving, impoverished, thirsty peoples in the third world. Instead of playing its fireman role, the United Nations ought to become, and will truly do one day, the main coordinator and assessor of the efficacy of the financial help provided to these countries.

"A deep reformation of the United Nations, writes Pierre Edouard Deldique, should also consider the creation of an "Economic Security Council", comprising diplomats representing the industrialised and non-industrialised countries, managers of enterprises, syndicates and non-governmental organisations, so as to create a more humane face for the economic globalisation. This council could control the IMF and the World Bank."[7]

The time will come when the world will solve economic and political problems troubling our planet by means of the UN, and not of the G7, more precisely G8, as a world forum of great powers. A time will come when the budgets for the United Nations' Programmes for Development (PNUD), of the World Organisation for Development and Industry (ONUDI), of the World Organisation for Agricultural Development (FAO), of the World Organisation for the Development of Education, Science and Culture (UNESCO), of the International Labour Organisation (OIT), of the World Health Organisation (OMS) and of other UN organisations will become independent and one of the major impulses behind the development of third world countries, the reduction of the economic gap between developed and under-developed countries, and, finally, the eradication of poverty.

Will that moment come in 15, 30, 50 years or more? This is not something to prophesize about, but has to do with the objective trajectory of our civilisation. The labours of the birth of the new world power and of the global rebirth of socialism would be that much shorter, the number of victims sealed in the foundation of our future would be that much smaller, the living witnesses of the birth of the new world would be so much more, and so more people would enjoy their sacrifices and dedication. Probably around 8 to 12 billion. Do not fear a population boom! Our planet will still have room for everyone.

References

1. Jean Ziegler, ditto, pp. 37, 38.
2. Lula da Silvia, http//www.latinreporter.com/argentine.
3. Jean Ziegler, ditto, p. 13.
4. Alexandre Adler, Comment sera le monde en 2020?, Robert Laffont, Paris, 2005, p. 74.
5. Jean François Revel, quote from Pierre Eduard Deldique, Faut-il supprimer L'ONU? Hachette, Paris 2003, p. 276.
6. Pierre Eduard Deldique, ditto, pp. 279, 281.
7. *Ibid.*

Epilogue

WORLDWIDE REVIVAL AND GLOBALISATION OF SOCIALISM UTOPIA OR OBJECTIVE TREND OF SOCIAL PROGRESS?

After six years of intense intellectual efforts in view of screening and choosing within the contemporary social development both the vital social relations permanently on the move of change, and the processes, categories and laws of social progress, and also the sketching, on such a foundation, of the design of our future, I am nearing the end of this summary on the revival and globalisation of socialism.

When I was writing these lines meant as a conclusion, to leave them to the present and future generations as a will of their future, I felt a certain unaccountable rush of the mind. Since the 1982s in my life and career, when the countdown of the remaining time started for me, I have been feeling morally content and grateful to Our Lord, the High and Mighty, for having given me enough power and inspiration to let me complete my reflections on the contemporary issues of social progress.

The readers with a pessimistic mindset and the non-believing antagonists of the social progress may raise the perfectly justifiable question: in the end, what are our predictions, utopia, extreme optimism, or the objective trend of social progress? Frankly, no true or objective analyst will ever be able to accept defeatism, pessimism or, even less, excessive pessimism. The philosophy of life, of success, of the chance and satisfaction of self-achievement lie in the great expectations, in the moderate optimism, which form the core and meaning of human life. With no hope, which is the last to die, and without optimism, that keeps alive our basic values, the present modern civilisation would cease to exist.

It is this moderate optimism, originating from the very sources of our hopes, from the very movements of social progress, which is the very result of these relations, which reflects the inner essence of these movements, as genuine relations of the economic basis and of the social superstructure under perpetual change, and which can become the fruitful force of social progress.

The secret of all objective analyses of the social progress, which results from the contradicting relations between the economic basis and the permanently moving and changing social superstructure, consists in the understanding of the Marxist concept, according to which the old social order does never disappear before within it the minimum material conditions appear and are formed for the establishing and existence of the new social relations.

"A social formation, wrote Marx, does never disappear before the development of all the production forces which it is able to comprise, and the higher production conditions are never established before the blooming of their material existence possibilities within the old society. Therefore, mankind does never set for itself other tasks than those it is able to achieve. Indeed, if we take a closer look, we will always find out that such a task emerges but where there already are the material conditions necessary for its fulfilment or, at least, where they are under way of being constituted."[1]

Hence, when we extrapolate the Marxist concepts on the proper course of social progress, we may say undoubtedly that the worldwide revival and globalisation of socialism are the result of the crashing discrepancy between the developed economic foundation and the backward social superstructure of the advanced and the underdeveloped countries. The ever harsher contradictions of these relations and, thence, their settling through a social revolution, mean the starting point of the social progress. This explains the striving of the disintegrating and excessively exploited society to solve these contradictions through a latent and peaceful social revolution, respectively by way of the large road of social progress or, where the necessary conditions are absent, through a violent revolution, and it also explains the wish to implement the material, social and political prerequisites for the revival of the new world.

The reinvigorating and globalisation of socialism is not merely an outrageously optimistic phrase or a commonplace utopia. We are not talking here about one more imaginary vision of the new society. The reinvigorating of socialism is obvious when we study not only how the implementation of the economic and social laws of social progress is going on, where the new social relations are under the way of being set up, along with minimum conditions for the achievement of the evolution triggered by these very new social relations.

Our projection of the future is based on three approximately real assumptions of the development of the production forces:

- the yearly increase of the GDP of the developed countries can vary within the range of the traditional and present rate of 1–3%,
- the yearly growth of the GDP of the medium-developed countries, such as China, India, Vietnam, Russia, Brazil, Iran, Venezuela, Cuba, Argentina, South Africa, and a number of other countries, may Range in the 6–10% range of the present rate of increase,
- the annual growth of the underdeveloped countries may vary within the economic increase range of roughly 4–5%.

The true future development of the production forces, in conjunction with the production relations, might add some adjustments to these movements, but can not bring about any radical changes of the social progress.

My predictions on the future have nothing in common with the fantastic unrealistic previsions of Jean Fourastié. When he detailed his previsions in a best seller that was famous at that time, "Major Ideas", Fourastié did not take into account the average yearly growth rate of the gross domestic product of approximately 2%, but instead the GDP increase in a certain history segment, namely the period of the years 1952 – 1960, when the annual growth rate of the GDP in the developed countries had attained 5 – 6%, due to some now recognised unusual circumstances.

Extending indefinitely the annual growth rate of the production forces, Jean Fourastié wrote:

"In the future years (for instance, a century from now), nothing will come to slow down the advance of the production factors; on the contrary, this progress will tend to accelerate following the outstanding development of scientific research; this will expand, gradually, to every nation on earth."[2]

Fifteen years later, Fourastié's unrealistic prognosis, extrapolating the "glorious years" for the next one hundred years, crashed down as a house of cards. The Western economy entered an era of crisis, decay and growth decrease. The underdeveloped countries entered the economy stage of general standstill and, a little later, the USSR and the East European countries entered the time of dissolution of the totalitarian system. The need for a new evaluation of the social movements, for a new evaluation of the nearing future, is unavoidable.

I have undertaken this labour of great responsibility and political risk with the understanding not merely of the social substantiation of my efforts, due to their contribution to the discovery of certain ways of the social progress and of the potentially imperfect conclusions, which require more scientific research work, but also of some impending failures in the discovery of the paths of such a long historical period, of the 21st century.

The main issue of the 21st century is not to find out whether the society is going to develop along the new ways identified by the present society in the evolution of socialism, or following the old roads of the decaying capitalism, embellished by cosmetic means, or of neo-colonialism. The ways of social progress are not the wishful thinking of the antagonistic social classes, but rather a natural historic process, which derives from the action of objective social and economic laws, so that the issue of choosing the path of social progress lies in the knowledge and bending of these laws to the will and goals of the progressive classes of society. In other words, the main issue of the future social progress is in fact not to know whether the society will evolve in the desired direction, but to know:

- If the political leaders of the left-wing parties, which are now in power, and those who are now preparing to take the power, will be able to achieve their socialist projects in a clever way, with no notable deviations and distortions, in compliance with the requirements of the people.
- If their actions are and will be in accordance with the historic, economic, sociologic and cultural conditions of the environment.
- If the old surviving classes, while defending their achievements, will be able to brake or to stop temporarily here and there the clock of history.

In our attempt to give an answer to the first question, starting from the historic experience of the dynamics of radical changes of the technological production ways, we may expect the failure of some left-wing parties in power.

Certainly, the development of the buds of socialism will not follow a straight course, at the same intensity, at the same pace and with the same rate of success in every country. It is possible that, in certain countries, the blossoms of the new production relations wither, and the failure of the leftist political parties be penalised by the voters. In this case, the social progress will be achieved by means of the procedure of alternation in power of the left-wing and right-wing parties.

The allegory told by Jesus Christ about a farmer and his crop, story retold by the Saint Apostle Mark in the Bible, is our compass in the process of evaluation and growing the buds of the young developing socialism.

"Behold, the sower went forth to sow; and it came to pass, as he sowed, some seed fell by the way side, and the birds came and devoured it. And other fell on the rocky ground, where it had not much earth; and straightway it sprang up, because it had no deepness of earth; and when the sun had risen, it was scorched; and because it had no root, it withered away. And other fell among the thorns, and the thorns grew up, and choked it, and it yielded no fruit. And others fell into the good ground, and yielded fruit, growing up and increasing; and brought forth, thirtyfold, and sixtyfold, and a hundredfold." (Mark, 4.3-9).[3]

The buds of socialism will grow differently, they will bring forth the best crop, or the less good, or the worst crop, depending on the relations between the objective and subjective factors, where the objective factors, that is the capacity of the humans to master the laws of development, play the leading role, just as confirmed by history.

Looking for the answer to the second question, we have to start not only from the older or more recent lessons of history. We have to start from the main ideas of the dialectic and historic materialism, according to which the social progress advances as a spiral, which means that it describes a sea wave like line, that it has high and low tides. It still has to face strong opposition from the old surviving classes. The causes of low tide are not as much of objective nature – for instance, the random immaturity of the material conditions for the emergence and development of the new social relations – as rather of subjective kind – the rush of the abolished dominant classes to prevent by force the social progress. Undoubtedly, with only few exception, the great ownership will never leave willingly and opposing no resistance its privileges as a ruling class, its benefits of luxury, and it will not give up its domination instinct typical for the powerful domineering the weak.

However, to a certain extent and in some instances there are four circumstances which could somewhat slow down the course of history, but not to stop it:

- Military raids of the great powers, with the vital interests of imperialism, against the national and social revolutions in the underdeveloped countries.
- Increasing of right-wing populism of the bourgeois parties, as an alternative of the revival of national-socialism, with the aim to gain over a part of the voters, to preserve the power along with its whole benefit system of the dominant classes.
- Corruption of some leftist political leaders, in view of attaining social peace, of achieving surface reforms and preservation of the old obsolete system.
- Increase of internal terrorism against the left-wing political parties and their leaders, of the multiple assassination attempts against political leaders and of

the common fighters for freedom, national independence, for the deletion of estrangement, for social justice.

Now-a-days, the world is no longer in the emergence age of capitalism, when the foundation of the new society was sealed with dozens of millions of casualties and dead, obscuring the roads of Africa up to the USA, when the bourgeois revolution killed millions of freedom fighters in Europe, North America and Latin America.

Nowadays, the world is no longer in the times of 1933 – 1945, in the age of the advance of fascism, of extensive extermination of leaders of the communist, socialist and labour movements, of extensive genocide against Jews, Gipsies, Poles, Serbs, and of treason of an important part of the socialist parties.

The neo-fascism, militarism and totalitarian system will never be able to destroy democracy, the unity of the people directed in a democratic way. The examples of France, Austria, Germany, Japan, Italy, Spain, Portugal, Russia, Poland, Hungary, Brazil, Venezuela and other countries will confirm the final victory of democracy over dictatorship.

The world is no longer at the moment when, after the Second World War, the French colonists in Algeria, Mozambique and Zambia, the Belgian colonists in Congo (ex-Zaire), the Americans in Indonesia, Colombia, Chile and other Latin-American countries killed millions of citizens of these countries, in an attempt to stop the course of history by military power.

The military interventions of France and the United States of America in Vietnam failed. The military intervention of France in Algeria failed, as did that of Portugal in Angola and Mozambique. The intervention of Belgium, France and other imperialist countries in Congo (ex-Zaire) failed, too. The same applied for the intervention of the USA in Cuba and Chile. That of the imperialist states in Haiti also failed. The intervention of the United States and England in Iraq and Afghanistan has almost failed. The military and diplomatic intervention of France in the Ivory Coast failed as well. Mao Zedong was right when, as a visionary, he made the world's nations attentive to the fact that imperialism is actually merely a paper tiger.

At present, the world is at a completely new crossroads of the history of the collapse of capitalism, of the failure of neo-colonialism and of the transit of most peoples and nations on our planet to the path of revival and globalisation of socialism. The world is on its way of reinforcing the unity of leftist parties and political movements, of sustaining the unity between left-wing parties and the civil society, between the left-wing parties, the Church and the State in their fight for national independence, social justice, social equality, wellbeing of body and mind for all citizens of society. The unity between the leftist political parties, between these parties and the population, between leftist parties, Church and State leads to the emergence of tremendous forces, like the atomic fusion which releases a terrible energy, needed for the revival and globalisation of socialism. We have now our own ideological bomb, which cannot be intercepted by the most sophisticated missiles of the decaying imperialism.

The power of arms is always less efficient than the authority and force of the ideas that are spreading through the popular masses, than the unity of ideas, theories and practice of the leftist political parties and peoples. So that I am bringing now my considerations to a close with the same words from Victor Hugo I quoted at the beginning of my book: "There is something stronger than all the armies in the world, and these are the ideas whose time of implementation has come."

References

1. Karl Marx, Préface de la (Foreword to) "Contribution à la critique l'économie politique", Editions Sociales, Paris, 1957.
2. Jean Fourastié, Idées majeures, Paris, 1966.
3. La Bible, Nouveau testament, Alliance Biblique Universelle, Paris, p. 32.

Index

N

R